Albert Camus
the Algerian

Colonialism, Terrorism, Justice

David Carroll

 Columbia University Press   *New York*

Columbia University Press
Publishers Since 1893
New York   Chichester, West Sussex
Copyright © 2007 Columbia University Press

Library of Congress Cataloging-in-Publication Data
Carroll, David, 1944–
    Albert Camus, the Algerian : colonialism, terrorism, justice / David Carroll.
        p. cm.
    Included bibliographical references and index.
    ISBN 978–0–231–14086–7 (cloth : alk. paper)—ISBN 978–0–231–51176–6 (ebook)
    1. Camus, Albert, 1913–1960—Political and social views. I. Title.
PQ2605.A3734Z62647 2007
848'.91409—dc22

                                                      2006030713

♾

Columbia University Press books are printed on permanent and durable acid-free paper.
This book is printed on paper with recycled content.
Printed in the United States of America
c 10 9 8 7 6 5 4 3 2

What they didn't like in him was the Algerian.

—Albert Camus, *The First Man*

For Suzanne

Without Whom None of This Would Have Been Possible

Contents

Preface   *A Voice from the Past*   xi
Acknowledgments   xv

Introduction   *"The Algerian" in Camus*   1
1   The Place of the Other   19
2   Colonial Borders   39
3   Exile   63
4   Justice or Death?   85
5   Terror   107
6   Anguish   131
7   Last Words   155
Conclusion   *Terrorism and Torture: From Algeria to Iraq*   179

Notes   187
Index   231

Preface

A Voice from the Past

> I want most earnestly to believe that peace will rise over our fields, our moun-
> tains, our shores, and that then at last Arabs and French, reconciled in free-
> dom and justice, will make an effort to forget the bloodshed that divides us
> today. When that happens, we who are both exiled in hatred and despair
> shall together recover our native land.
>
> —Albert Camus, "Letter to an Algerian Militant" (October 1955)

On January 4, 1960, at the age of forty-six, Albert Camus died in an automobile accident. Two years after his death, colonial French Algeria died as
well, when Algeria became an independent Muslim nation and a million
French Algerians, or *pieds-noirs*, fled their Algerian homeland. From that
moment, French Algeria, the land in which Camus was born and grew up,
no longer existed, and at the same time, the possibility of creating a postcolonial, multicultural, democratic Algeria of the type he advocated throughout his life was also destroyed. Camus' essays on Algeria were, for the most
part, criticized and dismissed during the war and then largely ignored after
independence. More recently, his Algerian essays and stories, if they were
discussed by critics at all, were attacked and used as evidence to prove that

Camus, no matter how often and passionately he denounced the lethal effects of colonialism and argued for equal rights for all Algerians, was himself in fact an unrepentant colonialist. This was, of course, just another way of silencing his voice and refusing to hear what it actually had to say about colonial injustice and the possibilities of a multicultural, democratic Algeria emerging out of the ruins of colonial Algeria.

With the passage of time, however, the general political atmosphere has sufficiently changed for Camus to be of interest once again to an increasingly large audience. It is, of course, not unprecedented for someone who was once attacked, silenced, and then forgotten in one era to be listened to again and found to have something important to say, something that needs to be said again, to or in another historical context. The project for the present book grew out of my sense that Albert Camus had been too hastily dismissed and that it is once again an especially appropriate time to reconsider his work, especially his political essays and literary texts dealing with colonial Algeria.

This is not to imply that the global political situation has not drastically changed since Camus' death or that the contemporary era is identical to the historical period in which Camus lived. There nonetheless exist sufficient connections between the postcolonial conflicts of the present era and the anticolonialist struggles of the 1950s and 1960s—especially, I would argue, between the Algerian War and the present "global war on terrorism"—to make it profitable and I would even say necessary to read Camus again. Already during the Algerian War, but even more vigorously from the 1980s on, Camus was attacked by postcolonial critics who did not agree with his position on the war and especially with his refusal to support the FLN's (Front de Libération Nationale) armed struggle for independence or justify its use of terrorism to achieve its goals. After the war, no one to my knowledge has challenged his criticisms of French counterterrorist tactics; in fact, his criticisms have been largely ignored.

From a narrow political perspective, many of the specific criticisms leveled against Camus' intransigency concerning Algerian independence could be considered valid. For example, it could be argued that Camus should have understood that recognition of and dialogue with the FLN, which had by 1956 succeeded in eliminating all competing Algerian nationalist opposition, was the necessary condition for ending the horrible bloodshed of the war. It could even be argued that his blanket denunciations of terrorism and proposals for moderate solutions to the war had by 1957 made him, if not an obstacle to the resolution of the conflict, then simply irrelevant to its eventual outcome, and that he was no longer listened to or taken seriously by either side. His most important contributions in the last years of the war were not political but humanitarian, for in a number of instances the letters he wrote demanding clemency for FLN militants who had been sentenced to death for their political activities resulted in their lives being spared. It may also be that his most important contribution to politics in general was his insistence that humanitarian concerns, the lives of individuals, had to come before political objectives.

For many years, I had for the most part agreed with the prevailing postcolonial critique of Camus' Algerian political and literary texts, holding the general position that, in fact, this present book directly challenges. Everything changed for me, as I believe was the case for many others, after I read Camus' autobiographical novel, *The First Man*, when it was published posthumously in 1994.[1] Reading the novel led me to question both my own assumptions about Camus and those of his most vocal critics and to reread all of his work, especially the texts dealing with colonial Algeria, which had been the focus of the most devastating critiques of his work. In rereading his essays on Algeria and the novels and short stories that take place in his homeland and discovering that they give a much more complex view of French-Arab relations under colonialism than has been generally acknowledged, I became convinced that what is most interesting in Camus' writings and missing from the picture of the "colonialist Camus" constructed by his most militant postcolonial critics is what Camus himself called "the Algerian" in him. Not a *French* Algerian in him who wanted Algeria to remain French at any costs, but rather the Algerian part of him, which continued to believe in the possibility of what he called "an Algeria of justice" emerging out of the destruction of the colonial Algeria of injustice and the violence of the war, a postcolonial Algeria that in fact never was to be.[2]

Thus even if, as many have argued, Camus was mistaken about a number of specific political issues, even if he made unrealistic demands on politics and proposed what most critics have argued were unlikely, if not impossible, resolutions to the violence and terrorism of the Algerian War; in other words, even if history has proven him in a number of important instances to have been wrong—whatever it might mean to be proven wrong by history—I am convinced that there is much that is right in his writings and that they can once again contribute to contemporary political debates by raising questions about the limits of politics in the never-ending pursuit of justice in a world still struggling to become truly postcolonial. The Algerian in Camus deserves to be listened to once again, and the pages that follow will attempt to demonstrate why. And if what Camus' Algerian voice has to say troubles us, forces us to rethink political issues we assumed had already been resolved, to question the basic assumptions and strategies of both sides of ongoing political conflicts, and to search for alternative ways to combat violence and pursue justice, so much the better.

Acknowledgments

My deepest thanks to Richard Regosin and Suzanne Gearhart, who read a number of chapters and made invaluable suggestions for improving parts of the book.

Parts of the following chapters have previously appeared in print, but all have been substantially expanded and revised. A small amount of material from the introduction overlaps with pages from "Albert Camus—Political Journalist: Democracy in an Age of Terror," the foreword I wrote for *Camus at* Combat: *Writing 1944–1947*, ed. Jacqueline Lévi-Valensi (Princeton, N.J.: Princeton University Press, 2006). The last half of chapter 1 is a revised version of "Guilt by 'Race': Injustice in Camus's *The Stranger*," *Cardozo Law Review* 26, no. 6 (2005): 101–113. Chapter 2 is a revised and expanded version of "The Colonial City and the Question of Borders: Albert Camus's Allegory of Oran," *L'Esprit Créateur* 41, no. 3 (Fall 2001): 88–104. Chapter 7 is a substantially revised and greatly expanded version of a section of "Camus's Algeria: Birthrights, Colonial Injustice, and the Fiction of a French-Algerian People," in "Camus 2000," special issue, *Modern Language Notes* 112, no. 4 (Summer 1997): 517–549.

Albert Camus
the Algerian

I would like to say to Camus that he is as Algerian as I am and that all Algerians are proud of him.

—Mouloud Feraoun, *Journal* (March 9, 1956)

Camus is an Algerian Writer.

—Mohamed Dib (March 17, 1995)[1]

"The Algerian" in Camus

Colonizer or Colonized?

> I am interested only in the actions that here and now can spare useless blood-
> shed and in the solutions that guarantee the future of a land whose suffering
> I share too much to be able to indulge in speechmaking about it.
>
> —Albert Camus, preface to *Algerian Reports* (1958)

Albert Camus was born in 1913 in what was then "French Algeria." Because he was born to parents who were legally French, he enjoyed from
birth the full rights and protections of French citizenship, unlike the overwhelming majority of Berber and Arab Algerians, who were denied citizenship and designated as indigenous "French subjects" or "nationals." His
father, Lucien Camus, who had spent part of his youth in an orphanage,
was barely literate and worked in different vineyards in Algeria until he
was drafted into the French army and died in France at the beginning of
World War I. Even though the ancestors on one side of his father's family were among the earliest French colonialists in Algeria, Camus seems
to have believed that his father's side of the family consisted exclusively of
Alsatians who had chosen to emigrate to Algeria in 1871, after the French

defeat in the Franco-Prussian War, rather than live in an Alsace occupied by Germany. This gave a patriotic and republican rather than colonialist justification for his father's family's presence in North Africa and corresponded to the fiction of Algeria in which Camus fervently believed until his untimely death.[2]

Camus' mother, Catherine Hélène Sintès Camus, never learned to read or write, and while Camus was a child she worked as a housekeeper to help support her family after the death of her husband. She came from a Spanish family who had immigrated to Algeria to flee the poverty of their Minorcan homeland only to discover the additional hardships and destitution that were the lot of many Spanish immigrants in Algeria. In a colonized land that was, at the same time, legally an "integral part of France," Camus was thus born into the lowest socioeconomic level of French-Algerian (or *pieds-noirs*) citizens. But in terms of the brutal dichotomy imposed by the colonialist system and because of the privileges that were an essential part of what it meant to be French in Algeria, his experience of colonialism was still not that of a colonized Arab or Berber Algerian.[3]

Camus' relation to both his French and Algerian identities, however, would turn out to be a more complex issue for this French citizen of Algeria than the stark opposition between colonizer and colonized might suggest. His father's death less than a year after Camus' birth left his family destitute, which meant that the actual conditions in which his family lived were closer to those of the powerless than to those of the privileged and thus not substantially different from those of the Arab families next to whom his family lived in Belcourt, a poor, ethnically mixed area of Algiers. In any case, they were far different from those of the rich French Algerian families of the strictly European sections of the city. It is also true that Camus' family, like other poor French Algerians, were still cut off from their Arab neighbors by culture, language, and religion, and also by the fact that they received the benefits, privileges, and legal protections of French citizens denied to Arab and Berber Algerians.[4]

French Algeria was divided into three *départements*, whose status was in principle the same as the other *départements* of mainland France. Yet the Algeria of Camus' youth was not French in the same way that areas of mainland France were French, and not even the most reactionary *colon* really believed that it was. The three *départements* of Algeria also differed from the majority of other French colonies, since Algeria was what was called a "populated colony"; that is, unlike most other colonies, it was inhabited by a substantial number of French citizens. At the time of Camus' birth in 1913, the French citizens of Algeria numbered approximately 750,000 and ruled over seven or eight times as many Arab and Berber subjects. The ratio of French to "natives" would steadily decrease during Camus' lifetime, largely because of the population explosion among Arab and Berber Algerians and a decrease in the rate of new European immigration, but until independence, the French population of Algeria considered Algeria to be not only an integral part of France but also, and more importantly, their homeland—or, as Camus put it, his "true country."[5]

The *départements* of French Algeria, in perhaps a more blatantly contradictory way than any other colony or *département*, were thus French and not French simultaneously, legally an integral part of the French Republic and, at the same time, an extension of the Republic outside itself, across the Mediterranean and into North Africa and the Muslim "Orient," a part of France inhabited by an overwhelming majority of non-French Muslim "natives" and ruled by a minority of French citizens empowered by French political, economic, legal, and penal institutions. The situation in Algeria was complicated even more by the fact that a substantial number of the French citizens of Algeria were themselves not descendents of French families from mainland France, but of Spanish, Italian, Maltese, Corsican, or Greek heritage, and after 1870, when Algerian Jews were granted French citizenship, of North African Jewish heritage as well. This meant that the question of national identity, what it meant to be French and how "Frenchness" was imagined and represented in political and literary texts, was more complex in the Algeria in which Camus was born and grew up than perhaps anywhere else in metropolitan France or in any other French colony or possession. It also meant that to be "Algerian" was an even more conflicted issue—not just for Berber and Arab Algerians, who had no officially recognized national identity, but for French Algerians as well.[6]

No native French Algerian, for example, could ever claim to be French in a narrowly nationalist sense and pretend to possess in Algeria, across the Mediterranean Sea and thus at a distance from the soil, monuments, traditions, and culture of mainland France, the imaginary identity that for militant nationalists every "true" French man or woman "naturally" had as his or her birthright and that made him or her what an "uprooted" foreigner could allegedly never be.[7] French Algerians could be French only in the way that an increasing number of French are French today, in a post-colonial world of hybrid identities and multicultural identifications—even if many, if not most, denied their own hybridity and displayed rather an exaggerated patriotism as concerns their "mother country."[8] In spite of the overall reactionary nature of politics in the colonies, however, it should also not be forgotten that from 1870 until the end of the Algerian War, it was republican and even socialist France that supported and believed most fervently in the colonialist project, not the antidemocratic, ultranationalist Right. Until General de Gaulle took power in 1958, when the Fifth Republic was formed, it was a series of Socialist governments that fought the Algerian War and authorized the torture of FLN suspects, summary executions, and the napalming of suspect villages—all in the name of democracy and the integrity of the French Republic and its people. As the then Socialist Minister of the Interior François Mitterand succinctly put it during his visit to Algeria in November 1954, soon after the first terrorist acts had been committed by the FLN at the beginning of their armed struggle for independence, "Algeria is France."

In reality, the Algeria that was France, a legal and integral part of the French Republic, was a land in which democratic rights were denied to the overwhelming majority of native Arab and Berber inhabitants of Algeria *in the name of democracy itself.* As compensation, these "French subjects" were given only vague and unfulfilled promises of assimilation into French culture and full citizenship in some distant, ill-defined future. If, under colonialism, all Algerians could be considered to have been exiled both from the land of their birth and from the French nation that claimed possession of Algeria—and exile is a dominant theme in Camus' writings—it is also true that they were not exiled in the same way or with the same economic, political, and cultural consequences, depending on whether they were French subjects or citizens, colonized or colonizers.

A substantial number of French Algerians, and especially the poor, uneducated *pieds-noirs* to which Camus' family belonged, even if the only official national identity they had was French, clearly considered themselves more Algerian than French and referred to France as if it were a foreign country. They did not say "we" but rather "they, the French," for example, when referring to the French people in general, because the French were for them a foreign people living across the sea in a land where French Algerians did not truly belong or with which they did not immediately identify. In Camus' own case, it was not until he had to flee Paris in June 1940 due to the arrival of German troops that he is reported to have admitted for the first time that he truly felt French.[9] His experiences in the war and in the French Resistance could also be argued to have reinforced his identification with the French of occupied France and his desire to participate in the struggle for freedom against Nazi Germany.

In spite of his strong identification with "the Frenchman" in him during World War II, "the Algerian" in Camus never disappeared, no matter how long he lived in Paris. Immediately after the war, Camus published a series of editorials in *Combat* arguing that the French could not continue to deny to the majority of the inhabitants of Algeria what the Resistance had fought to achieve in mainland France for all French: both freedom and justice. In 1945, and this would still be true in 1958, Camus did not take the terms "freedom" and "justice" in the context of Algeria, however, to imply immediate Algerian independence and autonomy from France. They rather meant for him that colonial Algeria had to be transformed into a true social democracy—which, in fact, was the political project he supported at that time for all of France. That is, fundamental reforms had to be made immediately to transform Algerian society into one in which Arab, Berber, and French Algerians would have equal rights and the same social and cultural status, one in which all ethnic and religious groups would live in harmony and that *all* Algerians could consider their "true country," no matter when or under what conditions they or their ancestors had originally arrived there. Already in 1945, a democratic, multicultural Algeria was "Camus' Algeria," the imaginary Algeria the Algerian in him argued should and could become a political reality.

Until his death and even in the midst of a horrible war, Camus stubbornly believed in this idealized vision of a multiethnic, multicultural Algerian people, of an Algeria with equality and justice for all Algerians. When, in the late 1950s, his hope for a peaceful resolution to the war without the participation of the FLN became increasingly difficult to imagine and impossible to sustain, he repeatedly lamented the failure of France to have begun working earlier toward creating a democratic Algeria. This is a vision he insisted could have been achieved by radical reforms and peaceful means before the outbreak of war, or even during its early stages, and without the horrible loss of life on both sides or the use of terrorism, on one side, and the torture and summary execution of FLN suspects, on the other.

With the escalation of terrorism and the brutal counterterrorist measures undertaken by the French army, Camus repeatedly warned that the most destructive elements of both sides—the most extreme and violent Algerian nationalists and the most reactionary, racist *pieds-noirs*—would ultimately determine the fate of the Algerian people. The inevitable result would be an even more repressive colonialist regime or a nominally independent state ruled by a brutal and authoritarian revolutionary council or military dictatorship. In both cases, justice would continue to be denied to the Algerian people—to Arab, Berber, and poor French Algerians alike, that is, to all those who for him were the true Algerians and who were paying the heaviest price throughout the war.

If the kind of democratic reforms Camus proposed for Algeria in 1945 had been undertaken immediately after World War II, it would not be difficult to imagine that the course of history in Algeria would have been radically changed and an independent Algeria born without the horrible bloodshed and suffering that was the result of eight years of devastating war. Instead, the increasingly brutal French oppression of the overwhelming majority of "French subjects" in Algeria and the horrible economic conditions in which they continued to live set the stage for the armed struggle that did in fact occur. What had been radical proposals for change in 1945 were by 1958 considered by most on the Left to be self-deluded musings over what could have been. But if Camus' idealism could legitimately be questioned in terms of its relevance to the political realities of the last years of the war, reading his political essays reveals that his commitment to justice in Algeria for all Algerians cannot be doubted.

It is also important to understand that Camus' perspective on Algeria, which was never exclusively or even predominantly *political*, was developed long before the Algerian War actually began in early November 1954. It was rather the result both of his own observations of oppression and injustice while growing up in Algeria between the two world wars and of his involvement in the French Resistance. What was common to his prewar and wartime experiences was his steadfast refusal to accept the political, cultural, and economic oppression of a people—whether of the French in occupied France or of Arab, Berber, and Jewish Algerians in colonial (or Vichy) Algeria—and his hatred of the racism that supported and legitimated such oppression. Camus was thus a *résistant* who never forgot "the Algerian" in him and who, even during his active involvement in the struggle against Nazi totalitarian oppression and the racist ideology that divided peoples into superior and inferior races, never accepted that colonialism, also rooted in fictions of cultural and racial superiority, could ever be justified or the injustices it perpetrated accepted.

From One Resistance to Another

In 1942 in occupied Paris, when a limited number of books were being published because of a paper shortage and all manuscripts had to receive the approval of Nazi censors, a young, relatively unknown Algerian journalist and writer named Albert Camus burst onto the French literary scene by publishing within a few months two important works: his first and still best-known novel, *The Stranger*, followed months later by *The Myth of Sisyphus*, an essay on "the absurd." Camus' national and, soon after the war, international reputation, which would culminate in his winning the Nobel Prize for literature in 1957 at the age of forty-four, thus began in the midst of one of the darkest hours of twentieth-century French history.

In the fall of 1943, Camus moved to Paris and became a reader for the Editions Gallimard. But it was only when Paris was liberated and the names of the contributors to the clandestine resistance newspaper *Combat* were finally revealed that the public discovered that one of its chief editors and editorialists was also the author of *The Stranger* and *The Myth of Sisyphus*. Camus very quickly became the living symbol of the young, politically committed writer who had risked his life in the struggle against racism and oppression and challenged existing social norms and values in his editorials, novels, and plays.

By the time of Camus' untimely death in an automobile accident in the midst of another especially dark moment in twentieth-century French history, almost everything had changed, at least as concerned his political reputation. No longer accepted by many on the Left as the noble defender of victims of oppression—a position he in fact mocks in his novel *The Fall*—Camus was treated by many of his previous admirers, and especially those former allies and friends who enthusiastically supported the armed struggle for Algerian independence, as a political enemy and an obstacle to peace and justice in Algeria. In the eyes of many of his former admirers, the heroic young *résistant* to Nazi oppression had disappeared at least a decade before and been replaced by a militantly anticommunist Nobel Prize–winning writer and public intellectual.[10] Rightly or wrongly, they felt Camus had changed political camps because his position on Algeria differed from that of the overwhelming majority of those on the Left, who belatedly—but, because of that, perhaps all the more fervently—attacked colonialism, supported the FLN in its armed struggle, and demanded immediate and complete Algerian independence. As the French were finally willing to recognize an independent Algeria in order to save both the Algerian people and the French Republic, they increasingly ignored Camus because of his opposition to the creation of an independent Algerian nation and his harsh criticism of the terrorist tactics and revolutionary-nationalist ideology of the FLN.

What his opponents disliked, he would assert in notes for his fictional autobiography, was above all "the Algerian" in him,[11] the part of him that even after living in Paris for a decade was still deeply attached to land of his birth and demanded justice for all Algerians, the part that did not believe, however, that independence and justice were necessarily the same thing. It is important to understand that the Algerian in Camus was the enemy of colonialism and the fanatic colonialists who defended "*Algérie française*" and continued French colonial rule. But the Algerian in him did strenuously defend the right of French Algerians to continue to live in a homeland that he insisted they had as much right as other Algerians to call their "true country." The "Algerian in Camus," in the sense I am using the term, does not, however, constitute an "Algerian identity" that would define Camus; it is rather the locus of a problem, of a split or conflict of national, cultural, and political identities that is expressed in his writings in various ways. Rather than the unity of a national identity, it evokes a fundamental relation to difference and otherness that is, at the same time, an integral part of a self that remains in large part a stranger to itself.

The Algerian in Camus should not be understood as an attempt to define *who* he really was, but rather as an expression of the alterity or hybridity of his conflicted identity, of a division at the very core of the self that constitutes an opening or receptivity to others. The Algerian in Camus is also an important component of his agnosticism, of his determined resistance to political and religious doctrines, systems, and ideas, the side of him that maintains a distance from—and a complicated, oppositional relationship with—national, religious, cultural, ethnic, and political identities, the side that resists oneness, sameness, uniformity, and all expressions of absolute truth. In Camus' terms, the Algerian in Camus is a Mediterranean: neither strictly French nor Algerian, neither European nor African, but both at the same time. The Algerian in Camus is also a rebel.

The Climate of the Absurd—What's Algeria Got to Do with It?

Camus, of course, changed in the eighteen years between the publication of *The Stranger* and his death two years before the end of the Algerian War. But what it meant to be a French Algerian had changed even more. With the French withdrawal from Vietnam in 1954 and the beginning of the Algerian War at the beginning of November of the same year, French colonialism was rapidly and violently coming to an end. The Algerian in Camus and the Algerian themes and topics in his writings, which during and immediately after World War II were considered positive aspects of his work, became during the Algerian War and are still considered by many critics today to be limiting, ideological components of his work. But no matter which side one takes in the decades-old debate over whether Camus' Algerian texts ultimately constitute a defense of or a critique of colonialism, a justification for or a rejection of colonial injustices, his writings in general and the political implications of his literary texts in particular, perhaps more than those of any other major French writer of the period, testify to the radical changes that occurred in French literature, culture, and politics during the troubled times from the beginning of World War II through the end of the Algerian War. In terms of no problem is this more true than the demise of colonialism in general and the long, agonizing death of French Algeria in particular.

When Camus published *The Stranger* in occupied Paris in 1942, however, the fact that this young, unknown writer was Algerian and that his first novel takes place in Algeria, with the Algerian landscape and climate playing a central role in the "tragedy" and revolt depicted in the novel, did not go unnoticed by Camus' first readers. It could even be said to have played an important role in the initial success of the novel. For the French living in occupied Paris, being a French Algerian was nothing to be ashamed of. In fact, Jean-Paul Sartre, the most important of Camus' earliest readers, published an essay on *The Stranger* and *The Myth of Sisyphus* in the review

Les Cahiers du Sud in February 1943 that repeatedly alludes positively to the Algerian dimensions of Camus' work.

Sartre begins his philosophical "Explanation of *The Stranger*" by agreeing with the consensus that it is "the best book in France since the end of the war" (the original French text says "since the armistice"), thus situating the novel's appearance and his own explanation explicitly within the context of the war, the German occupation, and Vichy collaboration ("the armistice").[12] Sartre also suggests that an important aspect of the novel's interest for readers living in France during the occupation under the conditions imposed by the armistice is precisely its foreignness: "This novel itself is a stranger. It comes to us from the other side of the Equator" (108 [99]; the French text says "from across the sea"). For Sartre, the novel does not merely have a "stranger" as its main character and his "foreignness" to French society as its principal subject. More important, the novel appears to have arrived in France from a foreign land located across the Mediterranean, a land of beautiful beaches and blazing sun where simple pleasures still exist, a land far removed from the war, occupied Paris, collaboration, and the continuing winter of French discontent. Coming from another place, the novel also arrives as if from another historical time, a time of simplicity, honesty, innocence, and moral courage, and in this way too it appears totally foreign to the French living in either occupied or Vichy France.

At the same time, Sartre asserts that the author and the novel, no matter how foreign they might appear to the French of occupied France, are profoundly French; Sartre even considers *The Stranger* to be the twentieth-century equivalent of Voltaire's *contes* (121 [121]). When Sartre discusses how *The Stranger* is related to *The Myth of Sisyphus*, he once again speaks of climate and geography, but now in terms of the absurd: "*The Myth of Sisyphus* might be said to aim at giving us this *idea* [of the absurd], and *The Stranger* at giving us the *feeling*. . . . *The Stranger*, the first to appear, plunges us without comment into the 'climate' of the absurd; the essay then comes and illuminates the landscape" (114 [110]). The Algeria of the novel and the idea of the absurd presented in the essay are thus doubly exotic to its Parisian readers: a climatic exoticism for readers dreaming of warm beaches and innocent pleasures and a philosophical-political exoticism that raises fundamental questions of existence and freedom in the stifling atmosphere of totalitarian oppression. Their foreignness, what could be called their Algerian dimension, is treated by Sartre as a breath of fresh air in the oppressive political and cultural climate of occupied, collaborationist Paris.

Camus' later writings will repeatedly confirm Sartre's early insight that climate and geography are as much philosophical-political issues in his work as they are natural phenomena. Even when Camus leaves the philosophical issue of the absurd behind, it is in terms of Algeria as a geographical, philosophical, and political landscape that he will repeatedly pose the problems of oppression, resistance, freedom, and justice. But in the last years of World War II, the Algeria of *The Stranger* was for Sartre and other readers not the site of colonial oppression but of the possibility of freedom and revolt. Sartre's "existentialist" interpretation of *The Stranger* had an important influence on readers of the novel and the essay for decades. It only began to be abandoned, although rarely if ever directly questioned, long after Algerian independence, with the growth of postcolonial cultural criticism in the last few decades. It is important, however, not to forget that the Algerian in Camus and his work was first seen in a positive critical light by one of Camus' most important and influential early interpreters, one who later, of course, became one of his most severe political critics.[13]

Postcolonial Controversies

> Given the collapse of systems of thought, the bankruptcy of ideologies, the incapacity of doctrines to enable us to foresee or even understand a world that is allegedly being changed . . . one has the right to ask in the name of what Camus's behavior was condemned. All of the old condemnations implied values that have today been abandoned.
>
> —Jean Daniel, *Le temps qui reste*

It would not be an exaggeration to say that many critics today still do not like the Algerian in Camus. Even though the question of Camus' relation to Algeria has divided critics for decades, most of the important postcolonial interpreters of his politics have paid at least lip service to the difficulties and contradictions a *pied-noir* on the political Left faced once a brutal anticolonialist war had broken out in Algeria. For example, Conor Cruise O'Brien, one of the earliest and harshest of Camus' postcolonial critics, admits that even though he is convinced Camus is militantly colonialist in his political essays, he considers Camus' literary texts to be more complicated and con-flicted.[14] From a very different if not opposite perspective, Michael Walzer characterizes Camus as "a good man" who "in a bad time . . . did better than most of his fellows."[15] Another influential critic of Camus, Edward Said, has used similar terms to characterize Camus, calling him "a moral man in an immoral situation."[16] Tony Judt praises Camus for being, along with Léon Blum and Raymond Aron, one of only "three Frenchmen who lived and wrote against the grain of these three ages of irresponsibility."[17] Whatever their ultimate purpose for doing so, all four commentators admit that Camus was a man of high moral principles, all acknowledge that the political situation he faced as a *pied-noir* during the armed struggle for in-dependence in Algeria was extremely difficult and painful and that he was highly conflicted over what he could and should do, and all are willing to praise his honesty and courage. But they definitely do not agree, at least not when the issue is colonialism in general and the Algerian War in particu-lar, as to whether or not honesty and moral courage were enough.

The general consensus among these four critics concerning Camus' moral character and personal courage in an "immoral situation" is thus somewhat deceptive, given that their political assumptions and critical goals are so different, if not opposed. O'Brien, for instance, attacks those critics who had ignored or depoliticized the effects of Camus' presentation of Algeria and Algerians in his fictions and essays and indicts Camus for what he claims is a defense of repressive French government policy in Al-geria.[18] He argues that underneath the mask of the progressive, antiracist, European humanist and defender of the oppressed can be found Camus' true face: that of a partisan colonialist. Walzer's purpose is the opposite: to "defend [Camus] against his critics," including or especially, one would imagine, O'Brien, "and at the same time free him from the bonds of myth" so that we can "learn from his experience something about the obligations and limits of the critical enterprise" (137).

Said, whose position is close to but not identical with O'Brien's, also feels that we can learn important lessons from Camus, but principally, if not exclusively, negative ones. Besides claiming that Camus was "simply wrong historically" (175), Said characterizes Camus' work as a determined defense of French colonialism in Algeria: "Camus's novels and short stories narrate the result of a victory won over a pacified, decimated Muslim population whose rights to the land have been severely curtailed. In thus confirming and consolidating French priority, Camus neither disputes nor dissents from the campaign for sovereignty waged against Algerian Muslims for over a hundred years" (181). Judt, on the contrary, exempts Camus, along with a very few other French intellectuals, from his otherwise sweeping and polemical condemnation of what he claims is the general irresponsibility of French intellectuals "from the end of World War I until the middle of the 1970s" (14). For Judt, however, no matter how "irresponsible" he alleges the French in general were, there "was never any doubt about Camus's sympathies," given his repeated attacks on "French policy and military practices in North Africa" (117). Judt argues that Camus' political position, even though it became increasingly outdated and unrealistic over the course of the war, never constituted an apology for colonialism.

On the "Camus-as-colonialist" side, then, O'Brien asserts that Camus supported "the substance, if not the details of the methods, of the French government's policy of pacification": "Despite his revulsion from the methods of the repression, his position was necessarily one of support for repression, since he constantly opposed negotiation with the actual leaders of the rebellion, the FLN" (90–91). Said's criticism is even more severe, since even though Camus was born in Algeria, because he was a French citizen and not an indigenous Muslim, Said denies him not only the right to consider Algeria his homeland but also even the right to identify positively with the Algerian landscape or describe it lyrically in his essays and fictional works. What Said curiously calls Camus' "realistic" descriptions of Algeria constitute a justification for continued French occupation rather than the expression of a subjective, emotional attachment to the harsh beauty of the land. For Said, Camus is quite simply not an Algerian, and thus the Algerian he would claim was a fundamental part of him is a usurper, which makes his claims on or for Algeria, even if fundamentally aesthetic, totally illegitimate.[19]

On the "Camus-as-anticolonialist" side, Walzer argues that Camus had valid reasons for opposing both sides in the Algerian War and thus considers him a courageous dissenter, a man of justice who, in the context of a war in which "madness was practical, moral sanity utopian," insisted on choosing "the least mad, the most just" of what for him were equally unacceptable alternatives (145). In a similar vein, Judt, who refers directly to Camus' political essays on Algeria more extensively than the other three critics, considers Camus' ambivalence on the Algerian War to be justified because it resulted from what he calls Camus' "search for an evenhanded application of justice. . . . Intellectual responsibility consisted not in taking a position but refusing one where it did not exist" (121). Overall, however, these four critics differ so greatly in their analyses and conclusions that it seems they are not even talking about the same person or the same body of work. It is as if their different readings had to do not with one Albert Camus but at least two and perhaps even four different Camus and thus with four very different and even opposed representations of Algeria and colonialism.[20]

The differences among these four critics—two who accuse Camus of being a colonialist apologist and two who defend what each considers to be his resistance to political dogmatism—are in fact symptomatic of the divisions among Camus critics in general, even if the influence of those critics who have treated Camus as a colonialist has in the last decades been far greater than those who have taken the opposite position. The goal of the present book, however, is not to rehearse and thus perpetuate what by now has become a somewhat tired debate over Camus and colonialism, but to explore the different and at times contradictory aspects of the Algerian in Camus and of the Algerian dimensions of his work, the way his writings present, comment on, and imagine alternatives to colonial injustice. Even though this book deals with questions similar to those raised by the critics mentioned above, it does so in large part by proposing readings of Camus' Algerian novels and short stories, namely, *The Stranger*, *The Plague*, three short stories from *Exile and the Kingdom*, and his posthumously published autobiographical novel *The First Man*. My purpose here is to challenge the reductive terms of the polemics over Camus' politics, and by doing so come to a better appreciation of both Camus' Algerian fictions and their political implications, not just in terms of the historical context in which they were written and first read, but in the contemporary political context as well.

The debates surrounding Camus' work have in my estimation for too long been focused on the question of whether Camus was a colonialist ideologue. To read him this way is also invariably to weigh some of the "evidence" found in his work more heavily than other evidence, especially if the goal is to make the strongest possible case against Camus—which means, in most instances, to argue that his refusal to support the FLN and his opposition to an independent Algeria under FLN control should be given much greater weight than, for example, his repeated denunciations of colonial injustices and demands for radical democratic reforms in Algeria. To have as a primary goal the construction of a case against Camus has meant that his literary texts have been read predominantly or exclusively in terms of their alleged political message, as a source of evidence for the anticipated verdict that Camus was a colonialist. The present work challenges this verdict, reinterprets the evidence, and offers alternative readings of Camus' literary texts to support its own claims for the critical interest of his writings and the importance of the fundamental ethical issues his texts raise.

I would even say that to judge and indict Camus for his "colonialist ideology" is not to read him; it is not to treat his literary texts in terms of the specific questions they actually raise, the contradictions they confront, and the uncertainties and dilemmas they express. It is not to read them in terms of their narrative strategies and complexity. It is to bring everything back to the same political point and ignore or underplay everything that might complicate or refute such a judgment. With the critic acting as prosecutor, judge, and jury, it is perhaps to make the strongest and most partisan case possible to readers who are themselves put in the place of the jury in a court of law or political tribunal. But what may very well be a strong case for a prosecutor or political militant is not necessarily the most convincing critical reading of either literary texts or complex political issues. I would argue that reading Camus without a prosecutor's mentality produces very different results from the verdicts of his harshest critics. This book urges readers, whether committed to postcolonial theories or not, to read Camus critically before, and even instead of, judging him.

Camus may not have found realistic solutions to the political conflicts of his own time or provided adequate answers to today's divisive political issues, but his writings raise fundamental questions concerning justice and the limits of political actions that can and should be taken in its pursuit. I believe that it is time we begin to take such questions seriously. I am thus proposing that Camus be read with an open mind concerning his relation to and perspective on colonialism in general and colonial Algeria in particular, neither mystifying his undeniable nostalgia for his "true country," his particular form of *"nostalgérie,"* nor dismissing the importance of his critique of both FLN terrorism and the French army's systematic use of torture, nor ignoring or undervaluing his insistent and passionate demands for justice for all Algerians. And above all, that before judging and attacking his writings, readers consider seriously his idea, no matter how unrealistic it might be, especially given what actually occurred in Algeria, of a hybrid, multicultural Algerian people and its implications for the postcolonial era or condition in which we now live. By focusing on the place of Algeria in Camus' work and "the Algerian" in him, and insisting especially on how he conceives of and deals with the issue of justice in the context of severe colonial oppression, I hope that what I would call Camus' defense of the rights of the oppressed will be better appreciated and his political essays and literary texts no longer treated lightly or dismissed. After rereading his political essays and literary texts, I am convinced now, even more than when reading *The First Man* for the first time, that Camus' is a voice to which we urgently need to listen once again. Or perhaps really for the first time.

Stranger, who could know what this word means. Stranger, to acknowledge that everything is foreign to me [*Étranger, avouer que tout
m'est étranger*].

—Albert Camus, *Carnets* (March 1940)

In a universe suddenly divested of illusions and lights, man feels like a
stranger.

—Albert Camus, *The Myth of Sisyphus*

The entire bureaucracy, the entire court system, all industry hears and
uses the colonizer's language. Likewise, highway markings, railroad
station signs, street signs, and receipts make the colonized feel like a
stranger in his own country.

—Albert Memmi, *The Colonizer and the Colonized*

CHAPTER ONE

The Place of the Other

Colonial Anonymity

> Colonization creates the colonized just as we have seen that it creates the colonizer.
>
> —Albert Memmi, *The Colonizer and the Colonized*

In his celebrated study of colonialism, *The Colonizer and the Colonized*, Albert Memmi describes how the colonial system deprives colonized peoples of their history, culture, rights, dignity, identity, and their very being:

> The colonized enjoys none of the attributes of citizenship; neither his own, which is dependent, contested, and smothered, nor that of the colonizer. He can hardly adhere to one or claim the other. Not having his just place in the community, not enjoying the rights of a modern citizen, not being subject to his normal duties, not voting, not bearing the burden of community affairs, he cannot feel like a true citizen. . . . Nationally and civically he is only what the colonizer is not.
>
> (96 [116–117])

To be what the colonizer is not only to be reduced to a state of political and cultural inferiority, both in the everyday lived reality of colonialism and in the colonialist imagination. To be what the other is not is in fact *not to be*.[1]

Postcolonial critics have for some time focused on examples of negative, stereotypical representations of colonized peoples in the literature of the colonial period in order to emphasize the nefarious effects of colonialism. But the absence of developed, individualized Arab characters in French colonial literature has also been considered symptomatic of colonialist values and prejudices. Militantly anticolonialist critics such as Connor Cruise O'Brien have in the case of Albert Camus treated the absence of individualized Arab characters in his novels and stories that take place in Algeria as indications of Camus' alleged colonialist sympathies and evidence that in his fictions he "implicitly denies the colonial reality and sustains the colonial fiction" (O'Brien, *Albert Camus*, 23). In the few instances when Arab characters do appear in Camus's novels or short stories, they function as insignificant elements of the décor, faceless, nameless, and anonymous, providing a small amount of "local color" to the stories but nothing more. Blending into the North African landscape, they are all easily ignored or forgotten, given no more importance in Camus' fictional universe than they had for French colonialists in colonialist society in general.

Camus' alleged *literary failure* to give an individual voice or identity to Arab characters in his novels or short stories or present them as autonomous human beings on a par with the French characters is thus taken by O'Brien and critics who have followed his lead to be a serious *political fault* as well. This is because the anonymity of the admittedly few Arab characters that appear in Camus' work—the two most important examples being "the Arab" who is murdered by Meursault in *The Stranger* and the unnamed "Arab prisoner" in Camus' short story "The Guest"—is treated as proof that in Camus' fictional universe Arab characters are not just *other* but also *inferior* to the point of being almost nonexistent. Or, as O'Brien succinctly puts it, readers are encouraged to consider the Arab character in *The Stranger* as "not quite a man. . . . The reader does not quite feel that Meursault has killed a man. He has killed an Arab" (25–26). Such criticisms, no matter how sweeping, cannot be simply dismissed, however, since even though the literary and political significance of the "evidence" used to indict Camus can be debated, the facts themselves seem undeniable.

The fundamental question raised by O'Brien's attack is thus whether the anonymity of the very limited number of Arab characters in Camus' fictions should be considered the sign of Camus' deep-rooted colonialist sympathies and prejudices, of his own acceptance of the inferior status of Arabs within French colonial society. Can it legitimately be used as proof that Camus supported both the myth and reality of colonialism and that he thus believed that the French political, economic, and cultural domination of Algeria and Algerians was legitimate and should continue? In order to answer this question, at the very least it would seem necessary first to analyze the specific place and function of the Arab characters in the fictional contexts in which they appear before drawing general conclusions about their political significance. Hastily drawn conclusions and sweeping generalizations about elements of a novel taken out of context risk distorting or simply missing the most important political implications of the work itself—perhaps even in some cases sufficiently distorting the work to make it representative of a political position it in fact opposes.

O'Brien does acknowledge that there are important differences between Camus' political journalism and his fictions: "Camus never did come to terms with the situation in question [colonialism in Algeria], and his journalistic writings are the record of his painful and protracted failure to do so . . . imaginatively he comes much closer to it" (26). To "come to terms with the situation" in Algeria, especially after the FLN's organization of armed resistance in 1954, does not for O'Brien, however, mean denouncing colonial injustices or advocating democratic reforms, which Camus regularly did in his many journalistic essays and editorials on Algeria from 1939 until 1958. It means for him rather something very different: actively supporting the FLN and its armed struggle for Algerian independence, which, it is true, Camus categorically refused to do.[2] What is missing from O'Brien's argument, however, is a sustained analysis of either what Camus actually wrote in his political essays or of how Camus' fictions "come closer" to doing what Camus' political essays allegedly never do. In fact, O'Brien's brief summaries of Camus' fictions tend rather to emphasize how they too "failed" and ultimately also constitute expressions of colonialist ideology.

O'Brien was not the first critic of colonialism, however, to claim that Camus' first published novel was in some way symptomatic of *pied-noir* attitudes toward Arabs. The celebrated historian Pierre Nora had already made such a claim about *The Stranger* in his study of *Les Français d'Algérie*, published in 1961, shortly before the end of the Algerian War.[3] In this early work, Nora analyzes—and given the terminology he uses, it would not be exaggerated to say "psychoanalyzes"—what he characterizes as the "delirium" of the entire European or *pied-noir* population of Algeria (46). The basis for this delirium is what he claims to have discovered in each and every member of the *pied-noir* community: the same deep-rooted, violent, racist hostility toward all Arabs. All *pieds-noirs*, without exception, are thus presented by Nora as being profoundly racist, even if their true feelings toward Arabs, he also argues, remain for the most part deeply repressed in their individual and collective unconscious, unacknowledged and un-acknowledgeable because of their violent nature. But they are nonetheless sufficiently evident in their behavior traits for Nora to observe and ana-lyze them while he was in Algeria teaching and compiling evidence for his study.

Nora makes a forceful case for the existence of all *pieds-noirs'* repressed racist hatred of Arabs, and his own portrait of the typical Algerian colo-nialist, a portrait that in many ways makes Memmi's portrait of even the most militant of the colonialists who accept colonialism seem tame, pro-vides the evidence to support his sweeping claim. For example, Nora treats the generally recognized openness and generosity of *pieds-noirs* as the op-posite of what it appears to be. For him, it is not generosity at all, but rather a symptom of a latent hostility directed against all internal and external outsiders, not just the Arabs living in Algeria, but also the French of main-land France. Surface traits of warmth, generosity, and hospitality, therefore, are considered by Nora to be nothing more than screens, symptoms of the desire to win the outsider (including the Parisian historian/analyst) over to their cause, a way of hiding under their apparent generosity and good will their true violent feelings and an entire reactionary political agenda.[4]

The picture of *pieds-noirs* that emerges from Nora's study, then, is of French men and women living a deeply divided life. In reality, they live in a French colony in which the overwhelming majority of inhabitants are Arab or Berber, but in their imaginations they live in a world inhabited exclusively by French *pieds-noirs*. Rather than confront what he claims are their deep feelings of racial hatred, Nora alleges that *pieds-noirs* flee from them: "Victims of troubled affectivity, Europeans have repressed the vio-lence of their feelings through a collective decision not to recognize the Arabs. Because of the colonial situation, they act simply as if Arabs did not exist" (184). They thus relate to Arabs not as individuals but as anonymous, interchangeable components of the collectivity referred to as "*les Arabes*" or "*les Musulmans*," which Nora treats as being symptomatic of their racism and hatred of the colonized Other.

The anonymity of Arabs in the *pied-noir* world is thus in Nora's analysis the screen for an even more violent, genocidal hatred, from which he claims no *pied-noir* is exempt:

> There is not one Frenchman who does not caress in the shadows of his unconscious this idea [genocide] as the extreme point of sadistic perversion. But they do not dare admit their desire. . . . Realizing this dream is impossible. As soon as the idea barely scratches the surface of consciousness, immediately the respect of metropolitan values of liberty, equality, and fraternity takes over. The French civilizing mission and French grandeur censor the desire for genocide that survives only as an absurd and amusing hypothesis.
>
> (187)

Nora does not explain how he has been able to penetrate this deeply into even "the shadows of [each French Algerian's] unconscious," especially since he acknowledges that the desire for genocide he claims to have discovered there, as soon as it begins to move toward the surface of consciousness, is immediately repressed by a French super-ego that represents the equalitarian values and ideals of Republican France. For Nora, the repressed desire for genocide nevertheless constitutes the horrible hidden truth of both colonialism in general and the desires of every French colonialist in particular. His study of the French of Algeria thus describes the profound identity crisis of a *pied-noir* community torn between the high equalitarian ideals of the French Republic and the repressed primitive colonialist desire for genocide.

Nora's study has a strong anthropological dimension and constitutes in large part an exploration of the customs and thinking of a people he presents as being completely "foreign" to the authentic French republican community of mainland France. *Pieds-noirs* appear in his study as a strange, exotic, and extremely dangerous tribe. They are a people with a smile on their face but murder in their hearts. They may claim to be participating in the "civilizing mission" of the "natives" of Algeria, but they are the ones who in fact lack civilization. They may be "French," but in name only. His condemnation not just of the colonialist system but of the *pied-noir* community in general is thus sweeping and uncompromising. *Pieds-noirs* in Nora's description are as barbaric and uncivilized as he claims "Arabs" are in the minds of the racist *pied-noir* community whose deep racist hatred he repeatedly brings to the surface and analyzes. *Pieds-noirs* are, in fact, everything the French are not—or at least everything they should not be—just as "the Arabs" are allegedly represented in the collective psyche of *pieds-noirs* as either nonexistent or the hated other, the opposite of what the *pieds-noirs* imagine themselves to be.

Near the end of his book, Nora presents what could be considered the most important piece of "evidence" for his case study of French Algerians: Camus' *The Stranger*. Nora claims that Camus' "genius" in *The Stranger* is to have succeeded in revealing what Nora rediscovered almost two decades later: the hidden desires of an entire *pied-noir* community, of all *French* Algerians without exception. Camus is treated in this way as a kind of "native informer," not just because of his modest birth, which makes him both economically and politically more disinterested in colonialism than the rich and powerful *colons* who benefit enormously from their privileged status in colonial Algeria. But it is also because Nora considers Camus to be a talented writer who is "exceptionally sensitive and cultivated" and thus "predisposed to sense the truth that his compatriots masked from themselves" (190).

The Stranger, which Nora characterizes as "the only great work written in Algeria by the only great French writer of Algeria," represents for him nothing less than "the exact reflection of the lived feelings of the French presence in Algeria" (190). Nora, like Freud, for whom poets delineated the "royal way to the unconscious," thus treats this literary work as a dream— or rather, a nightmare—that reveals the repressed truths of colonialist desire. And it is precisely because the work is a product of the author's imagination that it avoids the repression of the French-Republican super-ego. It is thus under the cover of fiction that the truth of colonialist desire and the colonialists' collective unconscious comes to the surface. What is most real is what is most imaginary, and thus the truth of the political is discovered in the fiction and literary imagination of the most sensitive and talented French-Algerian writer of his era.

For Nora, the most important "lived feeling" expressed in the novel is the desire for murder, which he finds just under the surface of almost every aspect of life in colonialist Algeria. By narrating the murder of an unnamed Arab by a French Algerian, Nora claims that Camus' novel serves a collective therapeutic function and succeeds in "liberat[ing] a latent aggressiveness" appropriate to "every Frenchman in Algeria" (191). Nora also argues that *The Stranger* constitutes a collective admission of guilt, "the troubling confession of a historical culpability which takes on the appearance of an anticipation" (191)—a phrase quoted by O'Brien to support his indictment of Camus as a colonialist writer, which is not Nora's purpose in his own study. Camus, it would seem, because of his rich imagination and talents as a writer, succeeds in Nora's estimation in expressing in his novel a generalized guilt that would only be felt long after the novel was in fact written—not until the very end of or after the Algerian War, and perhaps not then or even today.

O'Brien and Nora thus agree on the clinical/political evidence the novel provides, even if each uses the same evidence for different purposes. O'Brien uses it to indict Camus for being a colonialist writer who accepts the myth of and chief justification for colonialism, the superiority of the colonizers over the colonized. Nora finds in the novel evidence that allows him to indict an entire *pied-noir* community for its violent hatred of the colonized, while at the same time praising Camus' "genius" and honesty for expressing the blood lust of his people and portraying their guilt for their unjust treatment of Arabs—and even worse, for their repressed desire for genocide. But whether it is to Camus' credit or detriment, Nora and O'Brien agree that *The Stranger*, given the centrality to its plot of the murder of an anonymous Arab character, conveys in one form or another colonialist values and desires. It is for both of them a profoundly colonialist novel, with Meursault, the stranger, the embodiment of the colonizer, and his situation and actions in the novel representative of the attitudes and desires of an entire *pied-noir* community. The question that needs to be asked of such interpretations, however, no matter how much one might agree with their powerful denunciations of colonialism, is whether the novel as a whole really sustains them. Everything depends on what it means in the novel to be a stranger to society, an Other—and perhaps even more important, on the significance of the fact that Meursault is condemned to death in the novel not for the murder of an anonymous Arab but for occupying the place of the Other.

The Stranger Retried

Given the serious nature of the claims made by Nora, O'Brien, and numerous other critics who follow their lead, it would be impossible today to read Camus' novel and ignore the problem of how it relates to the colonialist context in which it was written and which it portrays.[5] In their haste to indict Camus, however, critics have tended to underplay or simply ignore the devastating picture *The Stranger* provides of what Memmi has called the "colonial relation," a hierarchical relation of oppression, forced dependency, and violence that is as evident in the microstructures determining everyday relations between colonizers and colonized as in the macrostructure determining the political, economic, and cultural domination of the colonizers over the colonized.[6] This banal, everyday violence is abundantly evident, for example, in the first part of the novel, in the growing hostility between Meursault's French friends and the Arabs who are following them. It culminates in Meursault's murder of an unnamed Arab on the beach. The murder may be depicted in the novel from Meursault's perspective as an unplanned, spontaneous, uncontrolled act, but without the sequence of violent events between two opposed groups, clearly identified in the novel as French and Arab, which sets the stage for the murder, it would never have occurred. And if it had not taken place, then Meursault would not have been arrested, tried, convicted, and himself condemned to death. To focus almost exclusively on the fact that in the novel a *pied-noir* named Meursault kills an unnamed Arab is to seriously reduce the complexity and interest of the novel and distort what it actually reveals about colonial Algeria—which in fact turns out to be quite different from what Nora, O'Brien, and others influenced by their interpretations have claimed.

The trial itself is one the most famous of all literature and has been analyzed repeatedly; the legal issues are as clear as they could be. An Arab with a knife in his hand is shot on a beach outside of Algiers and dies. There is no doubt that the main character and first-person narrator of the novel, Meursault himself, pulled the trigger of the gun that killed the man, or that after shooting his victim once, he shot him four more times after he had fallen. These are facts no one can dispute, whatever Meursault's motives and whatever the extenuating circumstances might have been, since we learn these facts from Meursault himself. We have no reason not to believe him, since his honesty and directness have been well established in the novel long before the shooting is narrated. Meursault is as reliable a first-person narrator as could be imagined, a trustworthy witness with no reason to lie about what happened. We thus accept his words as true, especially since he clearly admits his responsibility for the crime.[7]

The death of an anonymous Arab is of course crucial to the plot of the novel, but not because it is central to Meursault's interrogation both before and during his trial, which makes up the second half of the novel. Even though the shooting is the reason for Meursault's arrest, the victim of the crime and the crime itself are largely ignored or forgotten during the legal proceedings. And for decades, this paradox or inconsistency—the relative unimportance of the murder itself for Meursault's trial and conviction—has either simply been ignored by critics or explained away in various and conflicting ways. It would seem undeniable, however, no matter how the murder is explained, that Meursault would never have been arrested and tried had he not shot and killed another man. It is equally true that he would never have been considered a victim of the judicial system had the murder of "the Arab" not been largely ignored during the trial and if he had been judged and convicted for the crime he actually committed.

The more innocent Meursault is, in the eyes of the readers of the novel, the more guilty the society that condemns him to death must be, for only a petty, hypocritical, repressive, and unjust society could sentence a man to death for something as trivial as not crying at his mother's funeral. As far-fetched as it might seem when the reason for his condemnation is phrased this starkly, Camus himself strongly encouraged such a reading, when in his 1955 preface to an American translation of *The Stranger* he wrote:

> I summarized *The Stranger* a long time ago, with a remark that I admit was highly paradoxical: "In our society any man who does not weep at his mother's funeral runs the risk of being sentenced to death." I only meant that the hero of my book is condemned because he does not play the game. . . . He refuses to lie. . . . One would there-

fore not be much mistaken to read *The Stranger* as the story of a man who, without any heroics, agrees to die for the truth."[8]

To refuse to play the social game and to die for the truth could of course be considered commendable, even noble, acts, certainly far different than not expressing emotion at one's own mother's funeral. But it is still necessary to ask *what* truth Meursault actually dies for. The answer to this question will turn out to be very different both from what Camus' own statements would lead one to believe and from what most critics have alleged.[9]

It is crucial first of all to recognize that the narrative logic (or illogic) of the novel demands that the murder be committed and then ignored. For the murder is only a pretext for Meursault being arrested, interrogated, tried for a capital offense, convicted, and sentenced to death. Without the murder, his monotonous life, no matter how honest he was and how many social games he refused to play, would never have come to the attention of the police and never provided sufficient material for a novel. The murder once committed must then be forgotten, however, since it is only by having his crime ignored during his trial that Meursault, who is responsible for the death of another man, can be convicted for other, more superficial reasons and transformed into a victim of the judicial system and society as a whole. This is how an inconsequential clerk with few if any ambitions, only the most uncomplicated natural desires, and nonthreatening behavior becomes, in the eyes of the court, a serious threat to society and then, in Camus' words, a martyr to the truth, a rebel, and the very symbol of authentic revolt. This narrative (il)logic and legal absurdity, however, disguise (which is also a way of revealing) a historical-political insight of a very different nature and one that concerns not just the hypocrisy of modern society in general but more specifically the crimes and injustices of French colonial Algeria (and, as we shall see, of Vichy France as well).

Meursault's is a strange trial. During the proceedings, the judge and jury have to be reminded that a crime has been committed. But this is not done by the prosecutor, but rather by Meursault's own defense lawyer, who evokes the murder as a central part of his *defense* of Meursault. It is as if Meursault would have had a better chance of winning his case, or at least of not receiving a death sentence, if he had been tried for having killed a man, rather than for the crime for which he is in fact judged. As if Meursault could only be condemned to die if the crime he actually committed was largely ignored. And vice versa, that he could be declared innocent only if the crime of murder was the central issue in his trial. This is the strange and perverse logic of justice that the novel presents, and it is one of the principal points the novel makes about the fundamental injustice of the law—especially in a colonialist context.

The law has its own story to tell, and it silences or simply ignores the stories it does not want to hear, stories that do not conform to its protocols, stories that complicate proceedings and thus cannot be used to prove guilt beyond a reasonable doubt. These are stories that reveal guilt and innocence at the same time, not just of the defendant, but also of the prosecutors, the judge, the jury, the witnesses called to testify, the journalists covering the trial, and the spectators present in the courtroom. As Camus wrote in his essay "Reflections on the Guillotine," every society has the criminals it deserves, and no one is ever absolutely guilty or absolutely innocent. This is one of his arguments against capital punishment. *The Stranger* is already an indication of his conviction that no system of justice can be considered just or legitimate if it has recourse to this ultimate form of punishment, which Camus calls "the most premeditated of murders."[10]

The Function of Anonymity

As O'Brien observes, Arab characters in *The Stranger* are not given names other than the generic "Arab" and are portrayed as menacing enemies of the French characters in the novel—if not enemies of society as a whole, or at least the fringe Meursault and his friends represent. Arab characters remain nameless throughout the novel, both in life and, as concerns the murder victim, in death as well, since the victim's name is never revealed during the court proceedings. O'Brien is thus right to insist on the fact that Meursault does not kill a man with a name and identity; he rather kills "an Arab." This obvious point cannot and should not be ignored or denied, even if the sweeping conclusions O'Brien draws from the Arab character's anonymity need to be analyzed more carefully than they have been by the critics who have followed his lead.

The general problem of "Arab anonymity" is compounded in the novel by the fact that one of the unnamed Arab characters, the victim, plays an essential role in the development of the plot of the novel. Because he is shot by Meursault, not just once but five times, the murder has all the appearances of being a deliberate, premeditated execution, and not an act committed in self-defense. On the basis of these "facts," a case could be made that Meursault deserves the harshest punishment the legal system provides for premeditated murder: the guillotine. Meursault, however, describing the incident in the same neutral tone and with the same directness, simplicity, and naiveté as he describes his mother's funeral at the beginning of the novel, his affair with Marie, and every other aspect of his life, portrays the killing rather as the consequence of a chance encounter and the effects of the burning midday sun on his blurred consciousness.[11] So unless the sincerity and reliability of this first-person narrator are questioned in terms of every other aspect of his life, even those observations and admissions he makes throughout the novel that critics generally accept as true, there is no reason to disbelieve Meursault in this instance either. Within the fictional universe of the novel, his testimony has truth value, since he is a man with little to say but who, when he does talk, usually says only what he truly feels. He speaks the truth, as it is defined by his feelings—or by the absence of feeling.

During his trial, the only legally relevant statement Meursault makes in his own defense is to assert that he "had no intention of killing the Arab" (129 [1198]). He tries to explain that it was "because of the sun" that the murder happened, but having said this, he is immediately aware of how ridiculous his words sound when they provoke laughter in the courtroom (130 [1198]). But as ridiculous as it might seem in a court of law, this is precisely how Meursault, first-person narrator, describes the accident/murder in the novel before his trial, as it were, "as it was happening." He relates that he felt as if the sun was attacking him with its blinding rays of light and that he tried both to flee its attacks and defend himself against them. Thus, as a consequence of an unbearable North African sun, an unnamed Arab tragically dies.[12] There are also other, more legally convincing extenuating circumstances—especially the previous scuffle on the beach when his friend Raymond was wounded by the same knife used to threaten Meursault—so it would not be difficult to imagine that such a crime could have and should logically have been treated as manslaughter rather than premeditated murder—and thus not as a capital offense. And this would be true whether the victim of the crime was French or Arab, but in a colonial context, especially in the latter case.[13]

Meursault's ridiculous but truthful explanation for the murder is of course laughed at and ignored, even by his own defense lawyer—although Meursault will be condemned to die for even more absurd reasons. It is clear, however, that Meursault's destiny is to die—not for the crime he actually committed, whatever his motivations for shooting the gun and thus his responsibility for the murder—but for entirely different reasons.[14] Meursault's destiny and that of his Arab victim are in fact both tragic and inextricably intertwined from the moment Meursault wanders back to the spot on the beach where the original fight took place and fires the gun, killing a man whose fault is to be at the wrong place at the wrong time. Meursault's fault (and guilt) will turn out to be the same as his victims, as will be his fate.

Before the Law: Guilty and Innocent at the Same Time

> What a fate, to be condemned to work for a firm where the smallest omission gives at once rise to the greatest suspicion!
>
> —Franz Kafka, "The Metamorphosis"

A crucial reversal occurs in the second part of the novel: Meursault's political condition and social identity are radically transformed after his arrest. No longer ignored as an inconsequential French clerk living on the margins of society who follows the same routine every day and from time to time enjoys simple pleasures, he discovers that his very identity is being questioned when, as if in a story by Kafka, he finds himself before the law, guilty until proven innocent—and guilty even then. To be before the law is to be the victim of justice, whether one has actually committed the crime for which one has been accused or not. In a colonial society, it is structurally the situation of the anonymous, not the named, of indigenous colonized subjects rather than citizens, of Arabs such as Meursault's victim rather than Frenchmen such as Meursault. Arrested and accused of murder, Meursault loses his privileged place as a French citizen in colonial society and over the course of the second half of the novel is increasingly identified with and put in the place of the colonized Arab, the anonymous, indigenous Other.

To be before the law and thus subject to the judgment of society, of those who judge rather than those who are judged, is in *The Stranger* to enter the world populated almost exclusively by Arabs. Not only is this exemplified by the cell into which Meursault is first placed after his arrest, in which he is the only Frenchman. It is also emphasized when Meursault describes his fiancée Marie's first visit to the prison, when alongside a row of other visitors she is obliged to speak to him through a grill: "On my side of the bars were about a dozen other prisoners, Arabs for the most part. On Marie's side were mostly Moorish women" (90 [1178]). As a prisoner accused of a capital crime, Meursault loses not just his freedom but has his birthright and identity as a French citizen challenged. He loses the right to be on the French side of the bars colonial society erects not just between free men and prisoners but also between French citizens and Arab subjects. His place behind bars is in a world almost completely populated by Arabs.

Unlike the Arab prisoners and the colonized in general, however, Meursault's loss of the privilege of being French and thus on the other side of the bars could be temporary, for in principle it would be possible for him to regain his birthright, his identity, his civil rights, his freedom, and his privileges, as limited as they might be, by being declared innocent of murder and either set free or convicted of a much less serious crime, one that would not put his right to French identity into question. All that would have been needed was to show that there were extenuating circumstances for the murder and thus a justification for his act. But then the absurd nature of colonial "justice" would not be exposed as dramatically as it is in the novel. For in *The Stranger* the most profound change in Meursault's existence brought about by the murder is not really his loss of his freedom, to which he fairly quickly becomes accustomed. It is rather the loss of his birthright, which he must now prove in a court of law that he truly deserves. He must in court justify his very existence before a judge and jury and prove that he is equal to and of the same nature as those judging him. He must prove nothing less than that he is truly "French."

The possibility of being declared innocent, released from prison, and returning to French society, the possibility of becoming "French" once again, with all the rights and privileges granted to French citizens but denied to indigenous French subjects, is in fact presented to Meursault by the investigating judge in his attempts to convert him and save him from his fate. Meursault is a subject for conversion (or in colonialist terms, assimilation), which means that were he to declare his belief in the *Christian* God, he would regain his status as a *French* Algerian. Meursault's refusal to express a belief in Christ and accept the repentance offered him by the judge condemns him long before he is actually judged and sentenced in court. In rejecting Christianity, and when he later aggressively attacks a priest in his cell, he is in effect refusing French identity itself and the possibility of being assimilated (back) into French society, the only option, other than the acceptance of anonymity or nonbeing, of those whom the colonialist relation determines to be indigenous foreigners, strangers in their own land—all those who are not French "naturally" but have to prove that they are worthy of becoming French. For if Meursault will not accept Christianity, in the eyes of the judge and colonial society in general he clearly is not and cannot ever be French. He is rather treated like a Muslim (or Jew) and considered the dangerous enemy of Christian France: "Mr. Antichrist" (88 [1176]), as the judge scornfully calls him.[15]

This is why determining Meursault's guilt or innocence in terms of the actual crime of murder is not the central issue of his trial. The trial is staged rather to prove that Meursault is not French and in fact is not even human, not in legal terms but, more importantly, in moral, religious, and metaphysical terms. During his trial, Meursault is judged not for what he *did* but for what he *is*, for what the judicial system represents him as being or, over the course of his trial, transforms him into being through the prosecutor's reconstruction of his life and the stories told by witnesses. He is judged for his "soul," dark as it is claimed to be, for his strange "nature" or inner being, more than for his actions. He is thus not really condemned at all, as Camus claims, "for not playing the game" or for telling the truth—he in fact plays some if not most of society's games quite effectively, and he does not always tell the truth, lying to the police, for example, to provide an excuse for his dubious friend Raymond after he has beaten his Arab mistress.[16] Rather he is put to death for being inhuman, "a monster," one of "them," an alien enemy of the collective "us." It is above all for his threatening alterity, his strange[r]ness, that he dies.

During the trial and before he is sentenced, Meursault's individuality, whatever little there is of it and whatever it might be argued to be before he is arrested, is usurped. The trial from the start takes place largely in his absence, without his involvement, as if he were a spectator rather than the person on trial. When he is told by his defense lawyer "to shut up" for his own good, he reflects:

> It seemed somehow as if the whole case was being treated without me. Everything was happening without my intervention. My fate was being determined without asking for my say. From time to time I felt like interrupting everyone and saying: "After all, who is being accused here anyway? It's a serious matter to be the accused. And I have something to say." However, on second thoughts, I had nothing to say.
> (124, trans. mod. [1195])

Everyone has something to say about the person being judged except that person himself. And when he has something to say, it is considered irrelevant: no one listens and no one understands what he is saying. His words are given no weight, his explanations, such as they are, are ridiculed and ignored. It is as if he is speaking a foreign language no one else involved in the trial understands. A translated version of his life is put on trial and judged, but without his direct participation. Someone other than him, someone foreign to him, the stranger he has become is judged in his place.

The process of the distancing and even the elimination of Meursault from both his trial and his life is completed when his own lawyer in defending him speaks in his place, using the first-person "I," the "I" that dominates the entire novel and gives the novel the tone of an authentic, intimate, first-person testimony. Told that it is normal courtroom procedure for lawyers to speak not just in defense of their clients but *as their clients*, Meursault thinks: "I thought that this was to exclude me further from the case, to reduce me to nothing, and in a certain sense to substitute the lawyer for me. But I think by then I was already very far away from this courtroom. And besides, my lawyer struck me as ridiculous" (130, trans. mod. [1198–1199]). Meursault is condemned and will die as a man deprived by the law of his individuality, of his subjectivity, and even of the right to say "I." He dies as a man accused of one crime and judged, convicted, and sentenced for an entirely different kind of "crime," the crime of being *Other*.

He is condemned for what in the context of colonialist Algeria (and Vichy France) is his "race."

"Race" or the Soul of the Other

When I claim that Meursault is condemned to die because of his "race," I mean that he is condemned for what the court has decided he is, what "society," a particular society at a particular time and place, determines he is, no matter what he actually is, what he says, or what he has done. He is what the legal proceedings define him as being, and once defined, what he will continue to be until his death. In the eyes of the court and the general public, he is a monster, society's other, belonging to a species or race different from the "norm" or the "normal." "Race" in this sense is thus a construction that is determined by social, cultural, religious, political, and legal institutions, procedures, and authorities, which in the novel are those of colonial Algeria. "Race" is the collective identity that is projected or imposed on individuals and groups, which is then used to explain their behavior and values (or lack of values) and allow authorities to distinguish whether an individual is one of "us" or one of "them." And this same "fictive ethnicity" is used in courts of law as evidence of the guilt of an accused—who, no matter his crime, is in fact judged to be guilty of existing, of being who he is.[17]

After being interrogated at length by the prosecutor, not about his crime but about how he acted during his mother's funeral, Meursault begins to realize that he had become an "object of hatred" for the courtroom, not for having killed another man, whether intentionally or not, but for being the inhuman, immoral monster the prosecutor has accused him of being. He knows he will be found guilty, that he already is guilty in the eyes of the court and society in general, not for what he has done but for what he is, the object of their collective hatred: "I had a foolish desire to cry because I felt how much I was loathed by all these people. . . . I felt something then that was stirring up the courtroom, and for the first time I understood that I was guilty" (112, trans. mod. [1189]). Because he is feared and loathed as a monstrous Other, the negative of what it is to be French in Algerian colonial society and even the negative of all humanity, he is by definition guilty, no matter what he has actually done. As the extremist nationalist anti-Semite Maurice Barrès wrote concerning Alfred Dreyfus, he did not need to know if or why Dreyfus betrayed France, since Barrès knew "from his race" that Dreyfus was capable of betraying France and thus guilty of the crime whether he actually committed it or not.[18] Meursault's guilt is determined by the same perverse racist logic.

"Race," according to this logic, can be manifested in "biological" traits such as "blood," the color of skin, the shape of the nose, the texture of hair, and so on, or, as was the case for Barrès and other French nationalists of the late nineteenth and early twentieth centuries, in cultural factors such as religion, language, traditions, customs, and beliefs. In fact, with emphasis in different contexts given to either "biology" or culture, race is in fact always characterized by a combination or confusion of both "blood" and culture at the same time. In *The Stranger*, Meursault's "race" is constructed during his trial in terms of social-cultural norms, religion, and ultimately metaphysics—by the determination of nothing less than the nature of his soul. Or rather by the absence of a soul. Ultimately, race always comes down to the question not of the blood but of the soul of the Other.

The image of Meursault's "soul," which is the foundation on which the case made against him is constructed, is described by the prosecuting attorney in the following way:

> I tried to keep listening because the prosecutor began to speak of my soul. He said that he'd studied it closely and found nothing. . . . He said that in truth I had no soul at all and there was nothing human about me, not one of the moral principles found in human hearts, could be found in me. "No doubt," he added, "we should not reproach him with this. We cannot blame him for lacking what was never in his power to acquire. But in a court of law, the wholly negative principle of tolerance must give way to the more difficult but loftier principle of justice. Especially when the lack of heart such as is found in this man becomes an abyss into which the entire society can slip."
>
> (127, trans. mod. [1197])

By demonstrating that he lacks an essential human trait, although through no "fault" of his own but because of a deficiency he was born with and that remains in him, a deficiency that defines him as Other and by nature criminal, the court is called in the name of "justice" (rather than tolerance) to judge this lack as severely as possible. For the well-being of society it is asked to execute him "in the name of the French people" (135 [1201]). For French colonial society to be safe, Meursault can no longer be allowed to exist; it is as simple and grotesque as that.

The Stranger thus exposes the fundamental injustice of any legal system in which the death penalty is imposed and dramatizes what could be called the colonialist or racist dimension of what Camus called absolute systems of justice, where who or what you are, or rather, who society through its legal system defines you as being, ultimately determines your innocence or guilt. Through a tragic twist of colonialist fate, Meursault's destiny and that of the nameless Arab he murdered on the beach are inextricably intertwined at the end of the novel. For to be condemned to die in the name of the French people for *what he is*, no matter what crime he actually committed, is in fact to be judged and to die in colonial Algeria not as a French citizen but as an indigenous Arab subject. Meursault thus dies not for the truth and as the fictional embodiment of the absurd antihero who refuses to play society's games, but because he is judged to have no soul, to be not fully human. He eagerly looks forward to his own execution, though, expressing the desire to be hated by the very people to whose community he once belonged and who have judged him as no longer being worthy of belonging: "For everything to be accomplished, for me to feel less lonely, all that remained was to hope that on the day of my execution there should be a huge crowd of spectators and that they should greet me with cries of hatred" (154, trans. mod. [1211–1212]). Meursault in this way fully assumes the fate assigned to him by the court. He dies and wants to die in the place of the Other, as a stranger to the French, the negative image of what they are or imagine themselves to be. He dies and wants to die in the place of and as an Arab.

The Stranger was published in occupied Paris approximately two years after the Décret Crémieux was rescinded by Maréchal Pétain on October 7, 1940. Article II of Pétain's proclamation reads: "The political rights of indigenous Jews in the three departments of Algeria are regulated by the texts that determine the political rights of indigenous Algerian Muslims."[19] This meant that Algerian Jews under Vichy law were once again considered to be "indigenous subjects" rather than French citizens. In a novel published in occupied Paris in 1942, Meursault, as a hated indigenous Other, thus also dies as a Jew.

The colonial city revived and aggravated the social and spatial differences between communities and created the chasm that separated the affluent from the destitute, the center from the suburbs, and French citizens from native subjects.

—Omar Carlier, "Violences"[1]

I lived on the edge of an Arab neighborhood, at one of those hidden frontiers [*frontières de nuit*], at once invisible and almost impassable: the segregation there was as efficacious as it was subtle.

—Jacques Derrida, *Monolingualism of the Other*

From the banks of Africa where I was born, aided by the distance, you see better the face of Europe, and you know it is not pretty.

—Albert Camus, "Entretien sur la révolte" (February 15, 1952)

CHAPTER TWO

Colonial Borders

National Identities—When Numbers Don't Add Up

"Algérie, France: une ou deux nations?"("Algeria, France: One or Two Nations?")—this is the title of an essay by Etienne Balibar that asks what would appear on the surface to be a ridiculously simple historical-political question.[2] For if until 1962 France claimed and the international community generally recognized that Algeria was an integral part of the French Republic, the only possible answer to the question since independence would have to be that Algeria and France constitute *two nations*, for not even the most reactionary ex-*colon* or nostalgic *pied-noir* could deny that Algeria and France today constitute two separate, independent states.

For Balibar, such an answer, no matter how obvious, is inadequate and even misleading. This is because in a postcolonial context simple addition of national identities increasingly does not work, since what is being added are not only recognized national entities with determined geographical-political borders, but also shared sociopolitical spaces that cannot be adequately delineated by exterior borders. Balibar thus questions whether simple math (1 nation + 1 nation = 2 nations) can accurately account for the complexity of either social space or its historicity, and he provocatively asks whether "the spatio-temporal or socio-temporal idea of an irreversible duality [might be] the sign, not of decolonization, but rather of the persistent colonization of history?" (73). The "persistent colonization of history" would ironically result from the desire to break definitively with the colonial past and recognize the autonomy and integrity of a previously colonized people. Since Balibar's purpose is obviously not to attempt to legitimate after the fact either colonialism in general or the French colonization of Algeria in particular, his essay's title is intended rather to call attention to how, as an effect of their common colonialist history, Algeria and France both continue in the postcolonial era to be not just externally influenced but also internally constituted by each other.

1 + 1 does not equal 2, then, if long after Algerian independence each of the two nations continues to contribute internally to the constitution and identity of the other, if each constitutes a "foreign body" within the other that is at the same time an undeniable and integral part of the national body itself. Using what he calls a "numerical allegory," Balibar argues that Algeria and France added together "do not equal two but something like *one and a half*, as if each in being added to the other always-already contributed a part to the other" (76). Another form of allegorical math could very easily produce the result of two and a half or even three (or more), depending on how the "foreign body" within each nation is counted: either as something that makes each nation in itself more than itself (already at least one and a half in itself) or less than what it thinks itself to be—that is, either as a supplement or a deficiency (or perhaps both at the same time).

Recent conflicts in both nations over language, religion, and cultural practices have revealed how not just extremist political groups but also religious and political authorities on the different sides of the borders separating and linking the two countries continue to consider the different manifestations of this mutual constitution/contamination of national-cultural space as threats to national sovereignty and cultural identity. For both Algeria and France have in different ways repeatedly attempted without success to control, repress, or exclude the foreign bodies within them through a patrolling of both their external and internal borders and a more rigorous and at times violent imposition and enforcement of exclusionary nationalist-religious cultural norms. Balibar's "allegorical math" would suggest that such attempts, whether they take the form of repressive interventions of the army or police, terrorist acts of religious fundamentalists, or laws passed by duly elected officials, have failed in the past and will continue to fail in the future. It is too late, always-already too late, to impose a mythical ethnic, cultural, or religious homogeneity on either or both sides of national-cultural borders.

The willed forgetting or repeated denial of the historical and political consequences of colonialism on both sides of the different borders separating and linking France and Algeria, the general unwillingness to recognize and appreciate fully what Balibar calls each nation's "interior alterity [*altérité intérieure*]" (74), could be considered one of the most contentious issues facing not just France and Algeria but all modern nations in the postcolonial era.[3] The fundamental, constitutive role played by interior alterity within nations means that it is no longer sufficient to conceive of decolonization as the negation of what Balibar calls "the false simplicity of the number one," if it is only to affirm the equally "false simplicity of the number two" (78). The situation becomes even more complicated if the border separating nations such as France and Algeria from each other is what Balibar calls a fractal or "incomplete border [*une frontière non-entière*]" (76), a border that is neither completely open nor closed, one that both separates and distinguishes, on the one hand, and links and mixes together, on the other. The consequence of such open boundaries—open not by the decision of national authorities or the actions of armies but by the long-term aftereffects of colonialism itself—is that each nation's cultural identity is constituted in part by what Balibar calls "an interior difference" or "an essential non-contemporaneousness to self" (82). $1 + 1$ does not equal 2 because each nation, each people, each culture, as a result of its internal entanglement with the other, is in itself other than itself—more and/or less than itself. Postcolonialism in this sense signals the end of simple math as concerns closed national borders, homogeneous cultural identities, and continuous historical series.

In numerous essays and books he wrote before his death, Edward Said also questions the closed nature of the borders allegedly separating ex-colonizing and ex-colonized nations and the limitations of the oppositions assumed to define cultural identity. In his preface to *Culture and Imperialism*, for example, Said argues that critical analyses of relations between East and West should no longer focus exclusively on the history of Western imperialism, domination, and colonial expansion and the myths of Western superiority that support them. What also needs to be understood in the postcolonial era is that the history of imperialism produced varied and heterogeneous interconnections among different cultures. This means that what previously had been considered strictly external relations between distinct cultures in fact constitute internal relations *within* different but overlapping and mutually intertwined cultures: "*For the first time*, the history of imperialism and its culture can now be studied as neither monolithic nor reductively compartmentalized, separate, distinct."[4] The outside, the foreign, and the alien, which in principle are in opposition to the sameness or homogeneous identity of the inside, are in fact located within it, functioning as constitutive elements of the inside rather than intrusions from the outside. Cultural identity can thus not be taken as a given; it can no longer be assumed to be homogeneous or *one*.

Said thus argues that one of the results of *independence* is *interdependence*: "Partly because of empire, all cultures are involved in one another, none is single and pure, all are hybrid, heterogeneous, extraordinarily differentiated, and unmonolithic" (xxv). Following Said, it would be possible to claim that the continually increasing hybridity of cultures constitutes a or even the defining characteristics of the postcolonial era itself. Such mutual cultural entanglement does not eliminate borders (or differences) within, between, or among nations and cultures, however, but rather transforms the issue of borders and differences from being predominantly a question of the separation of the foreign from the indigenous or the outside from the inside into one of understanding the function and effects of hybridity or difference internal to (postcolonial) culture in general. The continuing tension between the desire for homogeneous identity and the effects of heterogeneity also highlights the persistence of internal exclusions within allegedly postcolonial nations and cities and helps explain why postcolonialism remains still today more of an unrealized project than a reality.

A Colonialist Allegory

If one accepts the arguments of Balibar and Said concerning cultural borders, the question of how or where to situate Albert Camus' work in relation to colonialism in general and to the border(s) between (and within) Algeria and France in particular may not be as easy to answer as critics of his work have argued. In an essay on Camus included in *Culture and Imperialism*, which is remarkably different in both tone and argument from his preface to the same work, Edward Said places Camus squarely on the French or colonialist side of the border, and he even criticizes what he calls Conor Cruise O'Brien's otherwise "agile demystification" of Camus for having misrepresented both Camus' relation to the non-European world and, even more importantly, the issue of "the frontier of Europe" in general:

> There is a subtle act of transcendence in O'Brien's notion of Camus as someone who belonged "to the frontier of Europe," when anyone who knows anything about France, Algeria, and Camus . . . would not characterize the colonial ties as one between Europe and its frontier. . . . Western colonialism . . . is first a penetration *beyond* the European frontier and *into* the heart of another geographical entity, and second it is specific not to an ahistorical "Western consciousness . . . in relation to the non-Western world" . . . but to a laboriously constructed relationship in which France and Britain call themselves "the West" *vis-à-vis* subservient, lesser peoples in a largely undeveloped and inert "non-Western world."
>
> (173–174)

Said's comments emphasize both the historical refusal of "the West" to respect geographic and political boundaries separating Europe from the lands lying outside its frontier and the constructed, artificial nature of the relationship it imposed on the "non-Western" areas and peoples it conquered and colonized. From the beginning of the imperial era at least, but undoubtedly even before, it is no longer a question only of exterior borders or frontiers, therefore, since by penetrating beyond its borders Europe also incorporated its frontiers within itself. The outside is now inside as the inside is extended outside.

European conquest and occupation of lands beyond its geographic borders and its domination of "non-Western" peoples and cultures cannot of course be disputed. At the same time, Europe's disrespect for borders or frontiers did not mean that borders were simply eliminated each time a European nation penetrated "*beyond* the European frontier *into* another geographic entity." Borders rather continued to be areas of dispute and violent conflict and were constantly relocated and redefined, both outside and within colonized lands and colonizing nations. This also suggests that what it meant to be either "Western" or "non-Western" was constantly changing as well. Cultures came in contact with each other and influenced or, according to ultranationalists, contaminated each other, although certainly not in the same way or on an equal, reciprocal basis, both because of and in spite of the colonial relation of dominance of European peoples and cultures over other peoples and cultures. If, as Said suggests, cultural hybridity, the sharing and mixing of different cultures across the borders that also separate them, should be considered the principal characteristic of the postcolonial world, in his own terms the process in fact began with the "first imperialist penetration" beyond the borders of Europe. Cultural hybridity could thus not be said to have appeared for the first time in the postcolonial world but was rather present (as both a possibility and reality) from the very beginning of the imperialist era—and, in fact, long before, from the beginning.

This would suggest that it would not necessarily be "an act of transcendence" to situate a writer such as Albert Camus on or in relation to "the frontier(s) of Europe," as long as it is acknowledged both how difficult it is to locate such a border before, during, and after colonialism and the way in which borders have both an external and internal cultural function. For no matter how oppressive French colonialism was, it could not and did not effectively efface "the frontier" between Europe and North Africa, but rather transformed and displaced it both outside and in. Given the complexity of the problem of national-cultural borders in such a context, it would perhaps make more sense to situate Camus' work not in relation to a single frontier between non-Western and Western, North African and European, or even French and Algerian national and cultural borders, but rather in terms of the different external and internal borders both separating Algeria from and linking Algeria to France, not just after independence but already during the colonial period itself. Camus could thus rightly claim to be *Algerian* or to have a profound and undeniable Algerian side, but "the Algerian in him" should not be conceived in terms of a hypothetical and fictive homogeneous geographical or national-cultural identity, no matter how either might be defined, but rather in terms of the conflicted history and hybridity of the term itself—again not just during Camus' life and before independence but after it as well.

In both his literary texts and essays, Camus' comments on the relations between "East" and "West" in Algeria and in the Mediterranean area in general are not of one piece: at times they are naïvely Eurocentric; at others, more critical and complex. Camus depicts the problem of the complex hybridity of both geographical and cultural identity in a colonialist context perhaps most explicitly in his descriptions of different Algerian cities, not just in various lyrical essays but in his fictional works as well, since Algiers is the setting of both *The Stranger* and a significant part of his posthumously published *The First Man*, and Oran, his least favorite Algerian city, is the setting of *The Plague*.[5] His descriptions of Oran in particular could, in fact, be the most telling indicator of Camus' contradictory relation to the internal national-cultural borders determined by colonialism in Algeria, in part because of his conflicted relations with the city itself and his different attempts to describe its hybrid cultural characteristics, but also because postcolonial critics have used his representation of the city in his allegorical novel of the French Resistance as particularly strong evidence of his alleged colonialist sympathies and prejudices.

In order to better situate Camus' representation of the city of Oran, however, it would be helpful to be able to compare it to the description of Oran in an overtly apologetic form of colonialist discourse. An excellent example of such an apology is the study of the geography and urban history of Oran written in 1938 by René Lespès, which considers Oran a model city and praises its rapid economic and demographic growth and overall success after a century of colonialism.[6] For Lespès, what distinguishes Oran from Algerian cities such as Algiers and Constantine and what he claims is the undeniable proof that Oran is the crowning achievement of French colonialism is that, unlike Algiers, for example, Oran was not an important city before the arrival of the French. Both during and after the Spanish and Ottoman conquests and occupations, Oran was a small fortress city with relatively few inhabitants, and it began to grow and prosper only *after* the arrival of the French. Lespès argues, therefore, that it is only *because of* French rule that Oran became a thriving modern metropolis in the 1930s, so successful that it represents for him the colonial city par excellence.

The ultimate sign of the great success of colonialism in Oran, however, is not simply the wealth of Oran's European inhabitants. It is rather the growth of the city's "indigenous population,"[7] which Lespès claims had been practically nonexistent before the arrival of the French: "The Oran of the French contains more Muslims that had ever been grouped there before our arrival" (109).[8] Oran is thus represented not as having been conquered, taken away from an indigenous Arab population, and then occupied by foreign French inhabitants. In Lespès' presentation, Oran is rather a city that was generously rescued by the French from more brutal and destructive foreign conquerors and then allowed to grow and prosper for the first time. For Lespès, the prosperity of Oran under French colonialism is the irrefutable proof of colonialism's success for both Europeans and "natives" throughout Algeria and the best justification for its continuation.

Lespès' defense of Oran and French colonialism is, however, more complicated than it might at first appear. For after praising the increase in its indigenous population and attributing this growth to French colonial rule, Lespès acknowledges that Oran still remains the most European of all Algerian cities. Oran is so European, in fact, that he admits that a visitor could walk through its streets and have the impression that no "Muslim natives [*Indigènes musulmans*]" inhabited it (133). Oran is thus a colonial city in which the colonized, although continually increasing in number, remain practically invisible, absent from the social and cultural life of the city, living within and yet apart from the city at the same time. Muslim natives of Oran in this analysis are thus simultaneously included within and excluded from the city, inside and yet still outside the interior boundaries that define the city in French colonialist terms. As their increasing numbers and prosperity are used to prove colonialism's success, their visible absence within this increasingly "European city" testifies at the same time to the effects of the exclusion produced within the city by its *internal* colonial borders.

But if Oran is the most explicitly European and thus least North African or Arab of Algerian cities, it is also paradoxically, Lespès acknowledges, "a Franco-Spanish city from the ethnic point of view" and "the least French of the three departmental capitals of the colony" (133). Oran, the crown jewel of French colonialism in Algeria, has clearly for Lespès succeeded in its "civilizing mission," but in doing so, in assimilating non-French subjects into a French urban space and/or simultaneously excluding/repressing from its European inner core and identity almost all signs of indigenous cultures, Oran has remained the least French of its cities, the city in which being French for the majority of its French inhabitants actually means being more Spanish than French. French cultural identity in Oran could thus be said to be based on the interior inclusion of its Spanish population and the internal exclusion of its Arab population.[9] The city's external and internal borders produce assimilation, exclusion, separation, and hybridity all at the same time.

With only one-fifth of its total population being of French ancestry, Oran is thus the Algerian city in which the most colonialist work had to be done on Europeans and non-Europeans alike to integrate diverse populations into French culture and in this way realize the contradictory ideal (myth) of assimilation that is at the very basis of French colonialist ideology. Lespès considers all colonial cities, given that they are always "populated with fairly heterogeneous ethnic elements," to be the best sites in which to pursue the colonialist ideal of "fusion and rapprochement" (469). But it is Oran that had most dramatically realized this ideal. And if assimilation had already been achieved for so many in this, the least French of all French Algerian cities, then he is also convinced that such success could eventually be achieved in all of Algeria, even for the "indigenous Muslims" of Oran, who in his version of history enter the city in significant numbers and prosper only after the French conquest and largely because of French rule. Even if, as he admits, they are still not yet integrated into or very visible in the city as such.

It is as if the Arab population of Oran is less indigenous to this city than anywhere else in Algeria and thus "more foreign" to Oran than "the French" are, even if the French themselves have predominantly Spanish origins and for this reason Spanish Algerians are presented as being the best representatives of what it is to be French. At this point in Lespès' descriptions and analyses, it is no longer clear which group is being assimilated into which or what the term "French" could actually mean in such a situation, since it is predominantly embodied by Spanish immigrants, most fully manifested in an Algerian city in terms of Spanish rather than French culture, and achieved by the exterior inclusion of Spaniards and interior exclusion of "Muslim natives."

But it is precisely because of its diverse populations and the relatively small percentage of French inhabiting the city that Oran is presented as the Algerian city where colonialist idealism met its most difficult test—and where for Lespès the triumph of colonialism was thus the most spectacular: "Oran testifies brilliantly of the success of urban colonization in Algeria. How could one not be led to recognize it as the chosen space in which the strongest and best distributed of French and neo-French populations are found?" (474–475). As Oran goes, then, so goes colonialism in Algeria, and for Professor Lespès, both Oran and colonialism were, by the mid-1930s, overwhelming successes.

In this analysis of a colonialist success story, Oran, the chosen urban space of French colonialism, is defined by borders that determine both a complex geographic and cultural identity that allow it to be distinguished from its rural surroundings and the other urban spaces to which it is compared. But at the same time, the city of Oran is a space in which French cultural identity is constantly at risk, constantly transforming others but in the process being transformed at the same time. Oran is thus complicated by the very colonial structure that allows the French both to dominate and oppress the colonized and assimilate others into French culture and society—not just its Spanish population but eventually, at least in principle, its Muslim population as well. The "success" of Oran and colonialism in general is thus revealed to be based on the contradictory postulate of the nonindigenous status of the indigenous population, just as the invisibility of "the natives" is necessary to highlight the indigenous nature of the Spanish cultural presence in the city and thus paradoxically the presence and dominance of the French and the success of French colonialism.

But as long as the Muslim population of Oran remains largely invisible, the process of assimilation would have to be considered incomplete and the success of colonialism in Oran, even in colonialist terms, far from total. But, as Albert Memmi and others have argued, successful assimilation is in fact a structural impossibility, for it would bring about the end of the colonial relation and thus the demise of colonialism itself. Colonialism was thus destined to fail, regardless of whether in its own terms it was considered to have succeeded or failed.[10] Oran in this sense is the site of this contradictory impossibility, the city in which success is failure and what it means in colonialist terms to be French is revealed to be a paradoxical hybridity of national cultural traits and an identity that does not add up.

Camus' Oran

If a colonialist apologist such as Lespès can obviously be criticized for his mystified view of colonialism, his study reveals and could even be said to revel in the contradictions of the general colonialist assimilationist project. What could be called Camus' "Oran problem" is of an entirely different nature. For Oran is also not just any city in Camus' essays and fictional texts, but the one whose descriptions have received the most attention and provoked some of the harshest criticism of his work. This is most definitely not because he presents in The Plague (or anywhere else) an enthusiastically positive view of Oran or treats it as the crowning achievement of French colonialism. It is rather because he allegedly does the opposite: he portrays Oran as an entirely French city and thus covers over its colonial nature and ignores or represses the existence of its indigenous Muslim population. If Lespès says too much in praise of colonial Oran, Camus allegedly says and shows too little, at least too little of its colonial nature, in his fictional depiction of the "same" city.

It is once again Conor Cruise O'Brien who, in his chapter on The Plague, presents the harshest criticisms of the novel and accuses Camus of justifying colonial injustices and colonialism in the novel simply by the way he describes Oran.[11] The main problem for O'Brien is that the Oran of The Plague is an exclusively European city, a city without Arabs or whose Arab population is for the most part invisible. Oran is described in the novel as a French city inhabited almost exclusively by French citizens, an Algerian city without the visible presence of indigenous Algerians, a colonial city apparently with no colonized people. O'Brien considers this to be not only a serious political distortion of the real, historical Oran, which of course it is, but also a symptom of what he alleges is Camus' general defense of French colonialism, which is reflected in the novel by his indifference to the plight of the Arab and Berber populations of his homeland and specifically the Arab population of one of Algeria's three principal cities. What is assumed by O'Brien is that such an omission, if it is *an omission*, is symptomatic and reveals what he claims are Camus' deepest colonialist political convictions.

The allegorical form of the novel does present certain problems for his argument, however, and O'Brien initially acknowledges that, since *The Plague* is what he calls a fable of the German occupation and the French Resistance, there is no compelling reason why it also should deal explicitly with colonialist oppression and injustice. He also recognizes that a fable follows a different logic, has a different purpose, and can have different historical and political implications than a historical or realist novel. O'Brien even admits that the novel's allegorical "strategy demands the disappearance of the Arabs, [since] it was metropolitan France, not Algeria, which was occupied by the Germans. . . . Myths and fables require a certain simplification, and it is therefore not surprising that Arabs should be kept out of the picture" (53–54). Whether the fact that Oran is not depicted in the novel as a colonial city is actually a "simplification" remains to be seen. But after having recognized what could be called the right of fable or allegory to simplification—what I would call the right to depart from, transform, and fictionalize historical reality—in a contradictory move, O'Brien then denies the novel the very right he had just granted it, because of what he claims are the nefarious political implications of this same omission or absence.

Because the novel briefly evokes the Arab quarter of Oran and its deserted streets in one of its descriptions of the devastation caused by the plague, O'Brien claims that it cannot then completely ignore the Arab population of the city and totally suppress the political issue of colonialism. And this is especially the case since the novel is an allegory of resistance to the oppression and deaths produced by political plagues. For O'Brien, it all comes down to whether colonialism can be considered a possible referent for the plague and, even more important for his indictment of Camus, whether Camus intended his allegory to apply exclusively to the Nazi occupation of France or imagined that it could also evoke other forms of deadly oppression as well, particularly colonialism. O'Brien himself is convinced that the allegory should definitely apply to colonial Algeria as well but that Camus, however, believed that it should not.

O'Brien boldly asserts, but provides no evidence to back up his claim, that at the time the novel was published (1947), certain "Arab Algerians," but not "Camus and his friends," believed that there was a connection between Nazism and colonialism and thus between the French resistance to the German occupation of France and Arab resistance to the French occupation of Algeria:

> There were Arabs for whom "French Algeria" was a fiction quite as repugnant as the fiction of Hitler's new European order was for Camus and his friends. For such Arabs, the French were in Algeria by virtue of the same right by which the Germans were in France: the right of conquest. . . . From this point of view, Rieux, Tarrou, and Grand [the "resistance heroes" of the novel] were not devoted fighters of the plague: they were the plague itself.
>
> (55)

Camus' characters (and by extension Camus himself) are thus for O'Brien not true *résistants* to oppression, injustice, and mass extermination, but actually carriers of death and agents of the plague in the form of colonialist oppression and devastation. In his argument, they are secret agents of injustice posing as agents of justice, perhaps the most hypocritical and dangerous kind of oppressors, which might help explain the harsh polemical tone of much of O'Brien's book. For the freedom they demand for themselves and for which they risk their lives in their struggle against the plague (in the form of Nazism), they allegedly deny to others' resistance to another form of the plague (colonialism). In this way, they condemn the indigenous colonized inhabitants of the city allegorically to oblivion and death. What "Camus and his friends" actually thought, wrote, and did to combat the plague of colonial oppression in Algeria is ultimately irrelevant for O'Brien, since for him there can be no question that the novel ends up spreading "the plague itself. "

In the most inflammatory remarks of his entire book—and of any of the attacks on Camus' writing of which I am aware—O'Brien links the novel even more closely to the Nazi oppression in general and the mass extermination of Jews allegorized in the novel in particular by calling the novel's silence concerning the Arab population of Oran "an artistic final solution of the problem of the Arabs of Oran" (56). Everything for O'Brien is thus reversed in the novel because of the absence of Arab characters, with the narrative of courageous, practical resistance to the plague actually a nefarious disguised form of the plague itself. Thus a novel, whatever its literary and political interest and limitations might be, which has been read by the overwhelming majority of its readers as a depiction of resistance to oppression, is in the final analysis for O'Brien the artistic expression of mass extermination. The novel describes the way a small number of individuals risk their lives in collective action in an attempt to save the entire population of the city from extermination. But in doing so, O'Brien claims the novel "exterminates" the entire Arab population of Oran.

Whatever the polemical force of O'Brien's attack on Camus and, more importantly, the critical and polemical force of the analogy he draws between colonialism and Nazism in general and its applicability to the novel, it is true that Aimé Césaire and other militant anticolonialist writers and critics also made use of a similar analogy well before O'Brien did.[12] It would probably surprise many of his critics to discover that Camus himself also used the same analogy, although not in as sweeping a fashion as O'Brien or Césaire. In an article he wrote for *Combat* in May 1947, Camus condemns the massacre of thousands of Algerian demonstrators and bystanders in the region of Sétif in 1945 (as well as protesters in Madagascar in 1947) and denounces the French use of collective punishment to combat mass demonstrations and civil disorder in its colonies. He was, in fact, one of very few voices at the time speaking out against such crimes and injustices.[13]

In his 1947 article, Camus denounces "the methods of collective repression" used in Algeria and characterizes the racist actions taken by the French as "a policy of terror" similar to that of Nazi Germany:

> Yet the facts are there, the clear and hideous truth: we are doing what we reproached the Germans for doing. . . . If the Hitlerians applied their shameful laws to Europe, the reason was that they believed their race to be superior, hence the law for Germans could not be the same as the law for enslaved peoples. If we French revolted against their terror, it was because we believed that all Europeans were equal in rights and dignity. But if Frenchmen can now hear of the methods

used in some instances by other Frenchmen against Algerians and
Malagasies and not react, it is because they are unconsciously certain
that we are in some way superior to those people and that it makes little difference what means we choose to demonstrate that superiority.

("Contagion," *Combat*, May 10, 1947;
in *Camus at* Combat, 291 [671–672])

Camus' condemnation of racism in this particular editorial and in fact
throughout his writings leaves no doubt as to which side he holds responsible for the "policy of terror" used in Algeria and other colonies. The charge
that "Camus and his friends" did not find colonial racism and oppression
repugnant and that he did not denounce them and see a link between colonial and Nazi racism and violence simply does not hold up to scrutiny. It
should also be noted that *The Plague* was published in June 1947, a month
after Camus wrote this article.[14]

The question remains as to whether it is legitimate to criticize an allegorical novel for being "historically inaccurate," or, in the case of *The
Plague,* for not giving a sufficiently detailed and accurate description of the
city of Oran and its different populations. The city depicted in *The Plague*
is obviously not the colonial city of Oran and shares little with it except its
name, geographic location, and general physical characteristics. The novel
also does not provide any indication of other aspects of Oran's long and
complex history or its different foreign occupiers. There are few traces not
just of its Arab population but also of the other ethnic groups that constitute this, the "least French" of all Algerian cities. Neither does this allegory
of resistance to oppression and extermination evoke any of the events of
World War II that most directly affected the city itself.[15]

But given the allegorical nature of the novel, it is still not clear that all
the historical and political events not mentioned in the novel, all the subjects not treated, make it either procolonialist or, as has also been claimed,
an ahistorical or antihistorical novel. O'Brien in fact does not criticize the
novel for not describing any of the events of the war itself. It is only in terms
of French colonialism in Algeria that he attacks the novel's lack of historical and political accuracy and what he feels are its dangerous ideological
implications. In O'Brien's reading, the allegorical border that separates the

fiction narrated in the novel and historical-political reality would appear to be legitimate, except when it comes to colonialism. In this one area he judges the novel to be ideologically suspect.

Other critics, however, including, surprisingly, the young Roland Barthes, well before O'Brien's book appeared, criticized the allegorical form of the novel and argued that even as concerns its principal historical referent, the Nazi occupation of France, the novel has antihistorical implications.[16] Camus, of course, never had the chance to respond to the kind of criticism made by O'Brien, but in his response to Barthes' criticism that the plague can at best have only an abstract relation to history because in the novel it does not have "a human face," Camus insists that the novel on the contrary, *as a fiction or allegory*, has an evident historical content and a direct relation to at least one clearly defined moment of history: that of "the European resistance against Nazism. The proof is that even though this enemy is never named, everyone recognized it" (*Théâtre, récits, nouvelles*, 1973). The fact that Nazism, unnamed and unrepresented as such in the novel, was easily recognized by readers as the principal historical referent for the allegory of the plague proves, Camus argues, that the allegory in fact has "a human face," as well as an obvious historical-political referent.

No more explicit reference to the events of the war was needed to evoke the oppressive historical reality and deadly effects of the occupation and the necessity for collective resistance. By not naming Nazism, by its absence as an explicit referent, the novel allows readers on their own to provide the missing name and construct the relations of the novel to that name and the historical events to which it refers. Camus insists that the absence of a named historical referent in an allegorical context does not thus constitute a denial of historical-political reality or a flight from history, but rather a nonrepresentational way of referring to, analyzing, and also questioning, if not resisting, historical-political reality itself.

Besides what he describes as his profound distrust or "disbelief" in historical realism, Camus also claims that the allegory of the plague relates to different historical-political contexts and referents rather than one alone, and this multireferentiality for him has a decided advantage over historical realism: that of at the same time applying to various forms of political oppression rather than only one.[17] When Camus wrote his response to

Barthes in 1953, and already in 1947 when *The Plague* was published, he clearly considered Stalinism another extreme form of political oppression that should be associated with the deadly characteristics of the plague. The question is whether other systematic forms of oppression such as colonialism should be associated with it as well.

Influenced by the fact that Camus a decade later would oppose the tactics of the FLN's armed struggle for Algerian independence, O'Brien claims that it is already evident in *The Plague* that Camus "intended" to exclude colonialism from the list of possible referents for his allegory of oppression. Given Camus' prewar journalism and especially the postwar editorials he published in *Combat*, in which he criticized French colonial oppression and injustice and repeatedly named the colonial system as the source of Arab and Berber oppression, humiliation, and destitution, it would seem difficult if not impossible to give much credence to O'Brien's assertion.[18] According to the logic of the allegory of the plague itself, colonialism would on the contrary have to be considered another of its possible historical referents, whether the novel does more than mention in passing the Arab inhabitants of Oran or not. To associate colonialism with the plague is consistent with the novel's multireferential allegorical form and with what Camus' essays on Algeria from the 1930s and 1940s repeatedly state. It is much more consistent in any case than the claim that the *résistants* in the novel to one form of the plague (National Socialism) are in fact secret agents of another form of the plague (colonialism)—or to claim that the novel itself encourages the first association but explicitly excludes the second. It is true, however, that unlike the obvious reference to "the European resistance to Nazism," which was immediately recognized by readers of *The Plague*, the references to both Stalinism and colonialism have not been sufficiently acknowledged by critics and too often, especially as concerns colonialism and following O'Brien's lead, vigorously denied.

By insisting so much on the importance of the location and inhabitants of the city in which *The Plague* takes place, critics have tended to overlook what I would argue is the novel's most important relation to Camus' perspective on colonial Algeria and his later position on the Algerian War. Based on Camus' experience in the French Resistance, *The Plague* presents an allegory of the struggle against oppression that is diametrically opposed to the form that the armed struggle for Algerian independence would actually take under the leadership of the FLN less than a decade after the novel was published. Camus' allegory of resistance in a novel that was largely written during World War II explicitly dramatizes the limits that he was convinced needed to be accepted by all resistance movements, no matter how oppressive and deadly the political plague being combated. It was when no limits were placed on the means being used that the form of resistance to one form of the plague became in fact the carrier for the next form, with the means of resistance themselves rapidly spreading the disease they were meant to combat.[19]

The chief organizer of the collective resistance to the plague, Dr. Rieux, who is revealed near the end of the novel to be the author of the "chronicle" narrated by the novel, gives a simple, commonsense, practical justification for resistance rather than a religious or political one: "The essential thing was to do your job well" (41, trans. mod. [1250]). It is also Rieux who, given the increasing number of deaths caused by the microbe, even before the true nature or even name of the disease is known, asserts that the situation already "permits no hesitations" and that debates over whether to call the epidemic the plague or not are "of small importance. . . . The important thing is to prevent its killing off half of the population of this city," to "take the responsibility of acting as though the epidemic were a plague" (49, 51, trans. mod [1257, 1259]). Rieux's position, which is in fact also Camus', is that in the face of oppression, no matter how overwhelming it appears to be, the deepest and most legitimate basis for resistance, the one that brings together groups of people with radically different religious and political beliefs, is the refusal to accept that a significant part of the population will be sacrificed to the plague. What is common to all the groups is the desire to save as many lives as possible.

The goal can never be "the salvation of man," an expression that Rieux explicitly rejects because it is "too big" and because he "would not go that far," but rather only "man's health," since "his health comes first" (219, trans. mod. [1397]). To work for the "health" of a community is an endless task, however, with no definitive victories and no guarantees or even a vague promise of a total cure (salvation) in the future. If the notion of resistance the novel presents has been mockingly characterized as a "Red Cross" morality, a more generous reading could find in its simplicity and practicality a recognition of the limits of all individual and collective action that is rooted in the awareness of the danger of promises of revolution or total salvation—whether in an afterlife, as Father Paneloux in the novel preaches in his first sermon, or through political action, as is the case with the different forms of what Camus in *The Rebel* calls redemptive politics.

What *The Plague* reveals about Camus' perspective on Algeria, therefore, is not a colonialist indifference toward the Arab population of Oran or any other Algerian city. His is rather a critical perspective that stresses at the same time the necessity for and limitations of all acts of political resistance to oppression, the obligation to put people's health first, before religion and before politics. In terms of the Algerian War, which would begin seven years after *The Plague* was published, it would not be a question for Camus of whether the resistance to colonial oppression was legitimate and necessary—there is ample evidence in his political writings that he felt it was both. The question for him would be what form that resistance should and could legitimately take, and whether it should be primarily oriented toward saving lives and concerned with the social and political health of the Algerian people as a whole. Or whether, on the contrary, through the use of unlimited violence and terrorism (which he considered political maladies, other extreme forms of the plague), it should promise not just an end to the injustices of colonialism but a total victory over oppression and thus a form of national-religious salvation—revolutionary redemption by whatever means deemed necessary and at whatever the costs in human lives and suffering.

Given these considerations, it would be difficult to characterize the modest "heroes" of the resistance to the plague in the novel as agents of colonial oppression. Except, as the novel asserts, if they are carriers of the plague they combat, so are we all. It is also Rieux's sense of the precariousness of "health" that explains why, at the moment of "victory" in the war against the plague and in the midst of the collective celebration and joy of the population of Oran after the deadly enemy has apparently been defeated once and for all and the barriers around the city finally removed, in the last lines of the novel he states that there is no "final victory" and that the "fight against terror and its relentless onslaughts" on the contrary is "never ending" (308 [1474]). For he knows that the terror of the plague can and will return once again: "He knew what those jubilant crowds did not know but could have learned from books: that the plague bacillus never dies or disappears for good" (308 [1474]).

There is one thing, therefore, that can be stated with certainty, one thing that Albert Camus (and "his friends") definitely did know, and knew long before he published *The Plague*: they knew that oppression and injustice also have a colonialist form, and that in Algeria, despite the victory over Nazi Germany, the plague in the form of colonialist injustice had not been defeated, the "health" of the Algerian people was deplorable, and Arab and Berber Algerians continued to suffer from economic and political oppression and die. The massacres at Sétif and Guelema in May 1945 were certainly overwhelming additional evidence—as if any more evidence was needed—of the increasingly deadly effects of the terror of the colonialist plague.[20] It would seem impossible to read *The Plague* and not come to the conclusion that the allegorical novel constitutes an unequivocal condemnation of such terror and gives basic, commonsense reasons for resisting terror in whatever form it appears—even or especially in its colonialist form.

Absence

Even if the absence of Arab characters in the presentation of the city of Oran in *The Plague* is in principle an issue worthy of discussion, a serious analysis of the significance and effects of their absence should also take into consideration the absence in the novel of other ethnic and religious groups as well. The Franco-Spanish population of the fictional, allegorical city, for example, is also not given the prominence it actually had in the historical city of Oran, but is represented predominantly by a small group of marginal criminals who try to arrange the illegal departure of people from the city after the official quarantine is imposed. Oranian Jews, who also constitute an important component of the city's diverse indigenous population, are also not mentioned in the novel. Regardless of the specific consequences within the novel of the absence of particular groups, it is important also to acknowledge that absence in its many different forms is in fact one of the principal themes of the novel and constantly evoked in the descriptions of the city and its inhabitants, whoever they are and whomever they represent. A serious analysis of the absence of any particular group would thus need to take into account the centrality of the problem of absence in general.

One of the most significant of the absences that define the city of Oran in the novel is the absence of beauty and nature. Oran is "ugly . . . without pigeons, without trees, and without gardens" (3 [1219]). In much the same vein, in "The Minotaur, or Stopping at Oran" (originally written in 1939 and republished in *Summer* [*L'été*] in 1954), Camus ironically describes how the citizens of Oran had succeeded in creating a barrier between themselves and the magnificent natural beauty of their surroundings, with the constructed, manmade ugliness inside the city successfully serving to obscure and even block out the natural beauty immediately outside the city's borders: "Compelled to live facing a glorious landscape, the people of Oran have overcome this formidable handicap by surrounding themselves with extremely ugly buildings. You expect a city opening on the sea, washed and refreshed by evening breezes. But except for the Spanish district, you find a city with its back to the sea, built turning in on itself, like a snail."[21] Before the plague in the novel results in physical barriers being constructed and policed to protect the outside world from being infected, Oran has in effect already turned itself totally back in on itself and closed itself off from the world of natural beauty lying just outside its borders.

The Oran of *The Plague* and Camus' essays is thus a city best defined not by what it is, but by what it is not, by what is kept outside its borders and indicated only by its marked absence inside. For Oran is not just a city "without picturesque sites, without vegetation"; it is also and more tellingly a city "without a soul" (*The Plague*, 6, trans. mod. [1221]). The absence of both created and natural beauty within the city is thus related to the most devastating of the lacks of the city: its inhabitants appear to lack the sensitivity, complexity, interiority, and consciousness that define what it means to be human. Oran is a zero-degree city for zero-degree, robotic, soulless inhabitants who are already culturally and aesthetically dead long before great numbers of them begin to be afflicted by and die horrible deaths from the plague. For the plague in the form of boredom and routine, death, in or as life, is already present in the city before the actual plague is recognized, named, and officially declared, long before the plague as such begins to threaten with its allegorical "final solution" not just one of the ethnic or religious groups of the city, but all of them.[22]

The soulless population of Oran thinks almost exclusively of making money and has time for little else, not even for lovemaking, which like other pleasures is described as "very sensibly . . . reserved for Saturday afternoons and Sundays," with all passions "violent and short-lived" (4 [1220]). Oran is also a city cut off from both national and world history, a city in which nothing really ever happens, a city that lives by routine and repetition. Oran is "a colorless place [*un lieu neutre*]" (3, trans. mod. [1219]) inhabited by a colorless, mediocre, "neutered" people lacking imagination and "without an inkling of anything different [*sans soupçon d'autre chose*]" (5, trans. mod. [1220]). The Oran of *The Plague* is thus an exemplary city in its mediocrity and in terms of what it lacks or excludes. It is presented as being representative not of the colonial city as such but rather of the emptiness characteristic of modernity in general, "a completely modern city" (5 [1220]). It would seem that even before the outbreak of the plague it would have been much better for *all* of the inhabitants of Oran never to have lived there at all.

And yet it is in this "*lieu neutre*," this empty, soulless, totally commercial, ugly, and thus for Camus most fully modern of all modern cities that an effective, practical resistance to the plague is organized, that a people comes alive in the midst of oppression and the threat of total extinction and struggles against a force so powerful that it initially seems fruitless to try to resist or attempt to defeat it. Given the general suffering, deprivation, and increasing number of deaths, a city and its people begin to organize to resist the horrible fate imposed on them by a superior force they do not understand. As we have already indicated, following Rieux, the inhabitants of Oran act not out of abstract ideological principles—whether religious or political—but out of practical necessity and a growing sense of solidarity with one another, for the plague infects all levels of society and all groups. It could even be argued that the emptiness of the city and its people, the absence of values, constitutes the grounds for the kind of practical resistance that is eventually organized by Rieux and the other characters in the novel. Theirs is resistance in its purest form, or more accurately, in its zero-degree form: a resistance to oppression and death with no other purpose or motivation than to save as many people's lives as possible and overcome the horrible isolation imposed by the "new order" in which they are forced to live under the occupation of the plague. Resistance would be meaningless if it were not first and foremost a resistance to all "final solutions," not just as concerns one group, but as concerns all the different populations of the *polis*. This is the strong antitotalitarian but also *anti*colonialist statement the novel makes; it is what Camus (and his friends) actually thought and knew about colonialism.

The woman who looks as if she has been suffering for three years from constipation: "Those Arabs, they mask their women's faces. Ah! They are not yet civilized!" Little by little she reveals to us her ideal of civilization: a husband who makes 1200 francs a month, a two-room apartment with kitchen and maids' rooms, movies on Sunday, and for the rest of the week rooms furnished by the Galeries Barbès.

—Albert Camus, *Carnets* (1940)

CHAPTER THREE

Exile

The Ideal of Freedom—"The Adulterous Woman"

In 1957, in the midst of the Battle of Algiers, when both FLN terrorism and the French army's violent repression of the civil population of Algiers, the systematic use of torture, and the execution of suspected members of the FLN were all at their peak, Albert Camus published a collection of short stories entitled *Exile and the Kingdom*. Four stories in the collection—"The Adulterous Woman," "The Guest" (*"L'hôte"*), "The Silent Men," and "The Renegade"—take place in Algeria and were written shortly before the outbreak of organized armed resistance. The publication of the collection precedes by less than a year the appearance of Camus' collection of essays *Algerian Reports*, in which he published his last public political statements on colonialism and the Algerian War. But if his collection of political essays was largely ignored when it first appeared and has still not been given the attention it deserves, the same cannot be said of at least two of his short stories from this collection, since they have been frequently commented on, especially in the last decade, when postcolonial critics have focused on Camus' position on the war of independence being waged in Algeria at the very moment his collection of stories appeared.

However, in his preface to the original French edition of *Exile and the Kingdom*, Camus does not explicitly mention either colonialism or Algeria, instead characterizing the stories as variations on the theme of exile, "which is treated in six different ways, from the interior monologue to the realist narrative" (*Théâtre, récits, nouvelles*, 2039).[1] These narrative variations on the theme of exile are also paradoxically explorations of the idea of unlimited freedom characteristic of what Camus calls "the kingdom," which he describes as being linked to "a certain stark, free life that we have to rediscover in order to be reborn. Exile in its own way shows us the path on the condition that we are able to refuse at the same time both servitude and possession" (2039).

The exiled "lords" of Camus' fictitious kingdom are thus the opposite of feudal lords because they possess nothing and rule over no one. For the same reasons, they are diametrically opposed to French *colons*, whose privileges and power are a direct result of their possession and exploitation of the land and the forced servitude of colonized Arab and Berber Algerians. This means at the very least that if the stories in *Exile and the Kingdom* are to be considered illustrations of Camus' contradictory relation to Algeria and thus as proof of his position on colonialism, the conflict between his literary variations on the themes of exile and freedom and the actual servitude imposed on Arabs and Berbers in his native Algeria needs to be analyzed with some care. Without such an analysis, it would be irresponsible to claim that Camus believed that freedom could coexist with colonialism or that his stories attempt to legitimize colonialist injustices and the oppression of Arab and Berber Algerians.

If exile could be considered the explicit, dominant theme of all the stories of the collection, the idea of freedom basic to Camus' notion of the kingdom is far less evident. "Freedom," in fact, is an allusive term in the stories and tends to be represented either negatively, by its loss or absence, or indirectly and metaphorically, existing not as a sociopolitical reality but as an imaginary, extrapolitical alternative to social constraints. The most striking example of the imaginary nature of the experience of total freedom is found in the first story of the collection, "The Adulterous Woman," which ends with the description of a French-Algerian woman's fleeting but powerfully sensual experience of absolute freedom.

To say that the main character's experience of freedom is imaginary is not to deny the specific sociopolitical context of this or the other stories in the collection, for the story is explicitly set in colonial Algeria, and its two main characters, Janine and her husband Marcel, are presented as having the beliefs, attitudes, and above all the prejudices of modest, petty-bour-geois French colonizers. They might even be considered fictional "portraits of the colonizer" comparable to those given in Albert Memmi's *The Colonizer and the Colonized*. In terms of its frank presentation of the distant, uneasy, and, at least as concerns Marcel, petty, aggressive, and racist relations with Arab Algerians, on its most explicit level the story constitutes an indictment of racism and the colonial society that has institutionalized it.

It would thus be absurd to imply or assert, as critics who have confused or conflated the voices, perspectives, experiences, views, and prejudices of the fictional characters in the story with Camus' own voice and views have done, that the feelings of fictional characters in "The Adulterous Woman" provide evidence of Camus' own attitudes toward Arab Algerians. For only if both the narrative perspective of the story and the specific source of the attitudes expressed in the context of the story are ignored would it be possible to attribute these attitudes to Camus and conclude, for example, that *he* felt that Arabs were deceptive, incompetent, or untrustworthy, as does the fictional husband Marcel in the story. Or that Camus felt uncomfortable traveling in close proximity with Arab Algerians, based on the fact that the story expresses the main character Janine's feelings of unease and distrust in the midst of their fellow voyagers, all but one of whom are Arab and who increase her discomfort by never looking at her.[2] It would be equally absurd to assume that Camus agrees that an Arab, who is described in the story as not acknowledging the presence of the two French travelers and thus not stepping aside for them or their baggage, is representative of all Arabs who "think they can get away with anything now," as Marcel asserts in the story. Or that Camus too "loathed that Arab's stupid arrogance" (20 [1568]), as Janine does. Or that for Camus, rather than for the characters in the story, all Arabs were indistinguishable, with the same "thin, tanned face that made them all look alike" (21 [1568]).

Articulating the fears and the petty, racist reactions and attitudes of fictional characters, rather than expressing Camus' own feelings or convictions, such descriptions demonstrate that he understood the effects of colonialist racism on the attitudes and behavior of ordinary French Algerians. If the statements and thoughts of the characters of the story reveal anything about Camus' attitudes toward Arabs, it is that Camus deplored racial prejudice, the ignorance, fears, and absurd sense of superiority on which it is based, and the destructive effects racism had on both colonizer and colonized alike. There is certainly ample evidence of his strong antiracist attitudes in this story and his other writings, as well as in his own life, to easily support such a claim.

Rather than demonstrate what Camus himself believed or felt about Arabs, then, the description in the story of a French Algerian woman's misunderstandings and prejudices indicate her separation from and fear of a people who do not have the same culture, religion, or language as she, a people with whom she has lived in close proximity all her life but of whom she knows almost nothing. The brief portrait given of Janine is that of a woman colonizer who has no place in the world of the colonized, a world she perceives as being dominated by proud, even "arrogant" Arab men in which "not a single woman could be seen" (21 [1568]). It is the portrait of a French woman who has no connection to the overwhelming majority of the people of her Algerian homeland, who speak "that language she had heard all her life without ever understanding it." She is also radically alienated from the land itself, especially the cold, hostile physical environment of the Algerian interior that does not conform to her dreams of "palm trees and soft sand" but is "merely stone, stone everywhere, in the sky full of nothing but stone-dust, rasping and cold, as on the ground, where nothing grew among the stones except dry grass" (9–10 [1562]). Her sense of exile could be said to be first and foremost that of colonizers in general, who are born and live as usurpers in a land that they claim as their homeland but that at the same time remains a foreign land.[3]

The fact that over the course of the voyage narrated in the story Janine becomes increasingly aware of her estrangement from Arabs and their culture, however, does not fully explain the extent of the experience of exile described in "The Adulterous Woman." For Janine's exile is also due to her alienation from the society and economic interests of the French colonizers of Algeria, even or especially from her own husband, whose "true passion [is] money" and whom "nothing seemed to interest . . . but his business" (8 [1562]). Her sense of exile is thus double and profound; it is the alienation of a French *woman* excluded from the worlds of French and Arab *men* as well as that of a *French* Algerian living in proximity to but at the same time radically cut off from the world and culture of *Arab* Algerians.

The portrait of Janine's husband is a more extreme, aggressive version of a French Algerian petty-bourgeois colonizer. And even if Camus claims in his essays on Algeria that the overwhelming majority of the poor and modest French inhabitants of Algeria were like his own family and not racist,[4] in this story he gives a powerful and uncompromising portrait of a *pied-noir* racist whose stupidity, pettiness, and aggressiveness are linked to his love of money and his overtly antagonistic relation to the land and its Arab inhabitants, who constantly frustrate him by resisting his efforts to dominate or exploit them. Marcel is the portrait of the colonialist not as master and ruler but as a once "courageous" *pied-noir*[5] who, because of his own inadequacies, repeatedly expresses resentment and hostility toward the land and the peoples who inhabit it.

Marcel's racism is evident in everyday relations with Arabs; it is the way he affirms his imaginary "natural" superiority over them. For example, when the bus in which they are riding breaks down and the Arab bus driver goes outside to repair it, Marcel asserts that "you may be sure he's [the bus driver] never seen a motor in his life." This is proclaimed immediately before the driver, who, unlike his two French passengers, speaks both Arabic and French, succeeds in getting the bus moving again (10 [1563]).[6] And pushing this portrait of petty, stereotypical racism to its limits, Marcel explains the inferiority of Islamic culture to French culture to Janine by claiming that the Koran prohibits pork because it "didn't know that well-done pork doesn't cause illness. We French know how to cook."[7] He also mocks what he perceives as the slowness of the Arab waiter in their hotel by evoking a stereotype of Arab behavior: "'Slowly in the morning, not too fast in the afternoon,' Marcel said, laughing" (15 [1565]). It is clear from this brief but unsparing portrait of a racist colonialist that Camus understood the effects of colonial racism all too well.

Much has been written about the detailed descriptions of North African landscapes that can be found in two of Camus' short stories from *Exile and the Kingdom*, and even more than in the other stories, the desert in "The Adulterous Woman" is not merely a background for the story but rather an active force, practically another character.[8] The landscape is not presented "objectively" or "realistically," however, but through the eyes of the two main characters and in terms of their hatred, fears, and, most important as concerns Janine, her desire for freedom. Marcel's relation to the land is as antagonistic and distorted as his relation to the Arab population in general, and he repeatedly "cursed this country" (10 [1563]) just as he viciously demeaned its people for not conforming to his will. Janine's relation is, as we shall see, completely different.

Sovereignty is a central issue in "The Adulterous Woman," but rather than being the justification for what Edward Said has called France's "ontologically prior" claim to Algeria,[9] it is the land itself—and not the French, nor Berber, nor Arab population—that is presented as sovereign, since it exists prior to and outside any other claim to priority or sovereignty, whether historical, political, or "ontological." It is Janine's sudden discovery of "the limitless expanse" (22 [1569]) of the North African landscape that sets the stage for her "adulterous" betrayal of her husband and her discovery of the possibility of freedom outside both the colonialist and French patriarchal contexts—which in fact are one and the same. Overwhelmed by the harshness, majesty, and limitlessness of the desert landscape she sees from an abandoned fort, Janine is described as being "unable to tear herself away from . . . a void opening before her," unable to "take her gaze from the horizon," where she discovers "there was awaiting her something which, although it had always been lacking, she had never been aware of until now" (23 [1570]). The "something" awaiting her is not a charted territory over which she imagines herself or anyone else to have sovereignty, but rather an open, uncharted, infinite space that is presented as the opposite of the social space in which she lives: a space not of distinctions, restrictions, possessions, hierarchies, exclusions, and prohibitions, but of infinite possibilities, open boundaries, and unlimited hospitality and freedom.

Diametrically opposed to the space *inhabited* by both colonizers and colonized in the story is the space through which nomads *wander*:

> Without homes, cut off from the world, they were a handful wandering over the vast territory she was discovering by sight, and which however was but a paltry part of an even greater expanse, whose dizzying course stopped only thousands of miles further south. . . . Since the beginning of time, on the dry earth of this limitless land scraped to the bone, a small number of men had ceaselessly trudged, possessing nothing but serving no one, destitute and free lords of a strange kingdom.
>
> (24, trans. mod. [1570])

The freedom of the destitute lords of this "strange kingdom" is a direct consequence of the absence of almost all possessions in their life and even of a sense of possessiveness, for the land the nomads wander through does not belong to them and is not theirs to possess or rule over. They rather share and belong to it.[10]

Just as the desert landscape is presented as a limitless expanse that extends as far as and in fact beyond what the eye can actually see, nomadic existence and the freedom it evokes are as borderless (and imaginary) as the nomad's wandering is endless. But the intimate relation nomads have with the land is at the same time a radical exile from the land—or rather a form of exile that represents the most profound sense of belonging, a belonging-as-exile. Their existence represents a form of freedom beyond or outside its institutionalized political states, the freedom of a people who never establish or institute themselves as *a* people. The sovereignty of these strange, distant lords is above all rooted in and takes the form of an absence or radical negation of sovereignty and possession in general.

The more a land is possessed and divided up, the more some are displaced from the land in order for it to be exploited and cultivated by others, the more some are made servants to the land and to those who possess it, the more external and internal borders are closed, the less freedom there is in a society. The more oppression and exclusion dominate, the further removed from the ideal of infinite freedom a people is—whether they are masters or servants, colonizers or colonized, oppressors or oppressed. This is the case no matter how their relationship with the land and with others was established and is perpetuated, whether through imperial conquest and occupation, economic exploitation, or both. What is thus evoked in the image of the nomads perceived in the distance by Janine (in fact more imagined than perceived, since they are barely visible) is what could be called a vision of impossible, total freedom, an imaginary, aesthetic ideal of freedom that could never be realized politically as such—an image or fiction of freedom that is the product of desire rather than a specific political reality or goal. It is an absolute form of freedom beyond all existing forms, one that cannot thus be ascribed directly to any particular society or form of government, whether modern or traditional—not even to actual nomadic cultures themselves.

Whatever the practical limitations of such an image of and desire for absolute freedom—assuming it makes any sense even to think about the political applicability of such a desire or ideal—it is most definitely the desire for a way of living with others and relating to the land that is in direct conflict in every imaginable way with the reality of colonialism and the parceling up, exploitation, and possession of the land colonial society guaranteed to colonizers and the servitude, oppression, and dispossession it imposed on colonized peoples. Colonialism would have to be considered the diametric opposite or absolute negation of nomadism and the ideal of total, unbounded freedom it evokes.

As an impossible horizon for Janine's life, the idea of infinite freedom is presented as a promise, something that she will never experience as such in or as her own life: "She knew that this kingdom had been eternally promised her and yet that it would never be hers, never again, except in this fleeting moment perhaps" (24 [1570]). The kingdom she perceives/imagines/desires represents a promise of radical change and liberation, the possibility of a way of living radically different from any Janine had ever experienced or even imagined. It is a promise or call that has been made from the beginning of time without ever being explicitly announced or previously heard, a promise that thus must be repeatedly made because it will and can never be completely fulfilled.

Janine's perspective on her own life radically changes after the exaltation of her first glimpse of the limitless expanse of the Algerian landscape and the ideal of infinite freedom it evokes in her. And at the same time, nothing changes in terms of her social condition. Her husband reconfirms the severe restrictions of her life by calling her "stupid" to be standing in the cold looking at a landscape he sees only as hostile, barren, and empty (25 [1571]), totally devoid of interest. When she finally turns away from the beauty of the desert landscape and lets herself be led by her husband back to their hotel and her life as a faithful French Algerian, that is, colonialist wife, in spite of appearances, something has changed in her: her sense of self. She is described as feeling a profound sense of loss as she returns to the hotel and as having a radically different sense of her own physical being: "She walked along without seeing anyone, bent under a tremendous and sudden fatigue, dragging her body, whose weight now seemed to her unbearable. Her exaltation had left her. Now she felt too tall, too heavy, too white as well for this world she had just entered" (25 [1571]).

The nomadic kingdom of total freedom she glimpses/imagines in the distance is a world that would in fact not be accessible to "too tall, too heavy, and too white" French men and women. It is promised to them only if they are first exiled from their size, their ethnicity, and their "Frenchness" and open to the desert's and its inhabitants' otherness, only if they discover in themselves a deep desire for freedom and accept the experience of the loss of self this desire implies, only if they refuse to exploit and possess the land and dominate and oppress the people who also inhabit and in fact have prior claim to it. The world glimpsed from afar is thus situated at the very antipodes of colonialism, well outside its borders, as a distant promise or unexplored possibility. It is an other world, the world of the Other, that is suddenly open to Janine, a world situated far beyond the horizon of the world in which she lives—and yet whose possibility is paradoxically within it as well.

In one of the most frequently analyzed scenes of Camus' entire corpus, later that same evening, responding to what the narrator describes as "the call of the night," Janine leaves the hotel bed she shares with her husband and returns to the fort that had offered her a perspective on the desert and its limitless horizon. Her return to the fort is the result of an explicit, conscious decision to revolt, for after her earlier brief experience she realized that ".she wanted to be liberated even if Marcel, even if the others, never were!" (29 [1573]). But at the same time, Janine is also described as returning impulsively to the abandoned fort as if she were unable to control her actions and had no choice but to return. Or rather, as if this were her deepest, most profound choice, initially made not by her conscious mind and will, but by her body, responding to an overpowering aesthetic or erotic impulse or desire.

Janine's uncontrollable need to return to the site from which, for the first time, she glimpsed or imagined a world of infinite freedom—and thus her choice to be "unfaithful" to her husband (and to her position as a French woman in colonial Algerian society)—are not political in nature, even if they do have obvious political implications. Described in explicitly erotic terms, Janine's experience is of a radical loss of self and not of possessing but of being possessed by the otherness of the night:

> Before her the stars were falling one by one and dying out among the stones of the desert, and each time Janine opened a little more to the night. Breathing deeply, she forgot the cold, the weight of others, her demented or rigid life, the long anguish of living and dying. . . . She

seemed to recover her roots and the sap again rose in her body, which had ceased trembling. Her whole belly pressed against the parapet as she strained toward the moving sky; she was merely waiting for her overwhelmed heart to calm down and for silence to grow inside her. . . . Then, with unbearable gentleness, the water of night began to fill Janine, drowned the cold, rose gradually from the obscure center of her being and overflowed in wave after wave, rising up even to her mouth full of moans. The next moment, the whole sky stretched out over her as she lay on her back on the cold earth.

(32–33 [1574–75])

The experience is at the same time erotic and metaphysical, an uncontrollable, orgasmic overflowing of Janine's body and being, which are both drawn to and filled with the obscurity and alterity of the desert night. For a fleeting but intense moment, Janine is possessed by Otherness; she loses all sense of herself and is Other.

But this overwhelming affect does not and cannot last. Afterward, nothing seems to have changed in her social situation, for as Janine says to her husband when she returns to the hotel in tears and rejoins him in bed: "It's nothing, dear . . . nothing" (33 [1575]). No matter how intense, the overwhelming experience of otherness is no more than a momentary break in her life, a brief but powerful adulterous encounter with what is most foreign to her existence as a married French woman living in colonial Algeria. The call to leave her husband's side and then the intensely erotic experience of infinite freedom itself come to Janine from outside her world, the world inhabited by French Algerians. It comes to her not just from the horizon of that world but from a more distant horizon beyond the horizon, from a world radically opposed to the colonial world in which she lives and to which she nevertheless returns. Her experience constitutes a call or promise of freedom rather than freedom itself, a promise, however, which as long as colonialism determines the relations between the French and Arab populations of Algeria, as well as between French men and women, can never be even partially fulfilled and thus must be constantly remade. The intense, erotic experience of impossible freedom is thus "nothing" at all in itself—nothing except the desire for a radically different life, the desire for freedom. A nothing that is everything.

Tragic Freedom and Absolute Hospitality—Host or Guest?

> A *hostis* is not a stranger in general. Different from the *peregrinus* who lives outside the limits of the territory, *hostis* is "the stranger whose rights are recognized as being equal to those of Roman citizens." ... A relationship of equality and reciprocity is established between this stranger and the citizen of Rome, which gives a sense of the precise notion of hospitality.
>
> —Émile Benveniste, "Hospitality"

> There is pure hospitality only when I welcome, not an invited guest but an unexpected visitor, someone who invades my privacy in a certain way, who comes to my house when I am not prepared for him.
>
> —Jacques Derrida, "Une hospitalité à l'infini"

> Camus does not say who is the host and who is the guest. That is his genius.
>
> —Jacques Derrida, "Être chez soi chez l'autre"

Undoubtedly the best-known story from *Exile and the Kingdom* is "L'hôte," whose title has been translated into English as "The Guest" but that could just as accurately (or inaccurately) be translated as "The Host," given that the word *hôte* in French, as in Latin, has both contradictory meanings.[11] The uncertainty of the meaning of the title is reflected in the way the story presents the complexities and ambiguities of its principal subject: the precarious and contradictory status of hospitality in a sociopolitical context of inequality and oppression. Hospitality in a colonial context would have to be considered an especially contentious issue, since its very possibility assumes that the most fundamental of rights, the right to call the land in which one is born one's homeland, to have the home in which one lives recognized as one's own, to be allowed to be at home in one's own home, is respected.

For how can one offer hospitality if one's home and homeland have been taken and are occupied by others, or if one's homeland is one's own only because it has been taken from others? How can one open one's home to welcome another if it has been taken away by another? And how can one accept hospitality under such conditions were it to be offered, if the host offering the hospitality has no legitimate right to be host and offer it? And by the same logic, if the guest should have been host and the one offering hospitality to the host, who then would have been guest rather than host?

To be denied hospitality by an ungracious host may well be a serious offense against the protocols of hospitality, but it could be considered a much less egregious offense or injustice than being denied the right to be host in one's own home and thus the possibility of offering hospitality to others. Colonialism reverses the situation of host and guest, because those who should in principle be at home in their homeland and in the position of hosts offering or refusing hospitality to strangers are precisely those who are treated as strangers in a homeland that is no longer theirs. They are thus at the mercy of their foreign hosts, the occupiers and usurpers of their homeland. They are "indigenous nationals" in a homeland that is no longer their own home, foreigners in their own land who find themselves in need of the hospitality of others in order to be at home in their home.

The desolate and destitute part of Algeria that is the setting for the simple, powerful story told in "The Guest/Host" is described as the homeland of both of the principal characters in the story—the French schoolteacher and the Arab prisoner. At the end of the story, it is a homeland from which they are both are radically exiled. Whatever the political and legal claims that might be made to defend the right of either or both of them to consider this desolate land their homeland, both face either imprisonment or exclusion from both their own communities and the land itself. And both find themselves living under the threat, if not likelihood, of death. The political question of who has the right to call Algeria their homeland is of course what was at stake in the war being waged at the very moment Camus' story was published in *Exile and the Kingdom*. It was a war that would resolve the question once and for all and result in Algerian independence and the mass departure of French Algerians from Algeria. But rather than focusing on the conflicting claims over the right to possess and rule the land, Camus' story points rather to the inadequacy and tragic limitations of all political solutions to conflicts among two peoples born in, living on, and having deep affective attachments to the same land.

As was the case with *The Stranger*, critics have often remarked that one of the characters in the story, the Arab prisoner, remains nameless and throughout the story is referred to only as "the Arab." The other two characters, the French schoolteacher and gendarme, have last names, Daru and Balducci, and thus have a status and a recognized personal identity that the Arab character lacks. Before deciding what the Arab character's lack of a proper name and anonymity might signify, however, it would seem advisable first to ask, as in the case of *The Stranger*, if there is any internal justification in the story for maintaining the anonymity of one of the characters, "the Arab," and thus his distance from the named French characters—even or especially from the French schoolteacher Daru, who acts as his nominal host and lodges and feeds him for one night.

In terms of the logic of the story and in order to highlight the conflicts and contradictions inherent in the colonialist sociopolitical context in which the story takes place and, more important, to make the distance between Daru and the Arab, the presumed host and guest of the story, remain as great as possible, the anonymity of the Arab is in fact an indispensable element of the story. For only if the distance and differences between Daru and the Arab prisoner are dramatically highlighted and maintained throughout the story can hospitality be offered in its most radical and contradictory form. Only with the maintenance of his anonymity and in an atmosphere of distrust, fear, and potential violence can the shelter, food, and eventually freedom the French schoolteacher/host offers his Arab prisoner/guest evoke a generalized, ideal form of hospitality, an *absolute* form of hospitality outside or beyond self-interest, sociopolitical differences, political disputes—and even or especially armed conflict.[12]

Ironically or rather, as we shall see, tragically, it is in the general context of colonial injustice and the increasingly overt hostility between the French and the Arabs of Algeria that "The Guest/Host" points to an absolute form of hospitality antithetical to colonialism. And it is thus significant that hospitality in the story consists in Daru welcoming into his home not a relative, neighbor, friend, or even an identifiable and therefore nonmenacing stranger, all examples of conventional hospitality, but rather in his offering shelter and comfort to a murderer who remains throughout the story anonymous, alien, and potentially threatening, even after he has been welcomed into and made to feel at home in the schoolteacher's "home," which is a room attached to the schoolhouse in which he teaches. The greater the distance and the more extreme the differences in culture, beliefs, and practices of host and guest, the more open, generous, and inclusive the hospitality offered necessarily has to be.

Freely offered, unlimited, absolute hospitality reverses the positions of host and guest, for when the host freely opens his house to his guest, the host in effect makes his guest master of his home and in doing so accepts being subservient to his guest. And the greater the distance and differences between host and guest at the start and throughout the story, the more unexpected and paradoxical ("absolute") the resulting experience of proximity will be. And more important for the "political implications" of the story, in a colonialist context the reversibility of the relation of host and guest would imply the interconnectedness, reversibility, and the equality of colonizer and colonized, no matter their very different status in colonial society. Such hospitality would constitute nothing less than an powerful indictment of the society in which it occurs.

The story begins with the description of a scene whose importance commentators have generally ignored. After a severe snowstorm and thus isolated in the schoolhouse in which he teaches and lives, the schoolteacher Daru observes the arrival of two unexpected visitors:

> The two men were now halfway up the slope. [Daru] recognized the horseman as Balducci, the old gendarme he had known for a long time. Balducci was holding on the end of a rope an Arab who was walking behind him with hands bound and head lowered. The gendarme waved a greeting to which Daru did not reply, lost as he was in contemplation of the Arab dressed in a faded blue jellaba, his feet in sandals but covered with socks of heavy raw wool.
>
> (88–89 [1613])

Daru does not recognize the prisoner being led up the slope on a rope, but because of the way he is dressed he can identify him as an Arab. Even though he clearly recognizes and names Balducci, whom "he had known for a long time," Daru does not, however, acknowledge his greeting. By ignoring his salutation, Daru distances himself from the French gendarme and his actions, and this distance will turn out to be much greater than that between Daru and the Arab prisoner, whose name he never learns. In the context of the story, addressing someone by his name will not necessarily be a sign of true recognition, respect, or solidarity. In fact, Daru's distance from and even opposition to the culture in which the names Balducci and Daru are indicators of identity and privilege will only increase throughout the story.

By not returning Balducci's greeting, Daru distances himself not necessarily from his old acquaintance Balducci himself, but rather from the French gendarme on horseback who is leading an Arab prisoner through the snow attached to a rope like an animal. The prisoner is not properly clothed for the harsh weather, and his hands are tied as he struggles to arrive at the shelter of the schoolhouse. To the French gendarme, as the agent of colonial (in)justice who is responsible for the prisoner's condition, the schoolteacher thus initially refuses recognition. For to respond to the gendarme's greeting in this context would be to accept and be complicit with the injustice being perpetrated on the Arab prisoner, no matter what crime he is accused of or has actually committed. To the Arab prisoner, the victim of the gendarme's inhumane treatment, Daru will on the contrary offer hospitality without preconditions or expectations of any sort.

From the beginning of the story, Daru is thus presented as distanced from both the French gendarme and his Arab prisoner, but in different if not opposed ways. For although he refuses to his fellow French countryman the basic courtesy of replying to his salutation, he unexpectedly and spontaneously offers hospitality to the prisoner and victim of the gendarme's mistreatment, an Arab prisoner whose name he never asks and is never told. From the very beginning of the story, then, the schoolteacher finds himself on the side neither of the victim of injustice nor of the gendarme responsible for it—neither on the side of French colonial law and practices that authorize French policemen to treat Arab prisoners in inhumane, unjust ways, nor on the side of the Arab prisoner, who Daru learns has committed murder, a violent crime he unequivocally condemns. It is also because of the murder he has committed that "the Arab" remains for him "the Arab" throughout the story, maintaining the anonymity of a criminal and potentially violent, threatening other at the very moment hospitality and freedom are generously and gratuitously offered to him and Daru's fate and the Arab prisoner's become intertwined. If Balducci treats his Arab prisoner as an inferior and menacing foreigner, Daru welcomes him into his home and, in spite of (or because of) his potential threat to him, treats him as a guest.[13]

The story from its very first scene thus already raises the question of whose side the French schoolteacher is on in the growing conflict between French and Arab, colonizers and colonized. Daru disapproves of the prisoner's crime and is described as feeling a spontaneous reaction of "sudden anger against this man, against all men with their filthy spite, their tireless hates, their blood lust" (93 [1615]). But when the gendarme evokes the possibility of an immanent revolt and claims that "we," that is, all the French, are in a sense already "mobilized" (92 [1614]) against "them," the Arabs, Daru refuses his demand to take official custody of the prisoner. The gendarme reminds him of his ethnic and national origins, of the fact that he is by birth and culture "one of us," French, and not one of the anonymous Arabs of Algeria who threaten violence and revolt. And because of what he is by birth, it is expected that he will act like "one of us," especially in volatile situations in which "they" are directly and violently pitted against "us." Or in the politicized language of the gendarme, which is that of the *colons*: "If there is an uprising, no one is safe, we are all in the same boat. . . . You're from here, and you are a man" (96 [1616]). Daru is from there, and he is a man. But by refusing Balducci's demand to treat the Arab as a prisoner, he also refuses to be forced into the same boat as the Frenchmen of Algeria in whose name Balducci speaks. He separates himself from and in fact opposes the "us" that he, like Balducci, nevertheless still uses to distinguish the French from the Arabs.

Who is Daru then? One of "us" (the French) but not in the same boat as other Frenchmen? Certainly not one of "them" (the Arabs), but he is increasingly implicated in the fate of the Arab prisoner, who is both a criminal and thus in principle deserving of punishment, but at the same time a victim of the injustices of French colonial law. After his initial refusal to recognize the gendarme, the agent of colonial injustice, Daru offers shelter and mint tea, traditional signs of hospitality in North African culture, to both Balducci, his old French acquaintance, and to the anonymous Arab prisoner—as if to show that as individuals, the one familiar, the other an unknown and potentially threatening stranger, they are equals. As if following an ancient ritual, Daru is described as kneeling down to free the hands of the unknown criminal, accepting him into his house and treating him as someone to whom he, as host, is obliged and indebted and to whom he kneels down in homage.

This symbolic reversal of the positions of host and guest, master and servant, and, in the story, colonizer and colonized is the sign of true hospitality and is of course diametrically opposed to the brutal colonial relation that determines the roles of colonizer and colonized. The striking image of injustice, the prisoner being dragged up the slope in the snow by a gendarme mounted on his horse, dramatically contrasts with the image of hospitality, Daru on his knees before the prisoner untying his hands and offering him tea and protection from the cold. The clash of images in the opening pages of the story could not be more stark.

Daru, in spite of himself and his best intentions, in spite of his repeated refusal to play the role of gendarme, which in the context of the story would be synonymous with assuming the role of being "one of us," that is, accepting the privilege of being "French" in colonial Algeria, cannot, however, avoid being placed in a position of dominance and authority, no matter what he says and does. Because of colonialism, he is and will remain "French" in all situations, whether he identifies with and accepts what it means to be French or not.[14] In resisting the authority associated with being French, although he is unable to avoid it completely, and by treating his Arab prisoner as a guest and refusing to protect himself in any way from the potential threat his presence represents, even though he is unable to identify with him and condemns his violent act, Daru's actions affirm what colonialism violently denies: that in spite of the colonialist system, which is based on the principle of the innate rights of the French to dominate, there exists nevertheless a fundamental equality of guest and host, the Arab prisoner and the French schoolteacher, colonized and colonizer. It is an equality that underlies the oppositions and hierarchies determined by colonialism and politics in general. Granting hospitality in this way in a colonial context is thus a profoundly anticolonialist act, even if it is the colonial system that places Daru in the position of being able to assume the role of host in the first place.

The Arab and the Frenchman in the story have no common national, ethnic, cultural, or religious affiliation or identity; they share only an affective attachment to the same homeland that unites and opposes them at the same time. Or as Daru puts it: "No one in this desert, neither he nor his guest [host], was anything. And yet, outside this desert, neither of them, Daru knew, could have really lived" (98 [1617]). Living in an inhospitable homeland and at the same time linked to and separated from each other—but ultimately less separated from each other than from their own increasingly closed and violent communities—they share only their differences, their strong affective attachment to the same land, as well as their insignificance in relation to it.

Hospitality as it is presented in the story can thus be seen as an expression of equality and reciprocity that occurs within a context of inequality and extreme oppression. Absolute hospitality thus constitutes an ideal diametrically opposed to the oppressive reality of colonial lived experience and the injustices the colonial relation produces and perpetuates. The hospitality of the host/guest, no matter how violent the general context in which the act of hospitality occurs, is at the very least an indication of the possibility of an alternative to colonialism that exists as a counter-force within the colonialist system itself.

The penultimate scene in the story is similar to the scene at the end of "The Adulterous Woman," except that the limitless space of the desert is familiar to Daru, is his homeland, rather than being totally alien, as the desert is for Janine: "Daru drank in, with deep breaths, the fresh light. He felt a kind of rapture before the vast familiar space. . . . Daru surveyed the two directions. There was nothing but the sky on the horizon. Not a man could be seen" (106–107, trans. mod. [1622]). Responding to the infinite space and in an ultimate act of generosity and hospitality, Daru offers the possibility of freedom to his guest [host] by releasing him and giving him the chance to choose his own fate: prison or freedom. In one direction, the horizon is limited, cut up, and occupied. It is where the town of Tinguit is located and where the French administration and police are expecting an Arab prisoner who has been charged with murder to be handed over to them by a French schoolteacher who is "one of them." In the other direction, the horizon is unlimited, for there live nomads who "will welcome [the prisoner] and shelter [him] according to their law" (107–108 [1623]), a law that offers more than what Daru could for one night: not just shelter and hospitality, but also freedom in exile.

Just as Janine returns to her husband's side after her aesthetic-erotic experience of total freedom, as if nothing in fact had really happened, the prisoner chooses the road to prison rather than exile and freedom. No explanation is given as to why he does this. It is an act that is not and cannot be explained. Whether this is because the freed prisoner has interiorized colonial law and himself feels he should pay for his crime—which is unlikely since he does not speak French, gives no signs of being assimilated into French culture, and feels he acted justly—or because he identifies with Daru, accepts his hospitality, and chooses prison in a reciprocal act of generosity in order to prevent his host from being accused by French authorities of freeing a dangerous criminal remains indeterminate. It is an ambiguous, contradictory, unexplained act that could be at the same time a sign of the acceptance of servitude by a colonized subject or a supreme act of generosity and therefore an affirmation of freedom on the part of an already postcolonial subject and host. In any case, Daru's hospitality and gift of the choice of freedom paradoxically results in the unnamed Arab turning himself over to French colonial authorities, with the possibility that he will be executed for the murder he has committed, especially during a period described as a time of growing tension between French and Arab communities. Exiled from his own community but offered the gift of freedom, the Arab accepts the gift but uses his freedom to give up his freedom.

The bitterly ironic conclusion to the story, which was added in one of the revisions Camus made before publishing it, is that Daru is directly threatened with death for his generous, hospitable act. For in the eyes of the militant Arabs, "the brothers" of the Arab he in fact freed, Daru is responsible for having handed the Arab over to French authorities. His hospitality, his good intentions, and even his generous liberating act all mean nothing in the violent atmosphere of colonial Algeria; all result in imprisonment and perhaps death, not freedom. Daru does not receive his death sentence, however, in a French court of law, as Meursault did in *The Stranger* and as the Arab prisoner who turns himself in to the French authorities very well might. Rather the schoolteacher on his return to his school reads his sentence on the schoolroom blackboard, scribbled clumsily between the French rivers he had drawn on the board for his students' last geography lesson: "You handed over our brother. You will pay" (109 [1623]). Daru is "objectively" an enemy of "the brothers" of the Arab to whom he offered his hospitality, no matter what he actually did, whose side he sees himself on, or what he refuses to do. He is an enemy of all Arab brothers because he is French, an enemy of the people he has taught to speak, read, and write French, people who because of him will also be able to recognize and name the four principal rivers of France and who condemn him to death in words learned from him or teachers like him.[15]

On neither side, at a time when political unrest and then war makes it necessary to choose one side or the other—to be either with or against "us"—at the end of the story Daru no longer fits in anywhere: "Daru looked at the sky, the plateau, and, beyond, the invisible lands stretching all the way to the sea. In this vast landscape he had loved so much, he was alone" (109 [1623]). If "the Arab" is equally alone, having chosen the path leading to prison, the "facts" in Daru's case are as incriminating against him as those against the Arab. Just as Meursault at the end of *The Stranger* occupies the place of the Arab in colonial society, Daru's fate overlaps with "the Arab's," the host's fate with that of the guest's, for each man, judged by the terms of justice of the other, is "objectively" guilty and at the end of the story finds himself alone to face punishment for his "crime." The ideal of hospitality and the possibility of freedom evoked by the encounter of the French teacher and Arab prisoner are thus both negated by the colonial system over which neither has any control and by the violent conflicts that pit "them" against "us" and prevent the continued reversal of roles of "them" and "us," host and guest, colonizer and colonized, which absolute hospitality in principle makes possible. To a colonial society, absolute hospitality, which consists of the mutual recognition of the freedom and equality of the other, represents in fact the greatest threat of all.

At the moment of the publication of this collection of short stories, political actions related to but more extreme than a gendarme's inhumane treatment of an Arab prisoner were being taken by "brothers" of the gendarme in the French army. More violent acts than murdering a cousin for having stolen food and threatening a schoolteacher were being committed by "brothers" of the anonymous Arab prisoner. Such actions were destroying or had already destroyed any hope of what increasingly appeared as the impossible reconciliation between the French and Arab communities of Algeria. At the end of "The Guest/Host," a very different form of solitude is imposed on the French schoolteacher than the kind he experienced at the beginning of the story, when a blizzard had isolated him in the schoolhouse. His exile from the French community, from his Arab and Berber students and neighbors, and also from the land itself is described as absolute and irremediable. Both the Arab Algerian and French Algerian end up perpetuating the cycle of violence they deplore, but they do it against their will and in spite of themselves and their brotherly, hospitable actions toward each other. At the end, they are not only alone but also enemy brothers in spite of themselves, condemned to solitude and death. Each is in some sense responsible for the death of the other, without meaning or wanting to be. Each is thus in part also responsible for his own death as well in a cycle of violence from which there is no escape, no neutral ground, no effective position that is also just.

The situation presented in the story is thus tragic, for there is no way for either character to escape from his fate, no place for either a French schoolteacher or an Arab prisoner except in one of the two warring camps. To be "French" or to be "Arab" is to be either executioner or victim of the other—or, in this case, both at the same time. To refuse this stark choice is not just to be alone and risk being irrelevant to the outcome of the conflict, but it is also, as the story shows, to perpetuate the very violence refused and negated in the act of absolute hospitality. "The Guest/Host" thus reveals that Camus clearly understood the impossible political position he was attempting to occupy both immediately before and during the Algerian War. The story also indicates his sense of powerlessness: neither he nor anyone else could intervene in a way that would stop or even mitigate the increasingly uncontrolled violence of the war that risked making victims of all Algerian civilians. For if even an act of absolute hospitality ends up adding to the violence of the conflict, if acts of justice end up provoking and in themselves constituting crimes, then the situation is truly tragic—not just for one side but for both.

For years I have been unable to see anything in capital punishment but a torture [*une supplice*] the imagination could not endure and a lazy disorder that my reason condemned. Yet I was ready to think that my imagination was influencing my judgment. But, to tell the truth, I found during my recent research nothing that did not strengthen my conviction, nothing that modified my arguments. . . . The death penalty stains our society.

—Albert Camus, "Reflections on the Guillotine"

CHAPTER FOUR

Justice or Death?

When "Justice" Makes You Sick

To kill or not to kill? For Albert Camus, the question of justice ultimately rests on this basic question of whether, outside actual battles fought between soldiers during war, taking the life of another human being can ever be justified. Convinced by both his deepest feelings and confirmed by his research that under no circumstances could murder be defended, he not only opposed capital punishment in the restricted, juridical sense of the term but also in a broader sense, which included political assassinations, terrorist acts, and the bombings of civilian targets, whatever the justifications given for them. Camus' opposition to allegedly "legal" or "justifiable" murder in general could in fact be considered the founding principle of his perspective on politics in general—and thus the basis for his condemnation of the injustices and crimes against civilians committed by both sides during the Algerian War. It is above all a principle that indicates the limits that he repeatedly argued judicial systems, nations at war, and revolutionary political movements needed to respect, no matter how formally democratic and fair the legal system, how just the war being fought, or how legitimate the cause being pursued. Camus strongly believed that murder could never be justified—in the name of either national security, independence, or justice. Murder is always a crime, whether allowed by law and performed under the authority of the State, authorized by military and civil authorities during war, or a part of the resistance to political oppression and the struggle for independence.

The polemical nature of Camus' opposition to political murder in *The Rebel* has led critics to treat it primarily as a component of his critique of totalitarianism and as an effect of the cold war on his thinking, a sign of his increasingly militant anticommunism. In fact, his rejection of capital punishment and political assassination predates World War II and is thus not just an important part of his attack on Nazism and Stalinist Russia in particular and revolution in general. It also informs his political perspective on how most effectively to resist colonial oppression in Algeria and radically change colonial society, even before the Algerian War began. Similar to the allegory of the resistance narrated in *The Plague*, his opposition to capital punishment has multiple sources, implications, and referents. This is because Camus' stance is not rooted in a political principle as such; rather, it is an expression of what could be called a "moral feeling," an innate sense of the limits of what human beings individually or collectively have the right to do to other human beings, whatever the legitimacy of the cause being pursued might be—or perhaps especially when a cause is in fact legitimate.

Near the end of *The Stranger*, after Meursault has been sentenced to death and while awaiting execution, he remembers a story that his mother told him about his father.[1] A slightly different version of the story is recounted at the beginning of Camus' essay against capital punishment, "Reflections on the Guillotine." The story is related a third time in his posthumously published autobiographical novel, *The First Man*. In the two novels and the political essay, the story describes the strong reaction of a father to what Camus calls "the most premeditated of murders."[2] But only in "Reflections on the Guillotine" is the story narrated in Camus' own voice and without the mediation of a fictional character. The mere fact that the story is recounted three times in his writings, and in both his first and last published novels, is sufficient reason to take it seriously. Its political implications in the context of the Algerian War are another.

Camus acknowledges in his essay that the story narrates his own father's reaction to an especially brutal and repulsive crime that had taken place shortly before his father left Algeria to fight and die in France at the beginning of World War I. An entire family of farmers, including young children, had been slaughtered by a deranged farm worker, who was immediately captured, convicted, and sentenced to be guillotined. Camus' father, whom he describes in his essay as a "simple, straightforward man," "a decent man [un honnête homme]," was so horrified and outraged by the crime that he told Camus' mother that decapitation was too good for "such a monster" ("Reflections on the Guillotine," 175–176 [Essais, 1021]). Camus' father felt so strongly that he decided to witness an execution himself "for the first time in his life."

Camus describes his father's reaction to what he witnessed in the following terms:

> What he saw that morning he never told anyone. My mother relates merely that he came rushing home, his face distorted, refused to talk, lay down for a moment on the bed, and suddenly began to vomit. He had just discovered the reality hidden underneath the noble phrases with which it was masked. Instead of thinking of the slaughtered children, he could think of nothing but that quivering body that had just been dropped onto a board to have its head cut off.
>
> (175 [1021])

Camus' father's silence and uncontrollable physical reaction to the spectacle of the execution speak louder than any words could. They are interpreted by Camus to be the irrefutable sign that this "new murder" or "ultimate justice . . . is no less repulsive than the crime" (176, trans. mod. [1022]). He argues that justice cannot be considered *just* if, in punishing a monstrous criminal for a heinous crime, it commits in turn an equally repulsive criminal act.

With the execution of the monstrous murderer, the first murder is supplemented by a second, this one committed by the State under the guise of justice and in the name of the people. Which is to say in the name of all French citizens and thus in his own father's name as well. His father's uncontrollable physical reaction to the execution is all the more significant for Camus because his father had been convinced that capital punishment was entirely justified, because of the viciousness of the crime and the innocence of the victims. Had he not been convinced, he would not have wanted to witness the execution in the first place. Justice for the innocent victims of the crime seemed to demand that the monster who had slaughtered an entire family pay for his crimes with his own head. But against his own powerful convictions, after watching the execution, his father *felt* something very different: disgust.

Supplementing his father's silence and interpreting his reaction, Camus states that what disturbed his father was not so much the horror of the actual beheading but rather the spectacle of the criminal's anguish immediately before he was decapitated. His anguish was so strong that it made his father forget the victims of the atrocious crime and transformed the perpetrator of the crime into another pathetic victim—a victim of justice itself. Witnessing the execution thus had the opposite effect from what his father had expected: instead of feeling the satisfaction that would have come from a sense that the victims had received just retribution and that the rule of law had been reaffirmed by the execution, he could not help identifying with the anguish of the murderer before his death and be affected by it. Rather than feeling satisfaction, he was repulsed by what he saw and vomited.

For Camus, his father's revulsion is in itself the sign that justice in such instances does not serve its principal function, which is "to bring more peace and order into the community," and that the new murder, "far from making amends for the harm done to the social body, adds a new blot to the first one" (176 [1021]). Camus refers to capital punishment as "a cancer" on the social body, but it is a cancer that society attempts to justify as "a necessity." He calls it rather an "obscenity" (177 [1022]). It is no wonder, then, that a decent man like his father would be rendered speechless, forget the victims of the original crime, and vomit after he had witnessed "the new murder" the state had committed allegedly in his name and in the name of justice.

A justice that horrifies and disgusts a simple, decent man, a justice that kills in the name of the people, a justice that makes good people forget the injustices and crimes of the past by compounding and perpetuating them is itself not merely unjust and criminal. It is also abject. As it did in the case of the father whom Camus never knew except through the few stories told to him by his mother, but especially through this particular story, Camus felt that it should make us all sick.

In his essay, Camus argues that capital punishment should be vomited out of the body politic, no matter what reasons are given to defend it or under what conditions it is carried out. And this is true not just when executions are decided by dictators, military officers, callous political leaders, or colonial authorities as the means to maintain control, reestablish order, or eliminate opposition, dissent, or revolt. It is equally the case when capital punishment is decided in democratic societies in legally constituted courts of law and used to punish monstrous criminals, or when individuals or groups are targeted by revolutionary groups in order to advance the cause of social justice and national independence. For it makes no difference ultimately whether the death penalty is decided during times of war or peace, or whether the verdict is voted on by a jury in a court of law and carried out according to the rules of a democratic legal system or decided by a revolutionary movement or national liberation front and used as a weapon against foreign conquerors, colonialist oppressors, or innocent bystanders. In all cases, the act itself is revolting; it should always make us as sick as it made Camus' father. In any case, it can never be justified. It is never just.

Camus firmly believed that any system of justice that punishes criminals by taking their life is unjust; any state or revolutionary party or movement that uses terrorism as the means to achieve its ends in fact perverts those ends, no matter how noble those ends might be. And any intellectual or politician who attempts to legitimize official or unofficial murders, no matter the social or political goals claimed to be served by them, is attempting to hide an "obscenity under a verbal cloak" (177 [1022]). Convinced that no compromise could or should ever be made when it comes to the basic question of life or death, Camus, unlike his father, did not remain silent about this obscenity. Rather he decided to "talk about it crudely" (177 [1022]), and he did so, not just once but three times, in works written at very different moments of his life and in vastly different political environments.[3]

Except for a brief moment of revolutionary fervor immediately after the liberation of Paris in World War II, when he supported the use of capital punishment in a limited number of cases, Camus consistently argued that there is no acceptable justification for capital punishment—or any other form of calculated murder. His disgust over both the executions themselves and the justifications for them is at the core of all his post–World War II political essays and constitutes the basis for his critique of both communism and imperialist forms of democracy, on the one hand, and his denunciation of terrorism, torture, and summary executions during the Algerian War, on the other. It could be argued that it was primarily his disgust at and refusal to accept all justifications for the murder of civilians during the

Algerian War that made it impossible for him to support either side, even the side that had justice on its side.

Premeditated Murder

> "I decided to have nothing to do with anything, which directly or indirectly, for good or bad reasons, causes or justifies murder."
>
> —Tarrou, in *The Plague*

In "Reflections on the Guillotine," Camus argues that there is no rational justification for capital punishment, since it is a form of "the law of retaliation" and rooted in "an emotion, and a particularly violent one, and not in a principle. Retaliation is related to nature and instinct, not to law. . . . Execution is not simply death. It is just as different, in essence, from the privation of life as a concentration camp is from prison. It is a murder . . . the most premeditated of murders" (197–199 [1038–1039]). The only way a state, political party, elected official, judge, or even a legally constituted jury could claim the right to execute criminals or enemies of the state in the name of justice, he further argues, would not simply be when the criminal of a capital crime was "absolutely guilty" of a heinous crime. More important, the decision to execute could be considered legitimate only if society and its political and legal institutions functioned perfectly and were in fact "absolutely innocent." But since no individual, class, group, government, political movement, or revolutionary elite, even when it represents and acts in the name of the victims of injustice, can ever legitimately claim to be "absolutely innocent," it follows that no one has the right to murder—no matter what the law allows. On the contrary, "the death penalty, which really neither provides an example nor assures distributive justice, simply usurps an exorbitant privilege by claiming to punish an always relative culpability by a definitive and irreparable punishment" (210 [1047]). If, as Camus claims, "every society has the criminals it deserves" (206 [1044]), a society that murders to punish murderers, a revolutionary movement that uses terror, executions, and assassinations as the means to achieve justice or independence, or even a nation that murders allegedly in order to punish past murders or prevent future ones is not just responsible for the premeditated murders it commits. It is also defined by them, since he argues that murder inevitably leads to more murder, terror to more terror—never the opposite.

Camus was not a pacifist, but in his post–World War II writings he consistently condemns premeditated murder and denounces what he calls the "era of murder" in which "state crimes have been far more numerous than individual crimes. . . . The number of individuals killed directly by the State has assumed astronomical proportions" (227 [1059]). He claims that faith in absolute principles or ideals always leads not just revolutionary movements, totalitarian states, and imperial or colonial powers but also democratic states to kill innocent civilians with impunity and then to justify the deaths as necessary means to allegedly noble ends. Unquestioned faith, not necessarily or exclusively in *spiritual* absolutes but in *historical* or *material* ideals that have been divinized, thus ends up also justifying or even being responsible for murder:

> One kills for a nation or class that has been granted divine status. One kills for a future society that has likewise been given divine status. Whoever thinks he has omniscience imagines he has omnipotence. Temporal idols demanding an absolute faith tirelessly decree absolute punishments. And religions devoid of transcendence kill great numbers of condemned men devoid of hope.
>
> (228 [1060])

For a political and religious agnostic such as Camus, absolute faith in the gods of religion, history, the internationalist revolution, or the nation-state has repeatedly proven to be one of the greatest threats to human life. Camus simply refused to believe in any spiritual or political ideal that had such lethal effects. The principle that human life comes before anything else, even before justice, means that murder is never just and can never be justified.[4]

Partial Amnesia

For a brief period immediately after the liberation of France at the end of World War II, however, Camus defended the execution of a limited num-

ber of French collaborators and traitors. His experience in the French Resistance and the extent of Nazi atrocities and Vichy crimes caused him to
accept briefly what in every other context he rejected. It is as if the memory
of his father's story, first published in fictional form in *The Stranger* in 1942,
had been forgotten, or more likely displaced or buried under more grip-
ping memories of horrible crimes and injustices that he could not ignore.
His father's story might even have seemed at that time trivial or irrelevant,
given the more powerful memories of Resistance comrades who had been
arrested, tortured, deported, or executed in the struggle to liberate France.
It is in fact the memory of the suffering of these victims that he argues in
numerous editorials should take precedence over all other concerns—even
over the repugnance or disgust that he claims he and others would feel
when these monstrous war criminals were actually executed. For a brief
time, then, all human life did not come for him before justice, but rather
the memory of the victims of unforgivable injustices did. As was the case
for his father before he witnessed the execution, he believed briefly that
the "monsters" who had committed such crimes should pay for them with
their own life.

Camus' acceptance of the death penalty for those responsible for the
worst crimes committed during the war also had a specific political justification, for as his editorials for the Resistance newspaper *Combat* indicate,
Camus, like many others on the Left, believed that, given the success of the
Resistance, France was on the verge of a socialist revolution. But to carry
out such a revolution and for France to remake itself and become a true social democracy, which is what Camus and his colleagues at *Combat* enthusiastically advocated, France first had to punish the traitors and criminals
responsible for the denunciation, torture, deportation, and murder of innocent civilians and Resistance comrades. This group of criminals included
officials of Vichy France, members of the French *Milice*, and opportunistic
or ideologically committed collaborators who encouraged and defended
the arrest, torture, deportation, or execution of Nazi and Vichy opponents
and Jews.[5] It is clear from his earliest articles on the purge trials, for example, that Camus felt that too many people had been tortured and murdered to spare those responsible for these crimes. For a brief time he thus
argued that capital punishment was justified and, unlike the execution of
the "monster" witnessed by his father, that executions could occur with-

out transforming horrible criminals into victims. In numerous editorials for *Combat*, he presents capital punishment not as the perversion of justice his other writings depicted it as being, but rather as the purest expression of justice—the form of justice necessary to honor the memory of the victims of Nazism and the Vichy State.

An unsigned editorial of this type that appeared in *Combat* during the period in which it was still being published clandestinely refers to the members of the French *Milice* as "rotten branches [that] cannot be left attached to the tree [but] have to be lopped off, reduced to sawdust, and scattered on the ground. . . . Courts-martial would be pointless, moreover. The *Milice* is its own tribunal. It has judged itself and sentenced itself to death. Those sentences will be carried out."[6] In such extreme cases, justice would thus be unproblematic and did not even need explicit laws, courts, judges, or juries to be implemented. This is because "the *Milice* has placed itself outside the law. It must be made quite clear that each militiaman, in signing his enlistment papers, is ratifying his own death sentence" (4 [128]). Justice for those so egregiously outside the law—not the law of the Vichy State, of course, but the higher law of justice itself—is thus argued to transcend any specific legal code. The perpetrators of the crimes know that their own acts judge them and by their crimes they have in fact already sentenced themselves to death.

Camus justifies his support of capital punishment for French collaborators found guilty of crimes of torture or murder not by legal or political arguments, but rather through emotional arguments and by describing in minute detail the atrocious nature of their crimes. It is as if the descriptions of the crimes themselves dictated the appropriate punishment. For example, in one of the earliest editorials he published in *Combat* after the liberation of Paris, Camus describes the discovery in Vincennes of the bodies of thirty-four Frenchmen who had been grotesquely tortured and mutilated: "We learn of comrades who had their guts ripped out, their limbs torn off, and their faces kicked in. And the men who did these things were men polite enough to give up their seats on the subway. . . . Who in such circumstances would dare to speak of pardon? . . . It is not hatred that will speak out tomorrow but justice itself, justice based on memory" ("The Age of Contempt," *Combat* [August 30, 1944], 20–21 [157–158]). Such "unbearable images" (20 [157]) rule out the possibility of restraint, mitigation, or pardon of any sort; they demand rather immediate, absolute justice, a justice dictated by the images of the atrocious crimes themselves and the memory of their victims.

In an untitled article written on the establishment of a High Court of Justice to judge Maréchal Pétain, Pierre Laval, and other prominent members of the Vichy government, Camus also expresses his support for the most extreme form of punishment for the crime of treason they committed: "If there are some cases in which our duty is not clear or justice is difficult to define, in this case we take our stand without hesitation. The voices of the tortured and humiliated join with ours in calling for justice of the most pitiless and decisive kind."[7] In numerous signed editorials, Camus presents the choice faced by the High Court and in fact by all French to be the choice between being on the side of victims or on the side of perverse torturers and executioners. And when the alternative is presented in this stark way, there is clearly no choice at all, no real judgment to make of guilt or innocence, since justice is obviously on the side of the victims and out of respect for them needs to be as harsh and pitiless as the crimes themselves.[8]

But even during this period, when Camus repeatedly argues that "the purge is necessary," he also urges that the principle of proportion be respected: "The point is not to purge a lot but to purge well. But what does it mean to purge well? It means to respect the general principle of justice without failing to make allowances in individual cases" (*Combat* [October 18, 1944], 77 [264–265]). If the principle of justice in such cases has to be "proportion," it would seem to be an extremely difficult if not impossible task, even under ideal conditions and even for the fairest, best-intentioned judges, prosecutors, and juries, to find a just proportion between, on the one hand, the memory of the suffering of the victims that would seem to demand the quickest and harshest form of punishment for those responsible and, on the other, the general repulsion that is felt by decent people when even a monstrous criminal is executed.

Camus leaves no doubt, however, that in such ideal circumstances at least he feels the decision to execute those guilty of the worst crimes would be just:

> We know full well that on the day the first death sentence is carried out in Paris, we will feel repugnance. At that moment we will need to remember the countless other death sentences imposed on men who

were pure and will have to recall so many cherished faces now buried in the ground and so many hands we once loved to shake. When we are tempted to prefer the generous sacrifices of war to the dark duties of justice, we will need to remember the dead and the unbearable image of those whom torture turned into traitors. As hard as that will be, we will know then that pardons cannot be granted.

(*Combat* [October 21, 1944], 82 [275]).

For Camus, the memory of the victims must ultimately triumph over and negate the repugnance that would be felt when executions occurred. Memory alone in such instances must determine what is just; repugnance, on the other hand, must be overcome or simply forgotten—assuming, of course, an uncontrollable reaction such as his father's could ever be overcome, ignored, or forgotten.

Thus Camus, even though he admits he has "no taste for murder" and that for him "the human person embodies all that we respect in the world," supported the death penalty for particularly atrocious war crimes. But only if justice is "prompt," if "all prosecution for crimes of collaboration end at some fixed date. We want the most obvious crimes to be punished immediately, and then, since nothing can be done without mediocrity, we want the errors that so many Frenchmen have indeed committed consigned to carefully considered oblivion" (*Combat* [October 25, 1944], 89–90 [288–289]). It soon became clear to Camus that in fact the opposite was in fact occurring: justice was most often rapid and severe for lesser crimes and painfully slow and indulgent for the greater crimes committed by Vichy officials and important industrialists. In Camus' own terms, justice was anything but proportional, which meant it could not be considered just. In reality, it very quickly began to disgust him.

Even if he continued to evoke the memories of the victims of Nazi and Vichy crimes, Camus' partial amnesia concerning his father's story—partial because he also continued to evoke his personal dislike of murder and the repugnance that he claimed all would feel when collaborationist criminals were executed—did not last very long. By the summer of 1945, Camus had changed his position on the necessity for the purge after he had been repeatedly confronted with its grotesque reality: "There can no longer be any doubt that the postwar purge has not only failed in France but is now completely discredited. The word 'purge' itself was already rather distressing. The actual thing became odious. . . . The failure is complete" (*Combat* [August 30, 1945], 249–250 [594]). In an earlier editorial, Camus had already attacked the trials for producing only "absurd sentences and preposterous instances of leniency. In between, prisoners are snatched from their prisons and shot because they were pardoned. . . . [Judges] will go on handing out death sentences to journalists who don't deserve as much. They will go on half-acquitting recruiters with silver tongues" (*Combat* [January 5, 1945], 163–165 [430–432]). The moment for a higher, moral form of justice rooted in the need to respect the memory of the "pure victims" of Nazism and the Vichy State, a "pure justice" demanded by their silenced voices and carried out in their name, had thus passed very quickly. But the obligation to honor the memory of the victims remained, even if in reality it proved to be a difficult, if not impossible, obligation to meet. Nothing in fact could make up for the suffering and loss of life of the victims—and, adding to the injustice, by making victims of criminals, their memory was obscured rather than honored.

In one of his many exchanges with François Mauriac, the conservative Catholic writer and fellow *résistant*, Camus summarizes his differences with Mauriac in the following way:

> Whenever I used the word *justice* in connection with the purge, M. Mauriac spoke of *charity*. . . . Some of us reject both the cries of enmity that reach our ears from one side and the tender solicitations that come to us from the other. Between these two extremes, we are searching for the just voice that will give us truth without shame. . . . This is what allows me to say that charity has no business here.
>   (*Combat*, "Justice and Charity" [January 11, 1945], 168 [439])

The "just voice" Camus claims he and others at *Combat* were searching for, however, was certainly not to be found in the purge trials, which revealed rather only partial or contradictory "truths" about the responsibility of both those who were executed and those who were not. The purge trials succeeded only in becoming increasingly "odious." And if "charity had no business" in them, justice was largely absent from them as well.

Camus is thus forced to admit "that it is probably too late now for justice to be done" and that the purge trials in general are examples only of "sick justice [*justice infirme*]" (*Combat* [January 5, 1945], 165 [432]). He will soon conclude that justice is always infirm when murders are committed in its name, even to punish murderers, and it is precisely in reference to his opposition to such "infirm justice" that Camus explains why he signed petitions to save the lives of two of the most notorious fascist literary collaborators, Robert Brasillach and Lucien Rebatet (the former was nonetheless executed immediately after his trial in February 1945; the latter's death sentence was commuted, and he was eventually released from prison in the amnesty of 1950). Camus' reason for signing both petitions was the same: he felt nothing but disdain for both Brasillach and Rebatet and considered their writings and actions to be criminal. But he also admits that he held the death penalty in greater horror than he did these two notorious literary anti-Semites and Nazi collaborators.[9]

The purge trials could be said to represent a turning point in Camus' relation to politics in that they vividly recalled his father's disgust with State murder. During the Algerian War, he would be harshly criticized for not supporting the FLN in spite of its use of terrorism against innocent civilians. He was attacked especially brutally in the press after he declared in Sweden a day after receiving the Nobel Prize that if he was forced to choose between justice and defending the life of his mother, he would choose first to defend his mother. Even though the statement was taken by many of his opponents as a sign of his colonialist sympathies and a defense of France's war strategy and right to continue to colonize Algeria, in fact it expresses rather his conviction that priority should always be given to protecting human life, to the life of his own mother, of course, but the life of all other Algerian civilians as well. Individual lives had to come before ideals, whatever the legitimacy of those ideals might be. There would not and could not be justice if the opposite were true, since no end could ever justify terrorist means. No ideal could legitimate murder, not even freedom and certainly not justice, for, as he learned in the purge trials, justice can never be total or "pure" without becoming unjust.[10]

For Camus, the failure of justice in the purge trials was thus both a sign and a cause of the impending failure of France to "remake itself" as a social democracy after the war. As he put it, "a country that fails to purge itself is preparing to fail to remake itself. The face that a nation wears is that of its system of justice" (*Combat* [January 5, 1945], 165 [433]). And the face of justice the French nation wore immediately after the Liberation was not just that of "confusion," but also the opposite of the impossible ideal of pure justice Camus evokes in his articles. It was, on the contrary, much closer to what his father had experienced when he witnessed the execution of a monstrous murderer before World War I: it was the face of infirm justice that would make any decent person sick. And during the Algerian War, given the systematic use of torture and summary executions to combat terrorism and reestablish order, the face of justice worn by the French nation would only become increasingly impure, infirm, and even grotesquely monstrous.

Thou Shall Not Kill

> Absurdist reasoning admits that human life is the only necessary good.... To say that life is absurd, the conscience must still be alive.
>
> —Albert Camus, *The Rebel*

"We live in terror," wrote Camus in "The Century of Fear," the first of the series of articles he published in *Combat* from November 19 through November 30, 1946, under the general title "Neither Victims nor Executioners" (*Combat*, "The Century of Fear" [November 19, 1946], 255–276 [604–643]). When he made this claim in 1946, World War II of course had already ended and Nazi Germany and Imperial Japan had been defeated. Soldiers were no longer dying in battlefields throughout Europe, North Africa, and the Pacific, and civilians were no longer living in fear for their lives in the cities that each side had targeted at different moments of the war. Camus' Resistance comrades and other political opponents of Nazi Germany and Vichy France were no longer being arrested, tortured, summarily executed, or deported to concentration camps to live and die under atrocious, inhuman conditions. Jews were no longer being deported to death camps and exterminated by the millions. Nazi oppression, torture, deportation, and mass murder were still painful memories of the recent past, but they were no longer part of daily experience. The terror of which Camus speaks in these editorials thus no longer had Nazi Germany as its unique cause.

Nevertheless, Camus insists in these articles that a reign of terror was continuing after the war because even if "fear can't be considered a science, there is no question that it is a method [*une technique*]" (257 [609]). And moreover, terror works by silencing opposition, preventing dialogue between opposing sides, and forcing people to choose one side or the other in an ideological battle that each side of the conflict presents as being between freedom and enslavement, justice and injustice, Good and Evil. The method in the madness of terror is to create a world divided between "us" and "them," the just and the unjust, friends and foes, true believers and heretics or renegades, a world in which each side is convinced it has justice and truth (God) on its side.

The primary source of postwar terror is ideology, or rather all of the "deadly ideologies" continuing to struggle for hegemony *after* the defeat of fascism. Ideologies are "deadly" for Camus first of all because he claims they have already been directly or indirectly responsible for the deaths of millions of victims who have in one way or another been considered enemies of or at least obstacles to the realization of political goals or ideals. And second, they are "deadly" because ideologies deaden the sensitivity and receptiveness of those committed to them and thus have the effect of transforming living human beings into what he calls robotic "abstractions." "There is no way," Camus argues,

> of persuading an abstraction, or, to put it another way, the representative of an ideology. The long dialogue among human beings has now come to an end. . . . A conspiracy of silence has arisen and continues to spread, a conspiracy accepted by those who quake in fear . . . and encouraged by those who find it in their interest to do so. . . . For all who cannot live without dialogue and the friendship of other human beings, this silence is the end of the world.
>
> (258–259 [610–611])

It ultimately makes no difference which side of the ideological battle one is on, since the nature of the battleground itself is the problem, so serious a

problem that Camus claims that the destruction of the conditions for dialogue among opposing positions through terror constitutes a threat to the
future of the human community as a whole. And it is the absence of dialogue and the treatment of all opposition and dissent as treasonous and of
all who disagree as mortal enemies that he claims lays the groundwork for
the legitimization of murder and is thus the deadly product of a general
climate of terror.

Camus' anti-ideological stance is rooted not in the belief that there exists an alternate form of politics that would be in itself completely pure
or nonideological, as is most often the case with those who are militantly
"against ideology." It is rather based on the conviction that because life has
precedence over politics, politics cannot be allowed to determine life. This
means that the first and most fundamental obligation of political activists
is not to defend their own position or tactics but rather to defend life, or, as
Camus puts it, "to save bodies," to keep living human beings from becoming corpses, sacrificed to one ideological ideal (or plague) or another. The
chief problem for him after the war is thus how to continue to be involved
in the struggle against injustice and oppression without committing, encouraging, or further legitimizing murder:

> The world that people like me are after is not a world in which peo-
> ple don't kill one another (we're not that crazy!) but a world in which
> murder is not legitimized. We are therefore living in utopia and con-
> tradiction, to be sure, since the world we live in is one in which mur-
> der is legitimized, and we ought to change it if we don't like it. But it
> seems that it can't be changed without running the risk of commit-
> ting murder. Murder thus leads to murder, and we will continue to
> live in terror either because we resign ourselves to it or because we
> seek to eliminate it by means that replace one form of terror with
> another.
> (*Combat*, "Saving Bodies" [November 20, 1946], 260 [614]).

No ideology and no form of political action thus escapes from this fundamental contradiction, since if actions taken to eliminate injustice risk producing further injustices, if attempts to destroy the world in which murder
is legitimized lead to and end up justifying additional murders, then a re-

jection of ideology, political activism, and perhaps even politics in general would seem to be the only way to avoid murdering in the name of eliminating murder and replacing one form of terror with another.[11]

However, Camus' response is not acquiescence, passivity, or indifference, since he rejects them as responses to what for him is the fundamental contradiction of politics itself. An awareness of the risk of murder implied in any militant political action that attempts to radically change society does mean, however, that no commitment to justice can ever be total, that is, exclusively political in nature. In both his postwar journalism and *The Rebel*, Camus repeatedly comes back to the same question: "Our purpose is to find out whether innocence, the moment it becomes involved in action, can avoid committing murder. . . . We shall know nothing until we know whether we have the right to kill the other before us, or to consent to having him be killed. Since every action today leads to murder, direct or indirect, we cannot act until we know whether and why we have to cause death."[12] Passivity is rejected because to decide not to act "amounts to accepting the murder of others" and to allow murder to retain what Camus calls "its privileged position" (5 [415]). In the political realm, you are damned if you act and damned if you don't. And yet one still senses in all of Camus' writings a fundamental imperative to act—but always within limits, always with the means to any end judged on their own rather than being justified by the ends they allegedly serve. If the means are not just, with the ultimate test being whether they are in themselves murderous or lead to and justify murder, then the ends they serve can never make them just.

To refuse either to live passively in a world where murder is legitimized or to agree that murders have to be committed and thus innocent lives sacrificed in order to eliminate murder may be utopian, but Camus claims it is to choose "relative utopia" over what he calls the absolute utopias constituted by both Marxist and capitalist ideologies: "It is a much lesser degree of utopia, however, to ask that murder no longer be legitimized. What is more, the Marxist and capitalist ideologies, both of which are based on the idea of progress and both of which are convinced that application of their principles must inevitably lead to social equilibrium, are utopias of a much greater degree. Beyond that, they are even now exacting a very heavy price from us" (*Combat*, "Saving Bodies" [November 20, 1946], 261 [615]). Camus clearly feels that the cost of "progress" in either Marxist or capitalist terms is too great a price to pay. For if human life must always come first and thus if murder can never be legitimized, then "progress" must always be judged first and foremost in terms of its immediate human costs. And when innocent lives are sacrificed, progress itself is illegitimate and neither progressive nor just.[13]

I would consider his refusal to legitimize murder—whether in the form of capital punishment, political assassination, terrorism, or counterterrorism—as the founding principle of Camus' critical perspective on politics, both his increasingly militant anticommunism and his refusal to defend the use of terrorism in the cause of national liberation in Algeria or torture and murder in France's counterterrorist strategy. In fact, even Camus' militant opposition to Communism had Algerian roots, as his experience as a Communist Party member in Algeria in the mid-1930s had already distanced him from the Communist International. By the time he was excluded from the Algerian Communist Party, he was already a critic of the Party's internationalist ideology and what he claimed was its blind faith in revolution, which he felt was the principal reason for its neglect of the actual plight of the Arab and Berber populations of Algeria and its refusal to support moderate Algerian nationalists and their demands for reforms. He was already at that time unwilling to put the project for an international proletarian revolution to be realized in an ill-defined future before the immediate problems of destitute Algerians in the present.

In an article he wrote for *Combat* soon after the liberation of France, after serious divisions among the communist and noncommunist elements of the Resistance had surfaced, Camus first reaffirms *Combat*'s position that "anti-Communism is the first step toward dictatorship": "We vigorously reject political anti-Communism because we know what inspires it and what its unavowed aims are" (*Combat* [October 7, 1944], 62–63 [237–238]). He then asserts that his colleagues' and his own differences with their communist Resistance comrades are not rooted in opposed social visions or goals, but rather in the unwillingness to accept what he calls communism's faith in dialectical history and "political realism":

> Most of our comrades' collectivist ideas and social programs, their ideal of justice, and their disgust with a society in which money and privilege occupy the front ranks, we share. But as our comrades freely recognize, their adherence to a very consistent philosophy of history justifies their acceptance of political realism as the primary method

for securing the triumph of an ideal shared by many Frenchmen. On this matter we very clearly differ. As we have said many times, we do not believe in political realism. Our method is different.

(63 [238–239])

The differences of "method" between Camus and communists (and later, his polemical exchanges with communist fellow-travelers and advocates of third-world revolution such as Sartre) would in fact be exacerbated during the cold war, when he in fact would become a militant anticommunist and critic of revolutionary movements.

It would be difficult to deny that Camus felt that the most deadly and thus dangerous form of "the plague" in postwar Europe was its Stalinist strain, although that was certainly not its only form. He continued to denounce another form, which was represented by dictatorship in Franco's Spain and about which Camus repeatedly wrote in *Combat* in order to call attention to the oppression of the Spanish people and criticize those democracies, especially the United States, that continued to support Franco (and other dictators throughout the world) for strategic reasons—that is, following what could be called democratic political realism.

The ultimate basis of Camus' political agnosticism and his determined opposition to all messianic, redemptive forms of politics could thus be argued in the final analysis to be neither an ideological or abstract ethical principle. It is rather a deep and at times uncontrollable feeling of revulsion at the spectacle of capital punishment, disgust not just at the sight but also even at the thought of legalized or politically legitimated murder. The thrice-repeated story of his father's rejection of the sick justice he witnessed in Algeria before World War I delineates the ultimate limit of the political for Camus, the line that he repeatedly argues no society or political movement should ever cross, a limit determined by the respect for human life that makes it impossible to ever justify murder.

For only when this primitive, abject, and fundamentally antidemocratic act against others is itself vomited out of the body politic, only when capital punishment in all its forms, including terrorism and counterterrorism, political murder, and the indiscriminate bombing of civilian targets during war, is treated as a crime by those on both sides, only when all religious and political justifications for the murder of others are considered unacceptable means to any end did Camus think that justice would finally be served. Only when human life in the present is defended before ideals or promises of justice in the future could a society rightfully claim to be free, independent, and democratic. To choose to defend his mother before justice was thus not to choose "French Algeria" before "Muslim" or "Algerian Algeria"—it was rather to choose human life before an ideal or promise of justice that legitimated terrorist acts against not just his own mother but all other innocent civilians as well, whether French, Arab, or Berber, Catholic, Muslim, or Jewish.

From the end of World War II until his death, Camus in both his literary and political texts repeatedly grappled with the contradictions of his anti-ideological position, struggling to reconcile his refusal to legitimize murder with an activist, socially responsible politics and, in each instance, to find a "third way" that would be able to effectively oppose injustices without supporting the deadly means used in revolutionary struggles for national independence—or the counter-revolutionary and counterterrorist means used against them. During the Algerian War, as we shall see in the chapters that follow, this proved to be an increasingly difficult if not impossible position to maintain.

It is important to recognize, however, that Camus developed his uncompromising position against terrorism and all other forms of premeditated murder not during and because of the Algerian War, but well before it began: in pre–World War II Algeria, because of his experiences in the Algerian Communist Party; during World War II, because of his experiences in the French Resistance; and in the immediate post–World War II period, because of his eventual disgust at the purge trials and sick justice. His rejection of capital punishment in all its forms affects the judicial practices of democracies as much as the terror used by totalitarian states, the repressive counterterrorist activities of imperial, colonizing powers as much as the terrorist acts of revolutionary movements of national liberation. The problem Camus faced especially during the Algerian War was how to make such a position politically effective. That he did not succeed in doing so does not, however, mean that he was wrong to have made the effort or that such a position should be considered irrelevant today. On the contrary, it may be more necessary to take his attempts (and failure) seriously today than ever before. For only the most fanatical ideologue would really ever choose to defend an ideal—even justice, independence, freedom—before defending (or at the sacrifice of) his own mother or other innocent victims. Only those totally indifferent to the anguish and suffering of others—even of those guilty of monstrous crimes—would praise rather than vomit at the sight of sick justice and any form of terrorism whatsoever.

Let me first say what everyone already knows, even the *colons* and the nationalists: that terrorist actions and repression in Algeria are two purely negative forces, both of them devoted to pure destruction, with no future other than the increase of furor and folly.

—Albert Camus, "Terrorisme et répression," *L'Express* (July 9, 1955)[1]

Innocents are blown to pieces. But which innocents? Who is innocent? Dozens of Europeans peacefully drinking in a bar? Dozens of Arabs strewn along the road near a blown-up bus? Terrorism, counterterrorism, terror, horror, death, blood, desperate cries, cries of atrocious sorrow, death rattles. Nothing more. Peace.

—Moloud Feraoun, *Journal* (October 6, 1956)

CHAPTER FIVE

Terror

Ends and Means

> Torture, ignominious torture, as horrible in Algiers as in Budapest.
> —Albert Camus, "Discours de la Salle Wagram" (March 15, 1957)

Albert Camus never wavered in his condemnation of terrorism—all forms of terrorism, even the form that is called counterterrorism. He could not accept that the murder of civilians could ever be defended as a legitimate means to an end, no matter how just the end was believed to be. This was the case whether terrorism consisted of placing bombs in cafés, racetracks, casinos, and offices to kill innocent men, women, and children in order to destroy the colonial system in Algeria and create a free and independent Algerian state, or whether it involved executing suspects, slaughtering demonstrators, and napalming suspect villages to ensure that Algeria would remain French. Whether it entailed the planned assassination of police, teachers, farmers, workers, and political opponents—Arab, Berber, or French—by the FLN, or the torture and murder of suspected terrorists and their collaborators—Arab, Berber, or French—by the French army. Terrorism for him could never be considered a justifiable means of self-defense or a legitimate tactic in a war of independence; it was rather a hideous and indefensible crime. Terrorism could never rectify past injustices or effectively counter other terrorist acts. Terrorism could not bring peace. It could only perpetuate itself.

In his political essays on Algeria, Camus repeatedly argues that the ends evoked to justify terrorist means, even if in principle noble or honorable, immediately become dishonorable with the use of ignoble means. To condemn some to die so that others would live as "new men," to commit unjust acts in the name of justice, to execute "enemies of the people" in the name of the people, to enslave in the name of independence, to torture in the name of democracy and the rule of law—these were for Camus unacceptable crimes, regardless of the ends they were alleged to serve. Ends they in fact never really did serve. Noble ends—independence, justice, equality, freedom—were inevitably transformed into their opposites—enslavement, injustice, inequality, oppression—when terrorism or the counterterrorist repression of terrorism constituted the means used to achieve them.

Violence against civilian populations was thus for Camus illegitimate, no matter who used it, why it was used, and what it was used for. Such violence, which should not be confused with armed resistance and guerilla attacks on military targets, was "fascist," even if it was being used to combat fascism, unjust, even if it was a part of a struggle against injustice, and equal to or worse than the worst excesses of colonialism, even if its purpose was to destroy colonialism. It was terrorist, even or especially when it was the tactic used to counter terrorism; no justification could be made for it.

Camus acknowledges in his preface to *Algerian Reports* that his stance against the terrorism of both sides of the war satisfied no one and would undoubtedly be rejected or ignored by both sides in the Algerian War. But he also admits that no position satisfied him either.[2] In his last public statement on Algeria, he once again presents a severe critique of colonialism and the unacceptable counterterrorist tactics being used by the French army to reestablish order in Algeria, which naturally made him the enemy of militant defenders of *Algérie française*. But he also attacks the leadership of the FLN and its equally unacceptable use of terrorism, which of course made him an enemy of the political Left in general and especially those who enthusiastically and uncritically supported the Algerian armed insurrection. His refusal to support either the French or Arab side in the war, to be one of "us" or one of "them," left him in a political no-man's land, as isolated as the schoolteacher Daru at the end of "The Guest/Host."[3]

A year before Camus published *Algerian Reports*, Albert Memmi had claimed that such a position was untenable and that "the role of the left-wing colonizer collapses" in what he called "an impossible historical situation." The result is that "the leftist colonizer . . . will slowly realize that the only thing for him to do is remain silent [*se taire*]."[4] Which is exactly what Camus did after 1958. As we have seen, Camus' most severe postcolonial critics find nothing contradictory or impossible about his situation, however, and therefore do not just criticize the political inefficacy of his position but also treat it as a defense of colonialism itself. In doing so, they ignore what Memmi and others on the Left, even if they ultimately chose to support the FLN, did not ignore: that supporting the FLN could not in itself resolve the contradiction of defending the tactics of a brutal and repressive undemocratic nationalist organization in order to achieve independence and freedom for an oppressed people.[5]

Camus simply rejected out of hand the notion that the FLN could be considered the legitimate representative of the Algerian people because of the nature of the organization itself and the terrorist campaign it had waged against the different civilian populations of Algeria since 1954—not merely against French civilians, which had received the most publicity in France, but against the other Algerian nationalist leaders and groups and innocent Arab and Berber civilians as well.[6] But to denounce only the terrorist practices of the FLN, on the one hand, or the indiscriminate bombings of villages and the torturing and murder of FLN suspects by the French, on the other, without immediately denouncing the crimes of the other side and implicating it as well in the escalating violence and terrorism was, he argued, of no assistance in bringing the war to a just end. On the contrary, it had the effect of encouraging and legitimizing further violence and terrorism, thus prolonging the war. This was the main reason Camus consistently rejected both the tactics and goals of both sides.

This is not to say that Camus did not take sides on the general question of the effects of colonialism in Algeria and of the responsibility of the French for the injustices and humiliation suffered by colonized Algerians for over a century. He repeatedly acknowledges in his essays that French colonialism was the principal cause of the misery of the Arabs and Berbers in Algeria, but he also expresses his deep concerns about the fate of all Algerians in an independent Algeria ruled by brutal nationalist dictators. Whatever its political limitations might be argued to be, Camus' was not the ignoble colonialist position some critics have claimed, however, even if as the war progressed his political perspective was increasingly difficult to maintain and his proposals for peace increasingly unrealistic. In hindsight, his analysis of the long-term effects of terrorism on the Algerian people could be considered prescient and, in fact, less mystified or illusory than the third-world revolutionary zeal expressed by numerous supporters of the FLN.

In his essays, Camus expresses a reluctance to speak about Algeria because of a fear that his criticisms of the criminal actions of either side in the war could provoke or be used to justify the terrorist acts on the other side and thus the murder of more innocent civilians. He acknowledges that this possibility imposes a limit on his political discourse and regrets that it did not impose the same limit on *all* political discourse and all actions taken by both sides in the war. In his mind, the recognition and acceptance of political limits, that is, of the basic principle that it is not possible to do everything even in the pursuit of the most noble cause, should have made even the most radical factions on both sides rethink their commitments, qualify their support for their respective causes, and at the very least reject the use of terror and all violence directed against innocent civilians. Camus attacks those on both sides who did not recognize or respect such limits, all of those who refused to acknowledge that in order for either side to succeed and defeat the other side, it would mean, as he put it, waging a "total war" against the Algerian people, a war that would destroy the very people in whose name it was allegedly being fought—and this was true whether Algeria would remain French or become independent at the end of the war. Camus did not understand or at least pretended not to understand why it was not obvious to everyone else as well that no cause was worth such a sacrifice.

Camus has nothing but scorn for the romantic and what he considered extremely dangerous praise of violence by intellectuals on the Left (and although he never names him directly in these essays, always using the phrase "Paris intellectuals," first and foremost Sartre), and he argues that their support for terrorism had devastating effects on both French and Arab Algerians alike. Nothing was less abstract and more real for Camus than the torture and execution of suspects and the collective punishment inflicted on the populations of entire villages, on the one hand, or the massacre of innocent men, women, and children in the streets and cafés of Algiers and the assassination of political opponents throughout Algeria and in France, on the other. Nothing was more destructively *political* in the worst sense of the term than both terrorism and counterterrorism, for in his view terrorism was destroying the fabric of Algerian society by threatening the lives of all Algerians and turning individuals and entire communities against each other.

Such actions were dangerous and destructive not just for their devastating effects during the war, but because he feared that they would also continue long after the war had ended, no matter which side emerged victorious. He was convinced that terrorism would have the effect of encouraging and justifying in advance future terrorist acts and perpetuate a cycle that would continue long after either Algerian independence or the defeat of the FLN had been achieved. A war fought and eventually won through either terrorism or counterterrorist repression and torture would thus never really be over. More than forty years after Algerian independence, it would be difficult to argue that Camus was wrong in having such fears.

Camus attacks especially severely the "Paris intellectuals" who defended the FLN's tactics but had no family or friends threatened by terrorist bombs. He claims that not only did these "Parisians" ignore or remain indifferent to the suffering of the poor *pieds-noirs*, but they were insensitive to the suffering of Arab and Berber Algerians as well, since terrorism especially threatened and took its victims among the Algerian poor, among Arab and Berber Algerians even more than French Algerians. The former, he claimed, were being sacrificed by those who justified terrorism as a necessary means to achieve independence. Algerians were not, in his mind, being liberated by such violence, but rather they were being further enslaved by it; they were not being born again as "new men," but rather being destroyed.

Camus thus repeatedly denounces the mass reprisal and torture of Algerians by the French and all attempts to legitimize such acts by claiming, as the army did, that they were necessary to maintain the integrity of the French Republic and keep Algeria French. He calls such acts *crimes*, the responsibility for which he attributes not just to the actual participants in torture and summary executions or the military and political officials who ordered or sanctioned the crimes, but in extension to all the French, including himself, in whose name the crimes were being committed. He argues that it was only in denouncing French counterterrorism that it was possible to have any credibility in condemning the terrorist tactics of the FLN as well: "Only from such a position have we the right and the duty to state that armed combat and repression have, on our side, taken on aspects we cannot accept. Reprisals taken against civilian populations and the use of torture are crimes in which we are all implicated. . . . We must refuse to give any justification at all to such methods, even efficacy" (preface to *Algerian Reports*, 114, trans. mod. [893]). As he had done a decade earlier when he rejected the argument that using an atomic bomb on the civilian population of Hiroshima could be justified because it shortened the war against imperial Japan, thus saving Allied soldiers' lives, Camus denounces the killing of civilians to win the Algerian war, no matter which side is responsible for the killings.[7]

At the same time and for the same reasons as he condemns the torture and the violent repression of Algerians by the French army, Camus attacks what were for him the equally unacceptable acts of terrorism of the FLN against both French and Arab civilians, which he considers to be crimes of the exactly the same nature and order as those committed by the French:

> To be both useful and equitable, we must condemn with equal force and in no uncertain terms the terrorism used by the FLN against French civilians and, to an even greater degree, Arab civilians. Such terrorism is a crime that can be neither excused nor allowed to develop. . . . There should be no way to transform the acknowledgment of the injustices imposed on the Arab people into a systematic indulgence toward those who indiscriminately slaughter Arab and French civilians without regard for their age or sex. . . . Whatever the cause being defended, it will always be dishonored by the blind slaughter of an innocent crowd when the killer knows in advance that he will strike down women and children.
>
> (115–116 [894])

If actions on both sides are considered crimes, only in the case of the FLN, however, does Camus evoke the cause of the struggle and explicitly acknowledge the legitimacy of the struggle against the injustices suffered under French colonialism by the Arab and Berber peoples of Algeria. But even the recognition of a legitimate cause could not for him and should not for anyone else, he argues, justify in any way the murder of women and children. His condemnation of FLN terrorism is on this general level therefore identical to his condemnation of the crimes of the French, whose cause—the perpetuation of colonialism—he considers unjust and illegitimate. Crimes for him remain crimes, murders remain murders, terrorism remains terrorism, no matter what cause they serve.

The Cult of Violence

Is freedom worth penetrating the enormous circuit of terrorism and counter-terrorism?

—Frantz Fanon, *Sociology of a Revolution*

Terror, counter-terror, violence, counter-violence: that is what observers bitterly record when they describe the circle of hate, which is so tenacious and so evident in Algeria.

—Frantz Fanon, *The Wretched of the Earth*

Certainly by 1957 and the beginning of the Battle of Algiers, Camus was part of an increasingly small minority of Algerian moderates who continued to argue for a resolution to the conflict that would put an end to colonialism in Algeria but not immediately create a totally independent Algerian state and empower the FLN. If his own proposals for peace could rightly be criticized as unrealistic, even if they do not in my evaluation constitute "a masterpiece of bad faith,"[8] his deep concerns about the long-term effects of terrorism and torture and the repressive nature of the FLN and the national revolution for which it was responsible should be taken seriously. In the debate over who was more right about Algeria, Camus or Sartre, for example, until quite recently very few would have said Camus. But forty-five years after independence, the response to such a question would appear to be much less clear than it might have seemed even ten years ago. As right as Sartre was about the systematic, oppressive nature of colonialism, he was nevertheless mystified and in fact dead wrong about the totally liberating, revolutionary effects of the Algerian War (and other anticolonialist struggles) and certainly naïve, perhaps intentionally so, about the nature of the FLN itself.[9]

There is still debate over whether either terrorism or torture was effective in advancing the cause of either side in the war, but there is sufficient evidence available to make a convincing argument that the cause of Algerian independence was in fact more hurt by terrorism than helped by it. One could also conclude that if France won the Battle of Algiers because of the oppressive tactics the French army used against the civilian population of Algiers and particularly the systematic torture of suspects, it could also be argued that it was also because of torture and other criminal acts it committed that the overwhelming majority of Algerians were driven to support the FLN and French public opinion eventually turned massively against the war.

This, of course, did not mean that both terrorism and torture did not have defenders outside the group of FLN leaders and militants who devised and carried out the terrorist acts or outside of the French government or the army officials who devised and executed the counterterrorist strategy that included the systematic torturing of FLN suspects. In general, those supporting either side's crimes defended their side's use of terrorism by projecting the responsibility onto the other side. The FLN thus defended its use of terrorism by evoking the use of torture and the summary execution of suspects by the French, just as the French army claimed it was forced to torture suspects in order to prevent more innocent civilians from being slaughtered in terrorist bombings. While French military leaders claimed that if the French really wanted Algeria to remain French then they would have to be given "carte blanche" and allowed to use all necessary counterterrorist means to accomplish that task, FLN leaders at the same time argued that the French had made the war a total war and that terrorism, no matter how regrettable, was necessary if Algerians were ever to be free. Each side could in fact be said to have been right in the narrow strategic context in which each articulated its justification for either terrorism or torture, and yet each was criminally wrong in a larger ethical context and in terms of both the short- and long-term consequences of their tactics. And tragically wrong in terms of the political, moral, and psychological effects of their use of terror and torture—not only on their victims but on themselves.

Frantz Fanon and Jean-Paul Sartre were two of the most widely read and influential intellectual supporters of the FLN, and both wrote what could be considered the most elaborate justifications for the armed resistance to colonialism in general and the unrestrained use of violence and terrorism in particular. Terrorism as such is not discussed at great length by either Fanon or Sartre, however, but it is for the most part subsumed within the general problem both do discuss: revolutionary, anticolonialist violence. Both claim that since for over a century colonized Algerians had been the victims of unrestrained, insidious forms of systematic, generalized violence, the use of an equally unlimited counterviolence was necessary for the Algerian people to achieve full independence and create their own national identity. All anticolonialist violence, including the use of terrorism, is thus argued by both Fanon and Sartre not to be the responsibility of those who devised and carried out the terrorist acts, but rather of the colonial system itself, which is considered the ultimate source of all violence, even or especially violence against colonialists themselves.

For example, in the first chapter of *The Wretched of the Earth* ("Concerning Violence"), which was originally published in 1961 months before his death, Fanon argues that violence is a constitutive, essential component of the process of decolonization itself. This is first of all because violence is present in the colonies from the very beginning, from the violent conquest and occupation of Algeria and throughout its ensuing long, antagonistic history: "Their first encounter was marked by violence and their existence together—that is to say the exploitation of the native by the settler [*du colonisé par le colon*]—was carried on by dint of a great array of bayonets and cannons. The settler and the native are old acquaintances."[10] With its source outside of itself, revolutionary counterviolence can thus never be questioned because it always increases in proportion to the violence it opposes and that in fact produces it: "The violence of the colonial regime and the counter-violence of the native balance each other and respond to each other in an extraordinary reciprocal homogeneity. . . . The development of violence among the colonized people will be proportionate to the violence exercised by the colonial regime being contested" (88, trans. modified [47]). The more violent colonialist oppression, then, the more violent the reaction to it must necessarily be. In this sense, anticolonialist violence can never be excessive or unjustified because it is only the reflection of the colonial violence that gives birth to it.

This means in effect that all violence is the responsibility of and justified by the repressive colonialist system itself. For every action, an equally violent counter-reaction. Fanon also argues that for the colonized, however, anticolonialist violence is also something much more significant: it is *in itself* already the sign of the colonized's freedom. The end of the struggle, freedom, is thus already present in the violent means used to achieve it: "Colonized man finds his freedom in and through violence. This rule of conduct [*cette praxis*] enlightens the agent because it indicates to him the means and the end" (86 [45]). The "circle of hate," of "terror and then counter-terror, violence and then counter-violence," can thus be broken only by continually increasing the levels of violence, which will be met with an increase in violence, until the cycle can no longer be contained and explodes, bringing about the birth of a new people and total independence (89 [48]).[11]

But the way out of the circle is the same as the way into it. It is always more of the same: more terror and violence, even if they now are alleged to serve the liberation rather than oppression of a people. And violence is in fact much more than a way out the circle of colonialist violence, for in Fanon's view the national revolution represents nothing less than the possibility of the total transformation and rebirth of the colonized as "new men":

> Decolonization is always a violent phenomenon. . . . [It is] the replacing of one "species" of men by another "species" of men. Without any transition, there is a total, complete, absolute substitution. . . . Decolonization is the veritable creation of new men. But this creation owes nothing of its legitimacy to any supernatural power; the colonized "thing" becomes man during the same process by which it frees itself.
> (35–37, trans. mod. [5–6])

Fanon's argument then is not just that, given the violent repressive nature of the colonial system, the colonized are forced to use unlimited counterviolence to free themselves from the colonial condition; it is also that violence in itself is the creative human force responsible for making out of a colonized "thing" an absolutely "new species" of man. Fanon's essay "Concerning Violence" is thus no mere strategic political justification for violence and terrorism; it is rather a metaphysics of rebirth and salvation. The truth may not set people free, but for Fanon, violence does.[12]

If the stakes are indeed absolute and nothing less than the creation of an entirely new species of man, then the means used to achieve this end must necessarily be without limits as well: "The colonized who decides to put the program into practice, and to become its moving force, is ready for violence at all times. From birth it is clear to him that this reduced world, strewn with prohibitions, can be put into question only by absolute violence" (37, trans. mod. [7]). It is precisely a project of total violence that Fanon, in his conclusion to *The Wretched of the Earth*, proposes for colonized peoples throughout the world, the goal being nothing less than the creation of a "total man": "Come, then, comrades, the European game has finally ended; we must discover something different. . . . Let us decide not to imitate Europe; let us combine our muscles and our brains in a new direction. Let us try to create the total man that Europe has been incapable of having triumph" (312–313, trans. mod. [230]).[13] Fanon's highly romanticized praise of violence and his faith that by means of absolute violence a new "total man" could be created could not of course withstand the test of reality. It has never been clear to me why Camus' view of the birth of a democratic multicultural Algeria has been generally considered naively idealist, at best the musings of a "beautiful soul" and at worst the cynical vision of a neo-colonialist, while Fanon's cult of total violence and the birth of a new "total man" on the contrary has been taken so seriously by so many.[14]

When Fanon addresses the FLN's use of terrorism directly, it is, not surprisingly, in an apologetic mode, at the same time regretting its use and justifying its necessity. He first points out that there exists a double standard in the evaluation of the tactics used by each side in the war and that colonized peoples who take up arms against their oppressors are somehow expected to fight their wars of liberation "cleanly, without 'barbarity,'" and to "practice fair play," while "its adversary ventures, with a clear conscience, into the unlimited exploration of new modes of terror. An underdeveloped people must prove, by its fighting power, its ability to set itself up as a nation, and by the purity of every one of its acts, that it is . . . the most lucid, the most controlled people." This, he adds, is of course "all very difficult," and especially during wars of national liberation they constitute unreasonable standards that cannot be met.[15]

Ultimately, it is in fact the difficulty of the decision and the care and restraint with which Fanon claims it was in each case made by the leaders of the FLN that reveals "that it had no choice but to adopt forms of terror which until then it had rejected":

> No one takes the step of placing a bomb in a public place without a battle of conscience. The Algerian leaders who, in view of the intensity of the repression and the frenzied character of the oppression, thought they could answer the blows received without any serious problems of conscience, discovered that the most horrible crimes do not constitute a sufficient excuse for certain decisions. The leaders in a number of cases canceled plans.... To explain these hesitations there was, to be sure, the memory of civilians killed or frightfully wounded. There was the political consideration not to do certain things that could compromise the cause of freedom. There was also the fear that the Europeans working with the Front might be hit in these attempts.
>
> (55 [38])[16]

Whether such "hesitations" were sufficient to justify the terrorist acts that were committed would still seem to be a legitimate question, however, especially given the extent of the terrorism and the number of victims, not just among French Algerians but Berber and Arab Algerians as well.

It should be noted that only one of the concerns listed by Fanon is not directly political but rather has to do with a concern for the suffering of the civilians killed or wounded by terrorist acts. But it is not clear that this concern has any more weight for him than the blatantly political concerns of not giving "a false picture of the Revolution" or not alienating "the democrats of all the countries of the world and the Europeans of Algeria who were attracted by the Algerian national ideal" and who actively supported the armed struggle against the French (55–56 [38]). Fanon is not explicitly claiming that any means can or should be used to achieve the glorious end of the revolution, but it would seem that any tactic decided by the FLN leadership after careful reflection and sufficient hesitation is most definitely justified, no matter its actual consequences, because of the "glorious" revolutionary ends it serves.

Whether really restrained in some or most instances and regrettable in others or not, Fanon's ultimate justification for violence, whether directed against combatants or civilians, is that it has in fact already produced "a new humanity" that had never existed before and would never have been born without bloodshed: "All the innocent blood that has flowed onto the national soil has produced a new humanity, and no one must fail to recognize this fact" (27–28 [10]). The most brutal and criminal acts against civilians during the war could only be justified by such a total, unquestioning faith in the revolution. And Fanon most definitely was one of the most enthusiastic believers in the righteousness of total revolution and the creation of a "new man" through total anticolonialist violence.

Jean-Paul Sartre was a fervent believer as well. He believed in the Algerian national revolution, for "if it triumphs, the national revolution," Sartre boldly asserts, "will be socialist," "a complete shattering of all existing structures."[17] And he also believed that third-world revolutionaries, not only Algerians but other colonized peoples struggling to free themselves from colonial oppressors as well, would, when successful, allegedly bring about salvation not only for themselves but also for Europe as a whole. Sartre had faith specifically in the "socialist fraternity" he predicted would emerge when "the last colon is killed, shipped back home, or assimilated" and in the better human being who would be created by means of the violence it was necessary to use to achieve liberation: "We find our humanity on this side of death and despair, they [the colonized] find it beyond torture and death. . . . Sons of violence, at every instant they draw their humanity from it: we were human beings at their expense, they are making themselves human beings at ours. Different human beings, of better quality" (149–150 [30–31]). It is one thing to argue that the colonialist system itself is the ultimate context and origin of the violence directed against civilians during the war; it is entirely another to mystify the creative power of violence and postulate that a superior form of humanity would be born from it.

Following but perhaps expressing a deeper faith in the redemptive power of revolutionary violence even than Fanon, Sartre argues that the violence that gives birth to and defines them as new and superior human beings is not the responsibility of Algerians themselves, since its origin is not in them at all. Rather, since "colonial aggression is internalized as Terror by the colonized," "it is not in the first place *their* violence that grows and tears them apart, but ours returned" (145 [26]). The same violence is thus for Sartre totally destructive when it "ravages the oppressed themselves" (145 [26]), but it is creative and redemptive when directed outward against colonialists. The obvious problem with Sartre's blanket legitimizing of unlimited violence against colonialists in general is that if the responsibility for all violent actions taken by Algerians in their struggle against the French (Sartre also makes no mention of FLN terrorism used against other Arab and Berber Algerians) can be attributed to the French and made their responsibility, then the FLN and the Algerians themselves are exonerated in advance for whatever they do. And according to this logic, the worse the terrorism actually becomes, the more it reveals the injustices and violence of the colonialist system itself and the more redemptive it is.

Violence also has a therapeutic value for Sartre in that it represents both a self-cure and the crucial step toward "man reconstructing himself" in general:

> The colonized cure themselves of the colonial neurosis by driving out the *colon* with weapons. When their rage explodes, they recover their lost transparency, they know themselves in the same measure as they create themselves . . . it leads to the progressive emancipation of the fighters, it progressively liquidates the colonial darkness outside them. Once it starts, it is merciless. . . . The fighters' weapons are their humanity. For, at this first stage of the revolt, they have to kill: to shoot down a European is to kill two birds with one stone, doing away with oppressor and oppressed at the same time: what remains is a dead man and a free man; the survivor.
>
> (148 [29])

The last sentence of the quotation is undoubtedly the most controversial Sartre ever wrote about the Algerian War, since he appears not just to legitimize terrorism as a necessary tactical weapon but also to call for the murder of French civilians as an essential step in the process of liberation.[18] When the price of justice and the birth of a "free man" is the murder of other men, women, and children, of anyone who is or can be labeled a *colon* or claimed to be serving colonialist interests, then no limits can be placed on violence or terror at all. At the very least, this should make one question whether there might not be a better way to give birth to free men and women—especially, as is the case here, when the "dead man" is not an enemy solider but a civilian who happens to be in the wrong place at the wrong time and is murdered as the representative of an oppressive system and thus sacrificed as a *sign* of oppression.

But if the superiority of the "new man" is inseparable from violence, according to this logic other more moderate, less violent ways of ending colonialism would not be revolutionary and thus produce only ordinary, "old," and much less free men. In his different essays, Sartre mockingly dismisses all moderate proposals for ending colonialism peacefully, since the Algerian War is presented by him, even more than by Fanon, as an all-or-nothing affair. In a burst of anticolonialist frenzy, Sartre accuses those who protest the terrorism being used against civilian populations in Algeria, those who demand that it cease and that less violent tactics be used in the struggle for independence, of being not just "well-meaning souls [*belles âmes*]" but "racists" (147 [28]). In an explicit reference to Camus, a year after his death, Sartre mocks "the non-violent" who are "neither victims nor executioners!" (150 [31]) and accuses them of preaching a nonviolence that is in fact protected by the violence of the colonialist system. For those like Camus, who were concerned that the cycle of violence would have devastating long-term effects or would never end, Sartre, on the contrary, *knows* that "it is the last stage of the dialectic" and reassures his readers that "violence, like Achilles' spear, can heal the wounds that it has made" (155 [36]). Violence, not time, he thus claims, will heal all wounds. I believe most would agree today that in Algeria (and elsewhere) this has definitely not been the case.[19]

The Madness of Truth—A Tale of Two Suns

> The land is savage and savagery is in the hearts of the men. The rebels burn farms and crops, cut telephone poles, slaughter the herds, assassinate, and castrate. The French army does the same.
>
> —Jean-Luc Tahon, "En 'pacifiant' l'Algérie. 1955"[20]

Today, the blinding sun of torture is at its zenith and illuminates the whole country; in this light, there is no laughter that does not sound false, no fact that is not made up to conceal anger or fear, no act that does not betray our disgust and complicity. Whenever two French people meet now, there is a dead body between them. In fact, did I say one? . . .

—Jean-Paul Sartre, preface to *The Wretched of the Earth*

Although it was written before Fanon's and Sartre's essays were published and as if anticipating them, Camus' most compelling response to what could be called the romantic cult of total revolutionary violence is not to be found in his essays on Algeria, but rather in what is perhaps the least understood, most enigmatic of his short stories, "The Renegade."[21] Camus is reported to have ironically described the story both as "the portrait of a progressive Christian" and "the story of a Christian who adopts Marxist ideology" (*Théâtre, récits, nouvelles*, 2044). In his essay on Camus, Edward Said claims rather that the story describes what Camus felt were the pathological reasons for and disastrous effects of a European in the colonies "going native." As Said puts it, "The Renegade" is the story of a missionary who, "captured by an outcast southern Algerian tribe, has his tongue cut out . . . and becomes a super-zealous partisan of the tribe, joining in an ambush of French forces. . . . This is as if to say that going native can only be the result of mutilation, which produces a diseased, ultimately unacceptable loss of identity."[22] Whether the story has to do with what Camus felt were the disastrous results of a progressive Christian—the main character is in fact anything but progressive—"going Marxist," or of a Frenchman "going native," as Said claims, Said and Camus do seem to agree that the zealotry, loss of control, and violent destruction of both personal and national-cultural identity of the main character constitute the principal subject of the story.

The "confused mind" in question is that of the zealous convert to the religion of violence, of the true believer who accepts no compromises in his beliefs, of the man who loses his old self and is "born again" in and because of his total commitment to a new Truth and the violence his new faith and total commitment demand from him. Whatever that Truth might be: that of a Marxist revolutionary or "native" believer in the Fetish, or even the Truth of the militant Christian himself, before going anywhere and becoming anything other than what he already was—only more so.

"The Renegade" is, in my judgment, Camus' most daring piece of writing, the most radically experimental of his experiments in narration from

Exile and the Kingdom. Even when compared to *The Fall*, which is considered by most critics to be Camus' most original and unconventional narrative text and which was originally intended to be a short story in this same collection, the narrative structure of "The Renegade" is even more complex. As an exercise in "interior monologue," it reads in places more like a text by Samuel Beckett than any of Camus' other stories or novels. The first lines of the story resemble passages from Beckett's *The Unnamable*:

> What mush! What mush! I must get my mind in order. Since they cut out my tongue, I don't know, it's as if another tongue has been constantly operating in my skull, something has been speaking, or someone who suddenly falls silent and then it begins again—oh, I hear too many things I however never say, what mush, and if I open my mouth, it's like the noise of pebbles rattling together.
>
> (34, trans. mod. [1579]).[23]

Like the voice in Beckett's novel, the voice of an other has invaded the voice of the missionary-turned-renegade and penetrated the deepest interiority of his interior monologue, so much so that the most interior of first-person interior voices is, in this instance, also the most exterior, alienated, and insane of voices.

This "something" or "someone" who speaks in and as the self is radically alien to the self, but at the same time is also paradoxically deeply within the self, an alien voice speaking as a disordered, confused interior voice, an alien tongue that has usurped the place of the original mother tongue. Mutilated, the tongue continues to speak, even if primarily with words that are "mush." This otherness or madness of the tongue is at the same time a difference, violence, or madness of or within the tongue from the very start, an otherness that makes the tongue, even the mother tongue, never completely original, never indigenous to the self—not just after mutilation, but before as well.

The "mush" in or of the voice reflects and conveys a disorder or confusion of the mind that it repeatedly attempts and fails to overcome: "Order, an order, says the tongue, and then simultaneously speaks of something else, yes I always desired order" (34, trans. mod. [1579]). The only way for the "confused mind" to compensate for its confusion is to add more mush to the mush already in it, more confused words to the confused words already coming out of its mouth, with seemingly no end to mush or confusion. The intensification and interiorization of violence in the story follows the same process, both the violence of the words said, thought, or hallucinated by the narrator (or by "his" voice, the other in him) and the violence of the world outside. For like confusion, the only way to combat the violence of the deadly struggle for dominance between "civilization" and "barbarism," Christianity and the religion of the Fetish, seems to be to perpetuate and escalate it. Inside and outside the mind of the missionary/renegade the same confusion, madness, and violence reign. Order and peace appear impossible to achieve once the cycle of confusion, disorder, and violence have begun—that is, from the very start.

Even if the violence and madness in his voice reflects the missionary's loss of an original "Western" self and results, at least in part, from his "going native," as Said argues, the desert land where the missionary's conversion/mutilation takes place has a role to play in his transformation or conversion. The desert is presented as a space of extremes, where blinding light gives way to total darkness, insufferable heat to unbearable coldness—with no transition between totally opposed extremes: "Day is breaking over the desert," says the voice of the self-proclaimed "dirty slave"; "it's still very cold, soon it will be too hot, this land drives men mad" (35 [1579]). Pages later, the same missionary/renegade describes the city of salt in the following terms:

> as if . . . they had cut out their white, burning hell with a powerful jet of boiling water just to show that they could live where no one ever could, thirty days' travel from any living thing, in this hollow in the middle of the desert where the heat of day prevents any contact among creatures, separates them by a portcullis of invisible flames and of searing crystals, where without transition the cold of night congeals them individually in their rock-salt shells.
>
> (42 [1583])

Madness is thus first presented as having an exterior, geographic origin, the result of living on the very limits of human existence, in the most extreme and inhuman of climatic conditions.

There are no shadows at high noon under this sun, and it is as if it were always high noon in the "village of salt" created and inhabited by the people of the Fetish. Except when the sun is totally absent and the darkest of nights prevails. But then too there are no shadows or nuances, only total obscurity. At the extreme limits of life, everything is either insufferably hot or unbearably cold, totally black or totally white, true or false. Everyone is either friend or enemy, believer or heathen, good or evil. Either one of us or one of them. The European outsider comes to the city to conquer and convert its inhabitants, and he in turn is tortured, mutilated, and enslaved as a threat to the truth, religion, culture, and very existence of a people. Those who cannot be enslaved or converted are destroyed.

The most desert of all deserts may drive men mad, and specifically white, European, Christian men striving to impose their Truth and mastery on the land and its inhabitants. But the madness of extremes is not that of the land alone. And it is certainly not exclusively or even primarily that of the fictive indigenous people depicted in the story as inhabiting the city and who are known for their extreme cruelty. For the violence and madness of extremes are already in whiteness, European-ness, Christian-ness, and man-ness themselves, already in the missionary *before* he arrives in this land of extremes, *before* he is mutilated, *before* he is forcibly converted to and becomes the slave of the Fetish, and thus *before* he "goes native."

For the missionary/renegade is already violent and mad before becoming violent and going mad in the desert, already devoted absolutely to an absolute Truth before changing beliefs and becoming devoted in the same uncompromising, absolute way to the Truth of the other he had previously combated. There is ultimately no real difference between his original faith in a militant, colonizing form of Christianity that forcibly converts others to its Truth and his forced conversion to the "primitive," violent religion of the Fetish to whom the missionary-renegade becomes devoted/enslaved. The violence depicted in the story is inherent in ideology and faith in an absolute "Truth" in general, in politics when it is practiced as a religion and religion when it is practiced and imposed on others as a politics. The "something else" that speaks in and through the voice of the missionary-renegade is the madness of extremism in general, of the terror at the heart of both politics-as-religion and religion-as-politics.

The struggle for truth is in fact a struggle for power and the desire for domination of one truth, one civilization, one culture, one god, one religion, one people—in the story, metaphorically one "sun"—over all others. Both the indigenous people of the land and those who come to conquer them and occupy their land are "people of faith." The missionary, for example, before mutilation, before conversion, before he had "gone native," "gone Marxist," or gone anywhere at all, was in the seminary already a true believer, a man who, once he had seized on an idea, "carried it to its end" (37, trans. mod. [1580]).[24] He had in fact already developed the following project:

> To join up with the most barbarous and live as they did, to show them in their own home, and even in the House of the Fetish, through example, that my Lord's truth was the strongest. They would insult me, of course, but I was not afraid of insults, they were essential to the demonstration, and by the way I endured them, I'd subjugate those savages, like a powerful sun. Powerful, yes, that was the word I constantly had on my tongue, I dreamed of absolute power, the kind that brings people to their knees, that forces the adversary to capitulate, that converts him in short, and the more zealous, the crueler he is, the more he's sure of himself, dominated by his own convictions, the more his acquiescence establishes the royalty of whoever brought about his defeat.
>
> (39, trans. mod. [1581–1582])

The logic is that of the clash of civilizations, religions, or ideologies. For only through the zealous, cruel, violent victory over the projected zealotry, cruelty, and violence of the Other can the power of European Christianity and its notions of love, charity, and forgiveness rule and its barbarous and violent superiority over an equally but differently barbarous and violent culture, religion, and Truth be ensured.

The madness of the missionary/renegade's project of subjugation and conquest of the Other reflects exactly and meets its match in the absolute Other it seeks to subjugate. And no matter how great the missionary claims the differences between good and evil, love and hate, "us" and "them," Christianity and the religion of the Fetish, and European civilization and North African "barbarity" are, his own madness and cruelty are not in fact the result of his having "gone native," and thus do not originate in his experiences with the "savage" natives. His madness is rather already that of the West (and Christianity) itself, in both its spiritual and political aspirations to conquer and rule in the name of love and charity; to subjugate in the name of progress, justice, and freedom; to impose its Truth where there is the most resistance to it; to bring the most radically other of all others to their knees. Disorder, violence, and madness are the essence of the project of conquest and domination, but under the cover of the announced desire for order, peace, and reason. Victory can occur only when all others have been subdued, converted, or killed—but given that the violence necessary to subdue provokes a counterviolence, no victory can ever be more than momentary, no conversion more than temporary, no death of one infidel sufficient to prevent the arrival of others.

The missionary can thus not really be said to "have gone native." He has rather gone to the violent extremes of himself and his own culture and religion. And it is because he fails in his attempt at conquest and conversion that he himself is conquered and subjugated by those he attempted to subjugate, converted by those he intended to convert, enslaved by those he attempted to enslave, and mutilated physically by those he intended to mutilate spiritually and culturally. In this way, his desire for power over this fictional "indigenous people," not of the darkest but of the brightest Africa, is reversed or redirected and becomes, after his forced conversion, a "mad" desire for revenge against the Christian god in whose name he once acted and the missionaries who still act in his name. His goal, after his mutilation and conversion, however, is no more insane or violent than his original goal of subjugation and conversion. The object of his hatred and violence has simply changed, for now he has a score to settle with the new missionary and his previous masters, with his teachers who deceived him, and with "filthy Europe" in general, which he now rejects as absolutely as he once embraced it.[25]

The struggle for total subjugation and absolute power is depicted in the story as an infinite cycle of revenge. A cycle in which "filthy Europe" sends its missionaries (along with its army and colonizers) to conquer and subjugate the non-European world to prove its own superiority and that of its Truth, only to find that its power is not exclusively its own and that subjugation can be reversed and its power used against it—both by those it has attempted to subjugate and those it has sent to subjugate them. And once the cycle of violence has started, there is no way out of it and no way to put an end to it, only increasingly more violence and increasingly more madness. Unrestrained violence assumes everything into itself, violence producing more violence, madness more madness. Without end.

Because the combat of absolute Truths has as its stakes the total subjugation of the other, it risks the subjugation of the self by the other. The master is as much slave to violence as is the slave in his attempt to reverse his condition. The missionary-renegade in his confusion or madness passes from one extreme to the other, from absolute mastery and conquest to total defeat and subjugation—but only to find mastery again in his enslavement to his new, all-powerful masters: "Lord! But what, which Lord, they are the lords. . . . They command, they strike, they say they are a unique people, that their god is the true god, and that one must obey. They are my masters, they do not know pity and, like masters, they want to be alone, advance alone, rule alone" (43–44, trans. mod. [1583–1584]). All that matters to this or any other unique, cruel, and powerful people is that they continue to advance on their own, that they continue to rule, that their god or Fetish (religion/ideology) receive total devotion and that they receive total obedience. This is all that matters until they in turn are defeated and converted to another god and subjugated to a different Truth by another "more" unique, violent, cruel, and powerful people. With each defeat/conversion, becoming other, but each time remaining the same, devoted to the same total violence. The choice is then always between total light or total darkness, mastery or enslavement, all or nothing, to possess the other and his god or be possessed by the other and his god. And to be nothing apart from these stark, absolute alternatives. This is the confused mind's, the renegade slave's true madness. And the master's madness as well. It is the madness of Truth and the politics of absolutes in general.

To believe in and be subjugated by the Fetish is thus the same as believing in and being subjugated to an all-powerful Christian God. It is ultimately then neither "to go Marxist," as Camus ironically suggested, nor "to go native," as Said has claimed, but rather to believe in and give oneself over to absolute Truth, whatever its form: Christian, Marxist, or that of the Fetish, the Truth of the West or of the East, "ours" or "theirs." The Fetish in the story is less the religion of the "absolute Other" than a mirror image of the dogmatic truth of "filthy Europe" itself. Both represent the "Truth" of religion when it is practiced as a politics, and of politics when it is imposed and practiced as a religion. The story tells of the madness of the state of violence when "power" constitutes "the malicious principle of the world," a principle not just to be accepted but also "adored" (53, trans. mod. [1589]). This is the principle of gods, religions, and political ideologies to which one gives oneself totally and thus by which one allows oneself to be totally subjugated and possessed. The madness of absolutes enslaves all those who believe in a truth as the Truth and who choose violence as their master to spread the Truth and ensure that its power be recognized. Of those who use terror to combat the cruelty and terrorism of the other and to justify their own violent conquest and conversion of the other. Of an other who is also always-already a projection of the self.

The missionary/renegade's "madness" (or the madness of "The Renegade") is thus the madness of all religious, cultural, and political absolutes, of all those who accept and believe in a truth as the Truth, all those who choose terror over dialogue and acceptance of difference, the struggle for the destruction of the other over the recognition of the other. The world of "The Renegade" is Camus' vision of sociopolitical hell, his most extreme depiction of pure political/religious terror, one in which power decides everything and where justice is sacrificed for the sake of "the Truth." Written just before the Algerian War began, it constitutes a nightmarish vision of what would be the madness and unrestrained violence of the war itself. There is perhaps no more powerful literary indictment of what could be called the terrorism of the Truth, whether the Truth is that of religion or politics, than this story. Truth in its extreme form does not set you free; no salvation is born in violence and terror. On the contrary, the Truth mutilates, enslaves, and kills. The Truth is madness itself; the total light of the sun blinds. The Truth is terrorist.

No colonization is human.

—Ferhat Abbas, *Autopsie d'une guerre: L'aurore*

CHAPTER SIX

Anguish

The Myth of Assimilation

There is no reason at all to believe that time cannot succeed in combining the two races. God in no way prevents it; only the mistakes of men could put obstacles in its way.

　　　　　—Alexis de Tocqueville, "Second Letter on Algeria" (August 22, 1837)

As for the failure of assimilation, I do not derive any particular joy from it. . . . However, it is clear that no one expressly desired assimilation in contemporary colonization, not even the Communists. Moreover, and this is the essential thing, *assimilation is the opposite of colonization.*

　　　　　—Albert Memmi, *The Colonizer and the Colonized*

Assimilation fully realized is quite simply the suppression of colonialism.

　　　　　—Jean-Paul Sartre, "Colonialism Is a System" (1956)

Very few today would disagree that assimilation, the proclaimed goal and chief justification for France's "civilizing mission" in its colonies, was a colossal failure. There is still debate, however, over whether assimilation was simply a cynical, duplicitous fiction that was intended from the start to mask the harsh colonial realities of racism, oppression, and exploitation, or a misguided republican ideal that had a positive effect, no matter how limited, on colonial policy and institutions and that served as a counterforce, no matter how weak, to some of the worst injustices of colonialism. In her study of French colonialism in West Africa, Alice Conklin argues that assimilation in fact was both a destructive ideological fiction and an authentic republican project at the same time. It was the way France attempted "to reconcile its aggressive imperialism with its republican ideals." Conklin thus disagrees with those scholars who "have too often dismissed the French *mission civilisatrice* as window dressing," especially if no attempt is made to understand "the insidious and persistent appeal of colonial ideology."[1]

From Conklin's perspective, assimilation thus served a paradoxical function. As a progressive republican principle that acknowledges, at least in principle, the original, "natural" equality of peoples of different regional, ethnic, cultural, and religious backgrounds, assimilation was considered the means of achieving social and political progress and equal democratic rights for all peoples—providing a way for those living under traditional religious and political oppression to enter the modern world and become free citizens. In reality, it was a promise that was never kept and that functioned in the colonies both to mask and justify the oppression of the colonized and the exorbitant privileges of the rich colonizers. Moreover, in colonialist discourse the failure of assimilation was most often not attributed to the laws, restrictions, and practices that made it almost impossible except for a small number of the elite among the colonized to achieve, but rather to the alleged inadequacies and ignorance of the colonized peoples themselves.

The concept of assimilation at the heart of the French colonial civilizing mission was of course rooted in an imaginary hierarchy in which European civilization and European cultures were projected as being superior to other civilizations and cultures and further advanced in the general meta-narrative of progress, with French culture and society, in large part because of the French Revolution and the declaration of the "Rights of Man," projected (by the French at least) to be at the very summit of that hierarchy. Colonized peoples in general, those to whom the promise of assimilation was made, were because of their culture considered to be behind and thus "inferior to" the French. Through the "civilizing" work of colonialism, this lag would be made up and inferior cultures would in principle be negated, transformed, and raised to a higher level as they were assimilated into French culture and overcame the limitations of their initial conditions. The desire to be French was thus for all intents and purposes assumed in colonialist ideology to be an innate, natural desire on the part of those who had not been born with this privilege, so that making it possible for others to become French was in principle a noble calling. Colonialists could thus see themselves as the missionaries of culture or civilization, spreading the good word of French culture, European civilization, and political progress in the form of democracy among those not fortunate enough to have been born with these gifts.[2]

If assimilation in reality was a lie, a false promise that was never kept, it was not by chance but because colonialist laws and institutions ensured that there would be two separate and unequal communities in the colonies and that each community would be defined primarily by the colonial relation as either colonizer or colonized.[3] As Albert Memmi and others have argued, one of the ways that colonialism in Algeria could have hypothetically ended peacefully would have been if assimilation had been seriously pursued and progressively achieved. To fulfill the promise of assimilation in the colonies would thus also have meant to bring about the demise of colonialism. This in itself explains why, in the history of colonialism, attempts to implement even modest democratic reforms that would have enhanced the mission of assimilation were invariably treated by colonial authorities and powerful colonialist interests as subversive threats to their existence and well-being and forcefully opposed. It also explains why, at the same time, such attempts were considered by progressive elements within the colonizers as well as moderate nationalist leaders among the colonized as an important part of a movement toward emancipation and national independence.

Whatever judgment is made about the limitations and naiveté of his political position during the Algerian War, it cannot be denied that from the time he joined the Communist Party in Algiers in the mid-1930s, Albert Camus firmly believed in assimilation and actively supported reforms that would have facilitated it. This was in part because he felt that the most progressive Algerian nationalist leaders and the majority of Arab and Berber Algerians believed in the promise. But it is also because Camus was convinced that it was only through assimilation that colonial injustices could be eliminated. Some of the first indications of his doubts, not about the principle of assimilation as such but rather about the sincerity of the French government to act effectively to achieve it, appear in his journalistic account of a trip he took in 1939 during a horrible famine through the desolate Kabylia region of Algeria. The trip brutally revealed to him the tragic consequences of the failure of assimilation and convinced him of the necessity of reversing the course of a century of neglect before, as he repeatedly wrote, "it was too late." All of his subsequent pleas for economic assistance and political reform could be said to grow out of this confrontation with rural misery, which was worse than anything he had ever witnessed in Algiers. If he stubbornly believed that it was not too late for France to reverse its course and begin practicing what it preached, he also demanded that France immediately live up to its responsibilities for the misery French colonialism had caused in Algeria.

Destitution

> Drought in the South—famine—eighty thousand sheep die. The entire population scrapes the earth looking for roots. Buchenwald under the sun.
>
> —Albert Camus, *Carnets III*

In the series of moving articles Camus published in the socialist journal *Alger Républicain* in 1939 under the title "Misère de la Kabylie" ("Destitution of Kabylia"), Camus describes his trip as "a journey through the suffering and hunger of a people. . . . Destitution here is not a formula or a theme for meditation. Destitution is. It cries out, and it drives you to despair."[4] In addition to demanding that the French government provide immediate additional emergency supplies to the people of Kabylia, Camus also argues for radical reforms to prevent future droughts or other natural catastrophes from having the same devastating effects. This, he argues, means eliminating the inequities and injustices produced by the colonial system, which greatly exacerbate the effects of natural disasters.

Camus' pleas were of course ignored, not only for the reason why demands and projects for reform in Algeria had always been ignored and would continue to be ignored until the Algerian War: the general indifference of the population of metropolitan France toward its Algerian colony and the powerful influence on both local and national politics of a small number of *grands colons* and extremist politicians. In 1939, it was also because France and the rest of Europe faced in Nazi Germany a more immediate and dangerous threat than the destitution in its colonies. Camus argues in his articles, however, that efforts to eliminate the destitution and suffering of the people of Kabylia could not be postponed until France and the rest of Europe countered the threat posed by Nazi Germany. Men, women, and children were dying in Algeria from starvation and disease, and this made the alleviation of their misery and the elimination of its underlying causes as pressing as any threat to national security, no matter how serious.[5] The choice before France was thus for him not a choice between defending itself against Nazi Germany or improving the living conditions of the colonized in Algeria. It was rather a question of how to do both at the same time. France, of course, did neither.

Camus argues in these articles that because the ultimate cause for the destitution of the people of Kabylia is the French colonial system itself, it is the responsibility of the French to act decisively and practice what the French apologists for colonization had always preached was the essential component of its "civilizing mission." In 1939, such a demand for assimilation and democratic rights for all Algerians was in fact more radical than Camus' critics have generally acknowledged. In any case, there can be no doubt that the *grands colons* of Algeria realized that Camus represented an enemy to their interests and that effective assimilation of all French subjects in Algeria would bring about the demise of colonialism and thus destroy their exorbitant privileges and the abusive economic and political power they exercised. This is why they continued to oppose even moderate reforms that would have led to the enfranchisement of a slightly higher number of Muslim Algerians.[6] It is thus highly ironic that Camus has often been criticized by postcolonial critics for the very same reasons he was criticized by the most zealous defenders of colonialism. Although rarely if ever acknowledged and certainly not analyzed at any length, at the very heart of the confusion and controversies surrounding Camus' Algerian politics is his very particular perspective on the question of assimilation.

One important difference between Camus' idea of assimilation and its strictly colonialist sense is that his is not based on the myth of the innate hierarchy of peoples and cultures. On the contrary, assimilation as Camus conceived it is based on the opposite principle: their fundamental equality and respective "grandeur." He argues that for assimilation to have a chance of succeeding, the dignity, cultural specificity, and, most important, the equality of the different populations, ethnicities, religions, and cultures of Algeria first had to be recognized, both in theory and in practice. This is why he considers evidence of what he claims is a movement toward the "greater independence" of the people of Kabylia to be not an obstacle to assimilation, but rather a positive step in the process: "And how, then, could I not have understood their desire to administer their lives and their appetite to become finally what they profoundly already are: courageous and self-aware men from whom without any false shame we could take lessons in grandeur and justice?" ("Misère de la Kabylie," 928). Camus' view is that only a noble, independent, self-aware people could be freely assimilated into the French people; only by remaining itself could it become other. Assimilation thus implies something very different for Camus than for colonialist ideology. Assimilation of Arabs and Berbers does not imply that Arab and Berber cultures and languages and the Muslim religion have first to be rejected for a Muslim to become "French." His notion rather implies that an Algerian would become French *as a Berber, as an Arab, as a Muslim.*[7] Today, this would be considered a multiculturalist position. In Algeria in 1939, it was considered a subversively anticolonialist position, even though or rather because it championed assimilation, the principle at the very core of French colonialism. And in fact it was.

Under the paradoxical conditions delineated by Camus, only a noncolonized people or a people who had never fully accepted their own colonization but remained "courageous and self-aware" under extremely oppressive conditions could be assimilated freely into another people and culture. In the same way, only a society that did not oppress and subjugate others could freely assimilate others into itself. It is thus only on the basis of anticolonialist principles or ideals that assimilation, the self-proclaimed goal of French colonialism, could occur. And this is why assimilation, the most "idealist" and fictitious of colonialism's self-justifications, could also be used as a weapon against colonialism itself.

When a small minority of people have the privileges of full citizenship and the overwhelming majority have only limited rights; when the culture, language, and religion of one community are recognized and those of other communities ignored or denigrated; when the most productive land has been taken away from the people who previously farmed it and given to others to exploit; and when laws applying to all communities are made by one community alone, are radically different for each community, and are applied more severely to the other communities than to the community making and enforcing the laws, then there is no way assimilation can succeed. Nor, from a strictly colonialist point of view, was it ever really supposed to succeed.[8]

For if Arab and Berber Algerians had in fact been allowed to become "French," that is, if all Algerian "subjects" had the freedom to become full French citizens equal to and with the same rights as all other French citizens without having to give up their religion, language, and culture, and if the majority then ruled in an authentically democratic state, then the colonial relation, as we have seen and as Memmi and others have argued, would have been destroyed, and there would no longer have been any colonized or any colonizers. And with the end of colonialism in Algeria and the overwhelming majority of ten Arabs and Berbers to one French, it would be not difficult to imagine that this demographic fact alone would have led to Algerian independence—although in a different form, with very different consequences for all of the different ethnic and religious groups in Algeria and with different nationalist leaders than when independence was actually achieved in 1962 after eight years of horrible war.[9] When the promise of assimilation was no longer believed in by moderate nationalist leaders, when the majority of the colonized no longer had any interest in becoming French, and as French colonialists continued to do whatever they could to prevent assimilation, then an armed struggle for national independence became the only alternative to colonialism. Camus' political essays on Algeria recognize this basic fact and use it to support radical reforms in Algeria, to prevent the worst from happening.

Independence

> We had been victims of a myth. In their turn, [the *pieds-noirs*] had been victims of a long mystification. They had been told for more than a century that Algeria, a French department, was only the prolongation of metropolitan

France. They believed it. When the hour of truth rang, for them as for us, they felt betrayed. Thus, they fought bitterly to make this aberrant fiction last.

—Ferhat Abbas (1981)

Even though Camus' pre–World War II series of articles on Kabylia are well known and acknowledged even by his most severe critics, it would most likely surprise most of those critics to discover that he continued to attack colonial injustices in the immediate postwar period, when he was editor-in-chief of the Resistance journal *Combat*. Colonialism in Algeria and European imperialism in general were for Camus never peripheral issues, neither before, during, nor after World War II. On the contrary, he was one of the very few voices in the immediate postwar period, when most of France was concerned only with rebuilding itself after the devastation of the war, to raise the issue of colonial injustices in Algeria. Camus argues in various essays that it is not only illogical and incoherent but profoundly unjust for the French, who had just regained their own independence and freedom, to continue to deny the same rights to Muslim Algerians, especially given that "hundreds of thousands of Arabs have spent the past two years fighting for the liberation of France."[10] For Algerians to have fought for the liberation of France during the war only to return to Algeria to discover that nothing had changed and that they and their families continued to be denied the rights of citizens was for Camus both the height of hypocrisy and a formula for disaster. He was right on both counts.

For him, the basic political issue was simple: freedom and justice could not be for some but not for others. In an article months earlier, Camus argues that France could not continue to have two different or even opposed policies concerning democracy, "one granting justice to the people of France and the other confirming injustice toward the Empire" (*Combat* [October 13, 1944], 71 [253]). His postwar essays provide ample evidence that he was in fact militantly *anticolonialist*, not just in terms of Algeria but also as concerns the entire French empire—in fact, as concerns all empires, including the rapidly expanding Soviet and American ones, and even in terms of what he feared was also an emerging Islamic empire. In another article, for example, he calls for "a policy of emancipation" in French Indochina: "Indochina will be with us if France leads the way by introducing both democracy and freedom there. But if we hesitate at all, Indochina will join forces with anyone at all, provided they are against us" (*Combat* [March 29, 1945], 183 [467]). France, of course, did not just hesitate but refused to implement policies of emancipation in its principal colonies, and thus independence in Vietnam and Algeria was achieved by other, more violent means and at a horrible cost in human lives—as Camus in 1945 predicted would be the case.

Camus' most developed analysis of the injustices of colonialism in his editorials in *Combat* is contained in the series of articles entitled "Crisis in Algeria," which he wrote after a trip through Algeria in April 1945 during another horrible famine. The series was published in *Combat* in May and June of 1945, immediately after the riots and massacres at Sétif and Guelema, which resulted in more than a hundred French deaths when demonstrations celebrating the end of World War II turned into riots. French men, women, and children were killed; some were savagely mutilated. In retaliation, thousands of Algerians were massacred by French civilians and the police.[11] The massacre of Arab Algerians by French authorities and civilians nine years before the organization of an armed insurrection by the FLN is considered by many to be the undeclared beginning of the Algerian War. Camus was one of the very few French journalists at that time who attempted to analyze and explain the cause of the riots and who defended the rights of Arab Algerians in an atmosphere of intense racist hatred and demands for revenge—on the Left as well as the Right.[12]

In the "Crisis in Algeria" series, Camus demands both that Algeria not be forgotten in the euphoria of the liberation of metropolitan France and that "the Arab people" of Algeria need to be recognized by the French:

> To begin with, I want to remind the French people of the fact that Algeria exists. . . . I want to point out that the Arab people also exist. By that I mean that they aren't the wretched, faceless mob in which Westerners see nothing worth respecting or defending. On the contrary, they are a people of impressive traditions, whose virtues are eminently clear to anyone willing to approach them without prejudice. These people are not inferior except in regard to the conditions in which they must live, and we have as much to learn from them as they from us.
>
> (*Combat*, 199–200 [499])

As in his essays before the war, recognition of the existence of "the Arab people" means recognizing Arab Algerians as a people different from but equal to the French—except in terms of the horrible conditions in which most are forced to live. Refusing to accept the indifference, if not racist hostility, of both metropolitan French and French Algerians toward people they generally considered, especially after Sétif, only as a "faceless mob," Camus warns of increased violence if their traditions are not respected, their virtues not recognized, and immediate steps not taken to radically improve social, economic, and political conditions in Algeria. As was the case after he had published similar articles in 1939, it was a warning few in France took seriously.

In his postwar articles for *Combat*, Camus argues that the French should be especially sensitive to the injustices suffered by Algerians for a very particular reason: "We cannot remain indifferent to their suffering, because we have experienced it ourselves. Rather than respond with condemnations, let us try to understand the reasons for their demands and invoke on their behalf the same democratic principles that we claim for ourselves" (201 [501]). His position on Algeria is thus the same as on Indochina: the colonized have the right to the same freedoms and the same justice as colonizers. Nothing could be more obvious for him than this simple democratic principle, and yet nothing could be further from the reality of colonialism.

It is clear from reading his postwar articles that Camus' position on assimilation had changed, in large part due to the fact that the moderate Algerian nationalist leaders he respected no longer believed in the promise themselves. Camus argues that it was the war itself that had drastically changed the thinking of moderate Algerians, and he disputes what he characterizes as a self-serving, hypocritical French government claim that 80 percent of Algerian subjects still desired to become French citizens. Even if this might have been true before the war, he argues that it is no longer the case in 1945, and "the primary responsibility for this is ours" ("Natives of North Africa Estranged from a Democracy from Which They Saw Themselves as Excluded Indefinitely," *Combat* [May 18, 1945], 207 [514]). The dashed hopes of Algerians at the end of the war, when their social and political conditions did not improve and when violence against them in fact increased with the horrible massacres at Sétif and Guelema, were for Camus the signs that a majority of Algerians no longer believed they would ever be granted citizenship and treated as equals of the French.

He recognized the serious consequences of the continued hostility of the *colons* to all reforms, the increasing violence of the most reactionary forces among Algerian colonialists, and the growing disappointment of the Arab and Berber moderates who had once believed in assimilation but were being forced by French policy to search for increasingly militant means to achieve freedom. Acknowledging the dangers of this increase in repression and violence, he considers not just the actual perpetrators of the crimes against innocent civilians but also French colonial policy in general to be responsible for the violence.

Given the general hostility among French colonialists to democratic reforms in Algeria, Camus uses a rhetorical device also found in a number of his other political essays: not a rhetorical question but rather what could be called a rhetorical "choice." In this case, it is the choice he claims the French need to make between colonialism and democracy. To choose the continuation of colonialism would mean that France acknowledges that it considers "Algeria to be a conquered land whose subjects, stripped of all rights and burdened with additional duties, would be forced to live in absolute dependence on us" (208 [515]). To choose democracy for Algeria, on the contrary, would mean that France "attributed to its democratic principles a value universal enough that it could extend them to populations for which it had responsibility" (208, trans. mod. [515]). Camus openly acknowledges that the choice is more rhetorical than real, since it is not still to be made by the French but is a choice that they have already made. For the citizens of the French Republic, in principle, although in the colonies not in practice, had long before already chosen democracy. This choice of democracy was then reaffirmed in the Resistance and at the end of the war in the restoration of the French Republic: "Having chosen, and so that its words would have a meaning, it was obliged to follow the logic of its decision to the very end" (208, trans. mod. [515]). The "logic" of the choice of democracy demands that all Algerians be given the same rights and protections under the law as other French citizens. In practical terms as well, Camus claims this is the only reasonable political alternative to the increasingly oppressive nature of colonial Algeria and the violence it provokes among the colonized.

Camus provocatively calls for the "reconquest" of Algeria this time, however, not through military means and in order to subdue a rebellious or resistant native population, but rather through authentic radical reforms that would guarantee the same freedoms for all Algerians and ensure that the entire population participated fully in society and with equal rights. That this would mean the end of colonialism did not of course escape him, for in another article in the same series he declares that he is "convinced that the era of Western imperialism is over" ("It Is Justice That Will Save Algeria from Hatred" [May 23, 1945], 216 [531])—a proclamation that was just a bit premature as concerns French Algeria.

Camus also acknowledges that the fundamental problem in Algeria was not just that the Arab and Berber populations of Algeria no longer believed in the possibility of their assimilation into French culture and economic-political life. Even more serious was the fact that they also no longer believed in democracy itself, especially given the grotesque form in which it had always been presented to them in the colonies: "But the Arabs seem to have lost their faith in democracy, of which they were offered only a caricature. They hope to achieve by other means a goal that has never changed: an improvement in their condition" (*Combat* [May 18, 1945], 210 [518]). The caricature of democracy that colonized Algerians are offered in Algeria makes "democracy" itself the problem, not the solution, for it is French democracy that is responsible for the denial of basic democratic freedoms to the overwhelming majority of Algerians. Democracy could thus be said to be paradoxically at the same time the cause of and solution to colonial injustice. Which means that the struggle to put an end to injustice in Algeria must take the form of a struggle both with and against democracy in the name of democracy.

The chief issue for Camus in 1945 was not *whether* the French should still work for democracy in Algeria but rather *how* best to work for it. He was convinced that if nothing was done and conditions continued to worsen that the violence would also increase—which is exactly what occurred. In Camus' view, though, neither France nor any other nation could claim to be a true democracy if it remained a colonial or imperialist power and subjugated and oppressed other peoples. No true democracy could deny to others the very freedoms it claimed for itself, but no true democracy had the right to impose by force their religion, culture, language, laws, or political system on another people either. Imperialist forms of democracy were thus for him no better than other forms of imperialism.

For Camus, the definitive sign that assimilation had finally been rejected by Arab Algerians was that the moderate nationalist leader Ferhat Abbas, who was erroneously blamed by French authorities and the press for the riots and massacres at Sétif, had rejected it. In a courageous and moving tribute to Abbas, Camus argues that even though Abbas had understood that a "politics of assimilation" had no chance of succeeding, at the same time he and the group he had founded, *Les Amis du Manifeste* (The Friends of the Manifesto), continued to occupy a middle ground between political extremes and had not yet been won over to the cause of what Camus calls "pure nationalism." After having "turned his back on assimilation," Abbas, Camus claims, "is calling for Algeria to be recognized as a nation linked to France by ties of federalism." The fundamental principle of the manifesto "takes note of the failure of [French] assimilation policy and the need to recognize an Algerian nation linked to France but distinctive in character" ("Arabs Demand a Constitution and a Parliament for Algeria," *Combat* [May 20–21, 1945], 212–213 [522–525]). Even though he does not explicitly support Abbas's nationalist-federalist position in this article, Camus does not criticize it either. In the essays he writes during the Algerian War, it will in fact be the position Camus himself maintains, even long after Abbas has abandoned it.

Camus points out that if the policy of assimilation was indeed doomed, it was once again not Algerian Arabs but the French administration and powerful colonial interests that had condemned it to death, through a long history of broken promises and repressive actions taken against moderate nationalists such as Abbas. To answer legitimate demands with "imprisonment and repression," which was what the French had done to Abbas after the massacres at Sétif, was, in Camus' words, "stupidity, pure and simple" (214 [527]). Democratic France continued to fight against democracy in Algeria and considered any demand for equal rights for all Algerians to be a threat not just to its colonial investments but to the very existence of the French Republic. For Camus, nothing could have been more stupid and dangerous than this. Nothing could have been less democratic and more likely to fail and encourage the emergence of leaders more militantly nationalist than Abbas. Camus was one of the very few French political journalists at the time to acknowledge the importance of Abbas's ideas, to defend them as a moderate, reasonable response to colonial injustices, and especially to consider them both Algeria's and France's best hope for a peaceful and just resolution to the increasingly violent conflicts such injustices provoked.

Given the continued mutual respect and admiration they felt for each other, in the midst of the Algerian War Abbas joined Camus in January

1956 in an "Appeal for a Civilian Truce." And after the escalation of French repression soon after the appeal had failed, Abbas fled Algeria for Egypt, where he publicly announced his support of the FLN and agreed to serve as president of the GPRA (Provisional Government of the Algerian Republic) from September 1958 until August 1961. Camus had to have clearly understood at that moment, if not before, what Abbas's decision meant for his own hopes that a compromise could be achieved among moderate Algerian forces on both sides: if the moderate nationalist leader he most respected had not only joined the FLN but had also agreed to preside over its provisional government, then there were no longer any moderate nationalist leaders left in Algeria with whom to enter into dialogue and form an alliance.[13] For the same reasons, the number of moderate *pieds-noirs* initially capable of forming such an alliance, always small in number, was also rapidly decreasing as the cycle of terrorism and counterterrorism continued. Camus' search for a moderate "third way" to resolve the Algerian conflict, at least after 1956, was increasingly desperate and unrealistic. But it was not procolonialist.[14]

Life or Death?

> France, we see, continues on. But behind it, Algeria dies.
> —Albert Camus, "L'Algérie déchirée," *L'Express* (October 1955)

> Ferhat Abbas and the Oulemas joining the FLN was a sign that should have made [Camus] reflect. . . . It is symptomatic that Camus speaks of "Arabs," then of "the Arab people," but never of the Algerian people. . . . That is his error. It escapes him that [the Algerian nation] is being formed in the fight against French occupation.
> —Jeanyves Guérin, *Albert Camus: portrait de l'artiste en citoyen*

Approximately a year before he went to Algiers to support the "Appeal for a Civilian Truce" organized by a group of his closest friends, Camus agreed to write a series of editorials on Algeria for the journal *L'Express*, in what would turn out to be another fruitless attempt to influence public opinion on Algeria. He also had a specific political goal as well: to facilitate the return to power of the moderate socialist leader Pierre Mendès-France, who Camus felt was the only politician who had a chance of ending the Algerian War in a way that would be fair to all Algerians.[15] Camus wrote for *L'Express* from May 1955 until February 1956, when he stopped writing, it having become clear that the Appeal for a Civilian Truce was having no effects on the escalating violence of the war and because Mendès-France had been thwarted in his attempts to become prime minister. The editorials have a double emphasis: an insistence on the increasing gravity of the situation in Algeria (amidst what Camus claimed was the general indifference of the metropolitan French) and the desperate hope that a moderate and just resolution to the increasingly violent conflict could still be found. Camus repeatedly states that it is the "last chance" for a peaceful solution to the conflict before the violence veers completely out of control and makes any compromise impossible. Once again, the "last chance" was repeatedly missed by both sides.

Camus' unwavering conviction was that Algeria and France in general, but more important, Arab, Berber, and French Algerians in particular, *could* never be separated from each other. As he put it in his "Appeal for a Civilian Truce," "French and Arab solidarity is inevitable, in death as in life, in destruction as in hope" (*Resistance, Rebellion, and Death*, 135 [*Essais*, 994]). The problem for him then was not *whether* but *how* best to create a society based on this solidarity. In spite of the increasingly deep political divisions that were greatly exacerbated by the war, Algerians in Camus' mind still had no choice, since, as he repeatedly put it, "in Algeria French and Arabs are condemned to live or to die together."[16] He could not believe that the overwhelming majority would not choose life over death.

Even during the worst moments of the war, Camus continues to describe French and Arab Algerians as being part of the same "Algerian family." This is a family, though, with no common ethnic or cultural background but constituted rather through a long history of living together/apart on the same land, in close proximity to but also radically separated from each other for more than a hundred years. Somehow this divided family had survived in spite of the economic inequalities, racial prejudices, and sociopolitical injustices suffered by the overwhelming majority of its members under the colonial system. Camus stubbornly persisted in the belief that this divided, dysfunctional family still had a chance of being reunited—or rather of being truly united for the first time—if the violence against civilians could be stopped and a dialogue begun between moderates on both sides of the conflict.[17]

Camus depicts the war in his editorials not as a political struggle for autonomy and national independence, but as a family tragedy, which explains (but not justifies) its unlimited violence: "All of the same tragic family whose members cut each others' throats in the middle of the night, without recognizing each other, groping about in the dark in a mêlée of blind men. . . . Soon Algeria will be populated only by murderers or victims. Soon, only the dead will be innocent" ("Trêve pour les civils" [Truce for Civilians], L'Express [January 10, 1956] [Essais, 983]). As the war continues to escalate, every Algerian, Camus claims, using the same terminology he used in his 1946 series of articles for Combat, "Neither Victims nor Executioners," is being transformed into either a victim or a murderer—or both at the same time. Only the murderers on one side or the other could emerge victorious in a total war of this type, with the result that the Algerian people as a whole would be the victims of a war allegedly being waged in their name, no matter which side ended up winning.

Camus' last political essays constitute a desperate plea to end this tragic cycle of terror. But at the same time, at his moments of greatest despair, he also seems resigned to accepting the inevitability of the tragedy. There is no evidence in these editorials, however, that he ever contemplated supporting the only practical solution to the war: direct negotiations with the FLN. A number of Camus' pieds-noirs friends on the Left did accept the inevitable in the hope that French Algerians would be able to live in an independent Algeria ruled by the FLN. But Camus never did. This does not make him a supporter of colonialism, but it does help explain why his last political essays seem the most pessimistic and at times bitter and have been generally considered even less relevant to the resolution of the war than his earlier writings.[18]

A Last Cry for Peace

> Whatever the ancient and deep origins of the Algerian tragedy, one fact remains: no cause justifies the death of the innocent.
> —Albert Camus, "Appeal for a Civilian Truce" (January 22, 1956)

On January 22, 1956, Camus traveled to Algiers to support the movement organized by several of his closest Algerian friends and deliver a speech published under the title "Appeal for a Civilian Truce."[19] Increasingly ignored by Parisian intellectuals and treated as a despised enemy by Algerian *colons*, only the FLN seemed to take the appeal at all seriously. But even if the motives of the FLN for doing so could very well have been primarily opportunistic, it is clear that the appeal, while not advocating national independence, tilts much more in that direction than in the direction of the continuation of colonialism in Algeria and the politics of proponents of *Algérie française*.[20] It was the latter in fact who threatened Camus' life and disrupted his talk, screaming threats such as "Death to Camus!" "Mendès-France to the gallows!" and "Down with the Jews!" outside the meeting hall where he spoke. These extremists understood what a civil truce would have meant to their cause. The FLN did as well, which is why it allowed its members to participate in the appeal and, without Camus' knowledge, provide security for him while he was in Algiers.[21]

With abundant evidence of the hatred and divisions separating the different sides obvious immediately outside the meeting hall, Camus nevertheless states in his speech that his goal that night is "not to divide but unite," to "bring together all Algerians, French or Arab, without their having to give up any of their convictions" ("Appeal for a Civilian Truce," in *Resistance, Rebellion, and Death*, 131 [991]). Camus insists that his speech has "nothing to do with politics," since he admits he is not a politician but rather a writer who has "devoted a part of his life to serving Algeria" and even more important, someone who was living "the Algerian calamity as a personal tragedy . . . incapable of rejoicing over any death whatsoever" (131–132 [991–992]). For Camus, what links the people assembled in the hall and by extension the great majority of those living in Algeria, what makes them all *Algerians*, is precisely their sorrow over the loss of innocent lives—regardless what justification is given for either the terrorist or counterterrorist acts responsible for the deaths. To be Algerian in his sense is to perceive the war as a tragedy for all Algerians because of the death of innocents, whatever one's political position is or whatever the eventual outcome of the war would be.[22]

Camus proposes in his speech no specific political solution to the war and no formula for creating an Algerian state afterward. He offers no vision of a hypothesized social or political unity that could be discussed and debated in the hopes of an eventual agreement, given that neither side recognized the political legitimacy of the other side and he himself did not support the FLN or its demand for immediate and complete Algerian independence. More political debate would only lead to the continuation and escalation of the war; an appeal to the sorrow of the Algerian people could, on the contrary, produce a civilian truce, which he argues would itself be a sign of unity and could serve as the basis for further dialogue.[23]

Camus argues that no matter how horrible the threat of violence all Algerians had to face, no matter how outrageous and unacceptable the injustices suffered by civilians on both sides of the war, no matter how increasingly evident the signs of hatred of each side for the other were, something fundamental was still shared by Algerians on both sides of the war, and this was what allowed him to speak as an Algerian both to and for other Algerians. What was shared was not something that is in its essence political, not a common idea of the people, the community, or the nation, for the differences between the political visions were irreconcilable, and the war was being fought precisely to determine which side's political vision would prevail and determine the future of Algeria. After 130 years of colonial oppression and two years of constantly escalating violence against civilians on both sides, it would not be an exaggeration to say that most no longer shared any common political ideal at all.

What Camus claims nevertheless still unites "French" and "Arab" men and women, what they continue to have in common despite their differences, and thus what makes it still possible for him to appeal to them collectively, are two sentiments: "love of our common land and anguish" (133 [993]). Camus does not address at great length Algerians' love of a common land, for in the midst of the horrors of war this most likely would have had divisive effects. It is rather the anguish of an entire people that is the principal subject of his appeal: "anguish faced with a future that is closed off a little more every day, anguish faced with the threat of a deteriorating struggle, of an economic disequilibrium that is already serious and getting worse every day" (133–134 [993]). He considers this common anguish the sign that on some level even the most militant factions on each side realize that the war cannot be allowed to continue to escalate and increase the number of innocent victims on each side. The common anguish of Algerians is also a sign of what could be called an affective consensus that FLN terrorism against French civilians, French torture and summary execution of civilian suspects, and the indiscriminate bombing of suspected FLN villages should be immediately stopped. Camus thus directs his appeal to that part of even the most militant members on both sides that he states still "will not indulge in murder and hatred and that dreams of a happy Algeria" (134 [993]). If he addresses the Algerian people primarily as a people of anguish, it is because during the war it is only their anguish that continues to link them to each other, that remains the last but most profound sign that those on both sides still believe that what he calls a "happy Algeria" is possible.

Because of the anguish that he claims is a constitutive part of every Algerian, Camus argues that it is still possible to agree at the very least that innocent human lives should be spared and that the protection of innocent civilians should come first, before any other principle or goal. On this basic point, as we have seen is the case in many of his post–World-War-II political essays, he simply asserts that there is not and cannot be any disagreement over this principle—life has to come before politics (and even justice). For, if it does not, if the ends of ideology justify the means of political (and military) action, then terrorism, unlimited violence, and total destruction are the inevitable consequences.

But Camus does not just speak *of* a common anguish; he also addresses his comments *to* it: "It is to this anguish we want to address ourselves, even and especially of those who have already chosen sides" (134 [993]). The anguish Camus claims is felt by all Algerians, especially the anguish resulting from the loss of relatives, friends, and loved ones, a deep anguish that no act of revenge, no form of terrorism, no ultimate military or political victory, and no success in achieving specific political goals could ever negate, diminish, or give meaning to, this anguish is for him the sign that there already exists a consensus that the violence and terrorism against civilians on both sides should be stopped and that political differences could eventually be overcome. Based on their common experience of anguish, the different communities could finally begin to work together for common goals.

Anguish is a deeply personal, solitary feeling of loss; one person's anguish is not another's. But one person's anguish can be recognized, even if not directly felt, by others, and in this way it can be shared, even if not experienced in the same way. Anguish has nothing, however, to do with the anger felt by crowds and mobs after a terrorist act has been committed or the mass hysteria that is publicly displayed in demonstrations and acts of collective outrage and revenge. Anguish is rather a feeling shared even more deeply and intimately with others because it does not justify revenge, since revenge cannot address or alleviate it. Anguish is the sign that something other than the struggle for and achievement of specific political ends is at stake in the struggle for justice, even at the most extreme and violent moments of war and revolution. Anguish indicates that the loss of family members, friends, and comrades can never be compensated for and thus never justified, whether in victory or defeat.

To recognize and address the anguish of others is also to recognize and address them as equals on a deep emotional level, regardless of whether they are friend or enemy, good or bad, one of us or one of them. To address anguish is to recognize the suffering and the right to anguish of others; it is to address others in terms of their losses and to acknowledge that their anguish is of the same nature and intensity as one's own. Private anguish that is recognized and addressed could become the basis, Camus argues, not of a specific political solution to the war, but rather of a general acceptance of the limits of what should and can be done in the name of the opposing causes defended by each side. The recognition of the anguish of others would be the first step in ending terrorism, the torture of suspects, the indiscriminate bombing of villages, and summary executions. But without such an acceptance of limits and with the continued denial of the right to and recognition of the anguish of those on the other side, the violence and terror inflicted by each side on the other side (and on factions on its own side) would not just continue but escalate. In terms of anguish, there can be no such thing as "collateral damage," since all damage to self and others is fundamental and of the same value and significance.

The only way to address the anguish of others, to speak of and to their anguish, is with the voice of anguish itself, that is, in a conditional, I am tempted to say, "literary," voice that is not entirely one's own, since no one can pretend to actually speak directly for or as the anguish of another. In any case, this is the voice Camus claims he would like to use: "If I had the power to give a voice to the solitude and anguish in each of us, that is the voice with which I would address you" (140 [998]). The voice of anguish cuts through the clash of ideologies and political, religious, and cultural differences, or the claims and justifications made by each side against the other, some more legitimate than others but all ultimately limited in the face of such anguish. Moreover, addressing and expressing their common anguish, it recognizes the responsibilities of both sides for the unjustifiable loss of innocent lives. To evoke such a shared voice, one that links Algerians together in terms of what separates them from and opposes them to each other, is in itself, if not the beginning of a particular form of dialogue, at least the sign of its possibility. Without such a shared/divided, conditional voice and the mutual recognition it implies, extremist politics and terror would continue to triumph and constantly increase, to the detriment and increased anguish of all.

Camus in his speech stubbornly refuses to abandon his conviction that "on the same land, one million Frenchmen established for a century, millions of Muslims, both Arabs and Berbers, settled in for centuries, and several strong and vibrant religious communities" could not, as he puts it, continue to "live together at the intersection of routes and races where history had placed them" (136, trans. mod. [995]). That shared history, Camus also argues, should not, however, be evoked as the justification either for continued French colonial domination and oppression or for the expulsion of French Algerians from Algeria. It is, rather, the sign of the possibility, up to then unrealized, of equal relations among the different peoples and cultures of Algeria. For Camus, the obvious cultural differences among the different populations constitutes not the justification for conflict but rather the basis for their living together in peace: "Our differences ought to help us rather than oppose us. As for me, here as in every other domain, I believe only in differences, not in uniformity" (136 [995]). To speak to and with the voice of anguish is also then to speak to and with the divided voice of cultural and political differences as well.

To believe in differences rather than uniformity is most definitely not to believe in the indivisible unity of a French Republic that includes Algeria as an integral part of itself but excludes the overwhelming majority of Algerians from citizenship. Nor is it to believe in the birth of "new men" through terrorism and a new and totally independent Algerian state composed of a unified Muslim people and with a single language, religion, and culture. It is not to believe in any political or religious ideology that considers difference to be a sign of inferiority or a threat to orthodoxy; any ideology or movement that legitimates injustices, crimes, terror, and war on the basis of a innate religious-cultural identity that defines and thus separates one group from other groups, one ethnicity from other ethnicities, one people from other peoples. It is rather to vigorously oppose colonialism and the oppression of the great majority of Algerians in the name of the integrity and grandeur of the French Republic and the fictional unity and identity of the French people. But it is also to reject the political program of the FLN and the fictive identity of the ethnic-religious Algerian state it is proposing, especially given the means being used to achieve it. Recognizing and speaking to/with the anguish of others thus means above all recognizing others' differences and their right to difference. It means recognizing their worth, equality, and right to life—and their right to anguish over the loss of life.

Camus' plea for a civilian truce thus turns both colonialism and the brutal anticolonialist war of national liberation on their heads, by making the radical differences among peoples living on the same land the principal reason for their reconciliation, the sign of a shared cultural nonidentity, of an "identity" experienced in terms of otherness, not sameness. Camus' "Appeal for a Civilian Truce" acknowledges the fundamental role of cultural differences within Algeria (and France)—within the Algeria that Camus imagined already existed in the anguish of Algerians and underneath the horror of terrorism and that he argues it is still possible to (re)create once terrorism, torture, and summary executions have ended. His is the dream of an Algeria in which political, cultural, and religious differences would play a constructive rather than destructive role—an Algeria in which past injustices would not serve as the justification for present or future injustices. Where the recognition of the suffering and anguish of others would peacefully unite rather than violently oppose peoples with different languages, cultures, and religions—peoples who nevertheless shared in spite of all their antagonisms and bloodshed both their anguish and their profound attachment to the same land. The failure to create such a multidenominational, multicultural society in Algeria was of course devastating for all Algerians, but, as Ferhat Abbas argues in one of his most pessimistic postwar statements, it could also be a sign of the impossibility of the project being realized anywhere: "If Algeria, and in a more general way, North Africa, was not capable of realizing a synthesis between the Muslim East and a renewed Christian West, then no other part of the world could hope to succeed" (*Autopsie d'une guerre*, 159). It would at the very least appear to be true that such a synthesis has not yet been achieved today, that the struggle even to find a peaceful and equitable coexistence between East and West is still a difficult, ongoing struggle.

Camus' "modest proposal" for a civilian truce was thus anything but modest. But when the French continued to torture and execute terrorist suspects, and then when the FLN once again began using terrorist bombs against civilian targets, it was clear that the appeal had been made in vain. Anguish was not listened to or addressed in the continued furor and folly of war, or if it was recognized, it was only "our" anguish and not "theirs," which meant that anguish was used as the justification for more violence rather than as the basis for dialogue and peace. Camus' pleas for a civilian truce clearly failed and turned out to be irrelevant to the last years of the war and its eventual outcome. One can only speculate what would have happened had Algerians gained their independence through earlier negotiations and before the escalation of terrorism and torture that characterized the Battle of Algiers in 1957. But any such speculations would necessarily have to acknowledge the role played by Camus in offering the possibility, no matter how unlikely, of an earlier and much less bloody resolution to the armed conflict and an end to colonialism in Algeria. For that is indeed what his plea advocated.[24]

It is too much to ask one's imagination to visualize one's own end.

—Albert Memmi, *The Colonizer and the Colonized*

CHAPTER SEVEN

Last Words

Camus' True Country

> The Mediterranean separates two worlds in me, one where memories and names are preserved in measured spaces, the other where winds of sand erase all traces of men within immense spaces.
>
> I have had a long affair with Algeria which will undoubtedly never end and which keeps me from being completely lucid. . . . [Algeria] is my true country.
>
> —Albert Camus, "Short Guide for Cities Without a Past"

Camus refers to Algeria numerous times in his essays as his "true country." But no matter how emotionally attached he was to Algeria, no matter how lyrically he describes its physical beauty and the generosity of its people, the Algeria depicted in his writings is anything but a *political* paradise. For as we have seen, in numerous essays from the late 1930s through 1958, Camus consistently denounces the radical separation between the "French" and "Arab" populations of Algeria and the oppression, humiliation, and exploitation of colonized Algerians as unacceptable injustices. It is true that Algeria is frequently represented in his work as a kind of *earthly* paradise, but even this picture is more complicated and nuanced than it might first appear.

For if Algeria appears in his writings as a nurturing Mediterranean land of great warmth and natural beauty, providing even the most destitute and oppressed Algerians with physical and aesthetic pleasures and momentary escapes from their destitution, oppression, and humiliation,[1] it is also depicted in the expanses of the high plateaus, mountains, and deserts of its vast interior regions as a hostile, inhuman land where the poor are engaged in a life-and-death struggle not only against the injustices and oppression of the colonial system but also against the land and climate. These same areas also possess a powerful and stark beauty for those who, like the schoolteacher and his Arab prisoner in his short story "The Guest/Host," feel they could never live anywhere else.[2]

The vast expanse of Algerian desert holds an important place in Camus' work as well, but it is also presented in two radically different ways. As we have seen, in "The Renegade," the desert is described as a climatic and sociopolitical hell whose unrelenting heat "drives men mad" (35 [1579]).[3] It is the site of unrestricted violence resulting from the clash of absolute Truths and competing religions and cultures, with the stakes of the struggle being domination or enslavement, salvation or damnation, life or death. And yet the North African desert is also described in both "The Guest/Host" and "The Adulterous Woman" as a limitless space of unrestricted freedom, an unstructured, open space inhabited only by nomads, whose meager existence and possessions make them "the lords" of a barren but majestic "kingdom" that is the diametric opposite of the divided, occupied space created by colonialist society. Camus' true country is thus at the same time both hospitable and inhospitable, nurturing and deadly, earthly paradise and inhuman hell, a complicated, internally divided land impossible to reduce to any one of its conflicting parts.

This land of extremes is also the birth land and homeland of different and at times violently opposed peoples who have ethnic origins and cultural identities as varied as the different geographies and climates of the land itself. Camus' true country is a country unwillingly shared by, unequally divided up amongst, and from the start violently contested by different peoples. For if, on the one hand, the land's richness, beauty, and warmth, and, on the other, its barrenness and the harsh living conditions it imposes on its inhabitants both contribute to making Algeria *his* true country and affective homeland, they are the very same elements that exile him from Algeria and make him (and every other Algerian) also a stranger in his own land.

Camus' Algeria is the homeland of a hybrid community that has not taken form or been realized as such, a community comprising different peoples who have no common language, culture, or religion but who do share a deep affective attachment to their birth land. This common attachment, which Camus presents as an indisputable fact, means that the attachment of no single individual or group is exclusive or can be privileged over any other. The legitimacy of an individual's or a people's claim to the land does not make any other individual's or people's claim any less legitimate.

For Camus, what could be called the right to affective attachment was not determined simply by longevity, by how many years, decades, or centuries a national, cultural, religious, or ethnic group could trace or project its own arrival and settlement in Algeria. He refused to accept any claim of a primary or exclusive right to the land based on the notion of a prior or more original possession of the land, any claim that Algeria was exclusively or primarily one national, religious, cultural, or ethnic group's rather than another's simply because one people settled there first, before others. To make such a claim would be to negate the history of all those who had arrived after the "original inhabitants" or "founding fathers" and would be equivalent to the chauvinistic claims of the "native French" who affirm their identity as true Frenchmen by tracing their ancestry back to the imaginary original inhabitants of France, "their ancestors, the Gaulois," and then use that fictive identity as the proof that those arriving in France more recently are not truly French.

Such fantasies of original ancestry or founding fathers are treated by Camus as dangerous nationalist fictions, the very myths that are exploited by racist, fascist, and extremist colonialist movements on the Right and nationalist-revolutionary movements on the Left. Given the ethnic and cultural hybridity of Algeria produced by its highly conflicted colonial history, Camus' Algeria is a land of cultural differences that no founding myth or nationalist project of unity (and thus exclusion) can effectively negate.

More fundamental and unalienable than any right founded in "first possession," longevity, conquest, or actual "legal" possession of the land is the aesthetic or affective right of attachment. Unlike nationalist myths, the right of affective attachment is not exclusive to any group, religion, or ethnicity. All Algerians, all the different ethnicities and cultures inhabiting the same land, whether they originally came to Algeria for legitimate or illegitimate reasons, or for both reasons at the same time, have the right to this right. Because no legal documents of residency are necessary to establish such a right, because it is grounded in no economic or political principle of possession or sovereignty, the experience of living in the land and being receptive to its both nurturing beauty and harsh climate constitutes the sole condition for the right to this basic right.

Whatever the strictly political limitations of Camus' imaginary construct of his true country or the problems with his vision of the Mediterranean in general as a multicultural, transnational site of cross-fertilization between East and West, an open space shared by Muslim, Christian, and Jewish religions, cultures, and traditions, a constant of his political essays on Algeria is his opposition to all myths of racial or cultural superiority and the related fictions of a continuous national history and homogeneous national identity.[4] Opposed to the economic and political realities of colonial Algeria, Camus in his essays and fictions constructs the image of a community whose identity as a people does not depend on the exclusion or oppression of any of its inhabitants, all of whom have or should have the same right to call themselves Algerians and claim Algeria as their true country. Algerians, no matter their ethnic background, religious affiliation, or cultural formation, no matter where their ancestors originally came from or with which ethnicity or nationality they are identified, are for Camus necessarily mixed. All in one way or another have disordered identities and in some sense are all "*métis*."[5]

Belated "Firstness"

> *The First Man* goes back over the entire route to discover its secret; he is not first. Every man is the first man, and no one is.
>
> —Albert Camus, *Carnets III*

As we have seen, Camus vowed that he would make no further public statements on Algeria after the publication of *Algerian Reports* in 1958. During the period of his self-imposed silence and until his death, he nevertheless continued to write about his true country. His writing, however, took the form not of political essays but of an autobiographical novel, *The First Man*, whose unfinished manuscript was found with his body in the ruins of the automobile accident in which he died. The Algeria he vowed he would no longer speak about publicly or in a political mode, he instead wrote about in a fictional mode. As he had throughout his life, he once again turned to fiction when politics offered only what he felt were unacceptable alternatives, tragic impasses, and increasingly lethal consequences.

In his autobiographical novel, Camus gives his most detailed and elaborate picture of Algeria and his idealized view of the French Algerians who had inhabited it for over a century and whose immanent demise the novel also recounts. In this sense, *The First Man* could just as appropriately have been called *The Last Man*. Jacques Cormery, Camus' fictional double,[6] who is described in the novel as "the first man," cannot, however, in any sense be considered an Algerian Adam, for his "original status" is highly paradoxical. He is not first in any chronological sense, nor is he the originator of the species. Nor is he even unique, since he is described as belonging to a "tribe," all of whose members are also first men. He is "first" in a land that for generations has been inhabited by others, a land where different peoples with radically different ethnic backgrounds, religious beliefs, and linguistic and cultural practices have lived together but also apart from and, most often, in conflict with each other. Some Algerian "first men" of course are more recent arrivals in Algeria than others, but because they are all in some sense "first," none can claim the right to have inhabited the land from the beginning or to have more right to inhabit it than others. None has the right to possess it exclusively. Longevity of habitation is thus no more legitimate a justification for an exclusive claim to the land than conquest, and neither can be evoked to legitimize the rights and privileges of some in order to deny those same rights and privileges to others.

To be an Algerian first man is to live in a land of different peoples so varied in cultural background that, no matter one's national heritage, language, religion, and culture, it would be impossible to project a *natural* cultural, religious, or linguistic identity for all. It is to be first in a land where no one is ever really first or where the claim to be first in any absolute sense is blatantly absurd, given the turbulent and constantly changing history of the land, its many conquerors, immigrants, and inhabitants. All first men thus share what could be called "belated firstness"—all are first, but only belatedly, after the fact.

Being first thus does not make any individual or group "Algerian Adams" or "founding fathers," for all are belated originators of a people who in fact would never grow or mature, "fathers" of a people who had and would continue to have no homogeneous national-cultural identity. Being a first man is thus to be at the same time originator and inheritor of a people who would remain virtual, more an idea or fiction of a people than a political reality. For a first man not only lives *as if* he had no predecessors, *as if* roots had little, if any, lasting consequences—both those of his own ancestors and those of peoples and cultures more indigenous or native to the land than his ancestors. He also bequeaths to subsequent generations the condition of "belated firstness," which is in a sense his only legacy, with all heirs of first men orphans, each generation of first men "lost and found children [*enfants trouvés et perdus*]" (*The First Man*, 194 [179]). The "gift" of belated firstness is thus projected both backward onto previous generations and forward onto subsequent generations.[7] If *being-first* were the characteristic of one generation, group, or man alone—or of one ethnicity, national group, culture, or religion—then the mythical first man of that ethnicity, group, culture, or religion would logically be the true and unique Algerian Adam, the founding father of all fathers, the first of the first. His people would be the original, true Algerian people. No such claim is or can be made for any first man in the Algeria depicted in the novel, however—not for Jacques Cormery and certainly not for French Algerians in general. Nor for any other individual or ethnic, cultural-religious, or national group.

Each generation of first men has to reestablish the roots that previous generations had failed to establish or that had been immediately destroyed, roots that remain for each generation, for each people, for all Algerians, always to be reestablished, as if for the first time. The novel's highly mythologized and tragic account of the struggles of the first French colonizers to Algeria consists of the fragmented, incomplete stories of the inevitably brief lives and then disappearance of each successive generation of first men. It is characterized by the constant lack of enduring traces of any past that would determine the present or give a specific direction to the future:

> All those generations, all those men having come from so many different countries . . . had disappeared without leaving a trace, closed in

on themselves. An enormous oblivion spread over them, and in truth, that is what this land dispensed. . . . [Each one, like his father who died in France in World War I] returned to that immense oblivion that was the definitive homeland [*patrie*] of men of [this] race, the final destination of a life that began without roots.

(193–194, trans. mod. [179])

The history of first men is thus a repetitive, cyclical history without a determined chronology or genealogy, one in which each generation starts anew, discovering and reestablishing itself in a land of absent and immediately forgotten ancestors. The destiny of first men is to disappear, to leave behind few if any traces, and then be immediately forgotten. It is history without any lasting familial, ethnic, cultural, religious, or national memory. First men are the nomads of history, not the founding fathers of a specific people or nation. *The First Man* is thus the story of the life and death of a people without a determined history and who never in fact became *a people.*

Becoming "French"—From Anonymity to Assimilation

Yes, I have a country: the French language.

—Albert Camus, *Carnets II* (September 1950)

The sparse, fragmented history of first men is dominated by absence, death, oblivion, and, above all, anonymity. Anonymity is both a threat to and the privilege of each first man and each generation of first men; it is a cruel fate to be struggled against and a modest but ultimately glorious destiny that provides each succeeding generation with the same unlimited possibilities. No generation is encumbered with the weight of previous generations and their legacy and traditions; no first man has a determining familial, national, or cultural identity. What Algerian first men have in common with each other, and with the land itself, is thus not a fictional "biological," cultural, religious, or national identity, but rather only "the mystery of poverty that creates beings without names and without pasts," a common "anonymity, on the level of blood" (194, trans. mod. [180]). They thus share and are defined only by what could be called a "biological" and cultural *nonidentity*. This is undoubtedly why there are no developed descriptions of *grands colons* in Camus' portraits of Algerians in this novel or anywhere else in his work, and why it is only the modest, poor, and destitute of Algeria who are for him the true Algerians and the true first men.

Camus' Algerians are predominantly modest or extremely poor "French" Algerians of diverse European ancestries who, like the mother of his fictional double in the novel and his own illiterate mother, "did not know the history of France nor what history was" and for whom France itself was "an obscure place lost in a dim night" (67–68 [68–69]). But Camus' Algerians also include the Arab and Berber "subjects" or "natives" of French Algeria as well, most often referred to in his works, as they were by *pieds-noirs* in general, simply as "the Arabs"—even though their stories are not told and they are rarely even given a name. Their history is even more obscure than that of the poor French because it is doubly ignored or repressed by colonial society. It is as if Camus' poor Algerians in general all shared the anonymity imposed on colonized Algerians by the colonial system, as if all had anonymity as their origin and their destiny, whatever the political and cultural differences that separated them from one another. If he was criticized for presenting in *The Stranger* and "The Guest/Host" Arab characters as anonymous figures, the fate of all first men, like that of Meursault, is to become "Arab." In any case, for Camus' Algerians the idea of the French nation remains distant and obscure, while their "native land," literally "the land of their flesh [*patrie de chair*]" (193 [179]), constitutes their immediate, concrete, and all-encompassing reality.[8]

The counterfigure to Camus' portrait of anonymous Algerians is the well-established, patriotic, middle-class French family, portrayed as being as foreign, unreal, and distant from Jacques' own family's experience as is France itself.[9] The most exotic of foreigners for Jacques is thus a classmate at the *lycée* who is a self-identified "true Frenchman":

> His family had a family home in France where he went on vacations ... with an attic full of old trunks where they saved the family's letters, souvenirs, photos. He knew the history of his grandparents and his great-grandparents. ... When he spoke of France, he would say "our country," and he accepted in advance the sacrifices that coun-

try might demand . . . whereas the notion of country [*patrie*] had no meaning to Jacques . . . for whom France remained absent.

(207–208, trans. mod. [190–191])

Family photos and fictions of the nation support each other and provide a clear image of who he is and what it means to be French. Jacques, who has no already determined sense of self, no sense of the nation, and no sense of belonging, is not just from a different social class than his French school-mate, but also of "another species," "with no past, no family home, no at-tic full of letters and photos." Unlike the self-proclaimed "true French," Jacques' family members and closest friends are "citizens in theory of a nebulous nation" (209 [192]). National identity for them is anything but a family affair.

If poverty is a "fortress without drawbridges" (145 [138]), first men are all entrapped in their poverty, poor in name, possessions, heritage, and mem-ory. It is above all poverty that produces and perpetuates anonymity and a sense of not belonging to any national chronology or family of names. Pov-erty also repeatedly interrupts the process of succession, the passing along from generation to generation of family and national identity and cultural possessions and traditions. Not only do first men have names that are im-mediately forgotten, but the same anonymity also defines both the harsh land where they are born and live and the unformed community of first men to which they belong. They belong first and foremost to a land, not a nation.

Neither the history of first men in general nor the story of the life of one first man in particular has a continuous, coherent, diachronic form, be-cause political and social conflicts, war, poverty, famine, and disease have disrupted the "natural," ordered, historical chronology that should have led from father to son and from one generation to the next. Fathers invariably die too young to establish any continuity: "The man buried under that slab, who had been his father, was younger than he. . . . Something here was not in the natural order and, in truth, there was not order but only madness and chaos when the son was older than the father" (25–26, trans. mod. [29–30]). The natural order of succession gives way to the madness and chaos resulting from the premature death of fathers and the gaps in chronology and reversals of generations it produces. Time is out of joint for all first men, who are never completely at home, not just in history in general but in their nation's, their family's, and even their own histories as well.

War

> Waves of Arab and French Algerians, dressed in smart shining colors, straw hats on their heads, red-and-blue targets you could see for hundreds of meters, went over the top in droves into the fire, were destroyed in droves, and began to fertilize a narrow stretch of land.... Each day hundreds of new orphans, Arab and French, awakened in every corner of Algeria, sons and daughters without fathers who now have to learn to live without guidance and without heritage.
>
> —Albert Camus, *The First Man*

Since the lives of first men leave few if any traces after them, their deaths have no meaning, even or especially when they die heroically for their own country. Or for a country that is not their own. As was the case for Camus' own father, his fictional double's father is one of the million and an half "French" soldiers who died anonymously in World War I, leaving behind only a meaningless inscription on a tombstone in a forgotten cemetery in mainland France. Whether they are legally citizens of France or colonial subjects of the nation for which they die, the corpses of Algerians are described as in the epigraph above as adding nothing to France's history but only fertilizing its soil (69–70 [70]). Thousands of Algerians died in France *"pour la patrie"* but far away from their true country, giving their life for a fatherland that was at the same time and to very different degrees, depending on whether they were French citizens or native subjects, not theirs (or their fathers' or mothers') at all.

The history of first men is predominantly a history of conflict and war. In World War I, they are among the millions of soldiers slaughtered mechanically and dying anonymously on the battlefields of France. But since they are Algerian, their history is also defined by daily violence and fighting in both declared and undeclared colonial conflicts, which are presented in the novel as being different from the wars fought between established states or nations. Colonial conflicts are characterized less by military battles between armies than by massacres, atrocities, and acts of individual vengeance committed against both soldiers and civilians. Part of Jacques Cormery's sparse family narrative is the story he is told of his father's experience fighting in Morocco and being deeply disturbed after witnessing the grotesque effects not of an act of war but of vengeance: "[The first sentry's] throat had been cut and that ghastly swelling in his mouth was his entire sexual organ. . . . A hundred meters further on, this time behind a large rock, the second sentinel was displayed in the same position" (65 [66]). In colonial conflicts, it is as if there are no limits imposed on violence, as if everything is permitted. It is as if such wars were fought by armies not just with the desire to defeat the enemy army but also out of a desire for personal and collective vengeance, which allowed for and even encouraged a form of violence beyond the violence of war itself. It is as if in colonial conflicts one was not just permitted to kill enemy soldiers but obliged to punish them after death. As if victory in battle was not the exclusive or perhaps even the primary or ultimate goal of such wars at all—as if the total destruction and humiliation of the other, even after death, in fact were.[10]

How is it possible to understand such acts? How should one react to a violence not just *of* war but outside and beyond war? The novel poses these questions, which were central to the debates surrounding the Algerian War in particular and which continue to be debated today in terms of ongoing conflicts and wars, but gives no single or definitive answer to them. Rather, in the novel Camus gives voice to two diametrically opposed positions concerning such excessive violence and atrocities. The first voice is that of Cormery's father, who on finding the bodies of the castrated sentries denounces those responsible for such outrages and accuses them of not being men (65 [66]). The second voice is that of one of Jacques' former school-teachers who fought in Morocco with his father and who explains that he disagreed with Jacques' father and told him that "for them [the Moroccans], that is how men should act, that we were in their homeland, that they were using any and all means" to defend it (65 [66]). For the teacher, the mutilation of the sentries' bodies was a condemnable act, but still understandable. For Jacques' father, it was incomprehensible, for no end could justify such means, no ideal could legitimate such atrocities, no defense of a homeland or struggle for independence could ever be considered just or even human if it depended on and legitimized such grotesque, inhuman acts. The problem the novel raises through this clash of opposed voices is thus not only the relation of ends and means but also what it means to remain "human" in the midst of war, especially an anticolonialist struggle for national independence. Remaining human for Jacques' father means above all that there have to be limits imposed on actions, even or especially in war, and that not everything is or ever should be possible, no matter the legitimacy of the cause being pursued or defended.

The emotional exchange that the novel describes between the two men (between Jacques Cormery's two fathers, the anonymous, dead father and one of the replacement schoolteacher fathers who at various moments supplemented the missing original) has to do with a question that every modern war, but especially anticolonialist wars of national independence, have raised: whether "inhuman acts" can ever be justified—either against enemy soldiers or innocent civilians. The debate is of course far from irrelevant today.

Responding to his friend's "explanation" of the Moroccans' acts, Jacques's father protests:

> Cormery's face took on a stubborn look. "Maybe. But they're wrong. A man doesn't do that." Levesque [his future son's future schoolteacher] said that for them, there were certain circumstances in which a man had to be allowed to do anything [and destroy everything]. But Cormery had shouted as if crazed with anger: "No, a man restrains himself. That's what a man is, or otherwise ... " Then he calmed down. "As for me," he said in a low voice, "I'm poor, I came from an orphanage, they put me in this uniform, they dragged me into the war, but I restrain myself.—"There are Frenchmen who don't restrain themselves," said Levesque. "Then they too, they aren't men." And suddenly he cried out: "Filthy race! What a race! All of them, all of them ... " And then white as a sheet, he went into his tent.
>
> (65–66, trans. mod. [66–67])

Albert Camus was most definitely the son of his fictional double's father. He did inherit something from the father he never knew (and the father he recreated in his novel): his disgust at "inhuman acts" and his refusal to justify them under any circumstances. No matter the cause or the ultimate goal, no matter the injustices already suffered or the inhuman, criminal acts already committed by the enemy, Camus, as we have seen, repeatedly argues in his political essays on Algeria that there needs to be limits placed on all actions, that all men have to restrain themselves, that everything is not and should not be possible. For if men do not restrain themselves, they lose their humanity and become part of a "filthy race"—no matter which side of the struggle they are on, no matter their "race," religion, or nationality. Without such restraints, all war becomes total war, and the mad vision expressed in "The Renegade" becomes in fact an accurate description of reality.

Both voices—the father's voice, which expresses disgust and unequivocal condemnation of the mutilations, and the schoolteacher's voice, which expresses the desire to understand and extend responsibility for such acts to both sides in the conflict—are components of what could be called the double voice Camus uses in this novel to address the issues of terrorism, counterterrorism, and colonial violence in general. The sentiments both voices express are part of the complex of contradictory sentiments he himself frequently expressed in his own voice and in his own name in his political essays on Algeria. And, as in the novel, the voice that condemns such atrocities invariably has the dominant, although not exclusive, role. There is invariably another voice in Camus' voice that recognizes and understands acts committed in defense of a homeland or as part of a struggle against injustice, even if this voice never silences or even dominates the condemnatory voice or attempts to justify unjustifiable acts that reveal the fundamental inhumanity of both sides in such conflicts. Camus claims in his preface to *Algerian Reports* that he admires, but from afar, those who have such devotion to the cause of justice that they are willing to do anything, even sacrifice their own family, for the cause. But, as he puts it in words very close to those he attributes to his fictional father in the novel: "I am not of their race."[11]

But what exactly is meant by "race" in this context, and who is really the "filthy race" denounced in the novel by Jacques Cormery's father? Who are "all of them?" Even from the father's perspective, the "filthy race" is composed not just of the actual perpetrators of the acts he denounces, that is, the Moroccans who killed and then maimed the French sentries as part of their struggle to liberate their homeland. Or by extension all Moroccans, all Arabs, all Muslims, all colonized. "All of them" is rather all of those men, in this context French and Arab alike, who either commit such acts or justify them before or after the fact. All those who are not "men enough" to "restrain themselves," even if they are convinced that their cause is just—or especially if in fact their cause is just. The words attributed to Jacques Cormery's father during a military campaign in Morocco set a limit on what "a man" can or should do. They set an absolute limit on violence and terror—whether during a declared war among established nations or a war fought by a colonized people against its oppressors and in the name of national independence and justice. To be "human" is to accept limits, and, first and foremost, the limits of the political, so that no atrocity of this type can ever be justified. There can perhaps be victory, but there can be no justice without such an acceptance of limits.

No matter how oppressed and victimized those using such tactics are, no matter how legitimate and just their defense of their homeland might be, Jacques' father's words deny anyone the right to commit such acts. Camus attributes these words to his fictional double's father, a simple, unsophisticated, barely literate man who considers all atrocities of this sort to be the work of men who are not really men. A man who turns white with rage when he witnesses atrocities, just as he became physically sick when he witnessed the execution of a monstrous mass murderer who he had previously been convinced deserved to die for his crimes. There are things a father cannot stomach. Nor can the son: neither Cormery, the fictional son, nor Camus himself.

These words, or words very much like them, are also Camus' first and last words on the subject of terrorism as well. Although they are not his only words. What Jacques Cormery and Albert Camus himself seem to have inherited from his/their father is their revulsion against acts of capital punishment, unrestrained violence, and all forms of calculated murder—whether strictly personal acts of revenge, planned military or paramilitary actions against civilians, or executions "legally" decided in courts of law. As we have seen, Camus argues in both *The Rebel* and "Reflections on the Guillotine" that for him it makes no difference whether acts of terror are sponsored and carried out by revolutionary movements in the name of national independence or by the state in the name of law and order. They are the acts of "a [filthy] race" of men of all national, ethnic, cultural, and "racial" backgrounds. Of both Europeans and non-Europeans alike, men of different political movements and parties, men from the Left as well as the Right, following different ideologies and pursuing different goals, whether just or unjust, but through unacceptable means. All nations, armies, police forces, governments, and religions can belong to "this race" when they exceed the limits of "the human," when they join the race of believers in absolute Truth, the race of both terrorists and counterterrorists alike.

In the same section of the novel (but in its discontinuous fictional chronology, occurring fifty years later), the exact words, "filthy race [*sale race*]" (75 [74]), reappear, in this instance screamed by a *pied-noir* worker after witnessing the effects of a terrorist bomb in the streets of Algiers. His words and the threat they contain are directed at an Arab worker who in fact had nothing to do with the bombing but simply happened to be in the area when the bomb exploded and wounded or killed the people waiting at a tramway stop. "You're all in it together, all you fucking sons-of-bitches," screams the French Algerian worker at the Arab Algerian. And then to show who he means by "you," after he has been restrained from attacking the Arab worker, he yells, "We should kill them all" (75 [74–75]). This overtly racist response to terrorism accuses not the fanaticism of specific individuals and political and military groups on both sides of the conflict for creating the climate of terror of which the bombing was a part, but one side, one "race," one people alone. It accuses this people of being "inhuman" and makes "them all," all "the Arabs," uniquely responsible for the violence of the war and for all acts of terrorism. At the same time, it legitimizes in advance any response the French might make to such terrorism, no matter how extreme, unjust, criminal, and inhuman it would be. Thus it represents the mirror image of the terrorism it claims to abhor, and it perpetuates and increases terror by justifying mass murder as a response to murder, even advocating genocide, the murder "of all of them." Terrorism, because it refuses to accept limits, has the murder of "all of them" as its ultimate, undeclared goal.

In the novel, Jacques rescues the Arab worker from the angry French crowd and in this instance prevents or at least delays the escalation of violence. This is exactly what Camus initially hoped his own and other moderate voices on both sides of the war would be able to do after armed conflict broke out in Algeria and the violence against civilians had escalated on both sides. Instead, as we have seen, each side continued to justify its own use of terrorism and its own crimes and acts of revenge by referring to the terrorism, atrocities, and crimes of the other side. Each decided to go beyond what "men" should do in order to respond to the terrorism of the other side. Each side, in Cormery's father's words, showed itself to be "a filthy race."

A particularly grotesque terrorist act is described in the novel by a farmer who refuses to move off his farm, even though he realizes his resistance to what he sees as the inevitable departure of the French is fruitless: "Life in that region had become intolerable. You had to sleep with a gun. When the Raskil farm was attacked . . . the father and his two sons had their throats cut, the mother and daughter raped over and over, then killed" (179 [167]). Camus clearly sympathizes with the small *pieds-noirs* farmers who were the victims of such atrocities, and he gives voice in this novel to their anguish and concerns for the safety of their families. Neither in this novel nor elsewhere does Camus justify the oppressive and what he calls equally criminal actions of the French army and extremist *colons*, however, but he clearly wants what he considers the legitimate fears of modest *pieds-noirs* to be taken seriously and for civilians, *all civilians*, to be protected from terrorist acts.[12]

Because of his deep concerns for the safety of French Algerians, Camus was never able to move beyond the contradiction of advocating peace and justice for all communities in Algeria, on the one hand, but refusing all direct negotiations with the FLN, on the other. Of wanting French and Arab civilians to be protected from harm, but refusing to approve of the French army's tactics and the crimes it committed, which the army and successive governments claimed were necessary to counter the terrorism of the FLN and protect the civilian population of Algeria. The novel proposes no way out of the dilemma, no political solution that could end the violence and the escalating cycle of terrorism. It rather narrates, before the fact, the last days of the French community of Algeria, anticipating an end that had not arrived by Camus' death, but did occur not long after it.

The Origin of Violence and the Pursuit of Justice

It is not necessary to agree with all of their analyses or conclusions to acknowledge that Fanon and Sartre were not wrong to attack the systematic oppression and violence of colonial society or to defend the right of colonized Algerians to struggle against the French in order to institute an independent Algerian state. But this does not mean that one is obliged to accept their claim that the violence of the colonialist system itself, because it predates and is thus considered the origin of the violence directed against the French, legitimizes and excuses in advance all terrorist actions taken by the colonized in their struggle for independence and justice. What is most problematic and dangerous in their arguments is that they both make total violence, and thus terrorism, a virtue, the necessary means not just to independence but to the birth of "new men." What should already be clear is that Camus' "first man" is the antithesis of the "new man" of Fanon and Sartre.

Unwilling or unable to support a political solution that would end the war by legitimizing terrorism, that is, by either recognizing the FLN or defending the repressive, criminal counterterrorist tactics of the French army, Camus, as if acknowledging the impasse his own political stance was unable to break out of, through the voices of different fictional *pieds-noirs* characters in *The First Man*, situates the violence of colonialism as well as the counterviolence of the Algerian struggle for independence within a historical process of long, even mythical, duration. For the violence associated with the struggle for independence is presented both as directly growing out of colonialism and at the same time as not being entirely specific to the colonial era alone, but part of a longer, repetitive historical cycle, one whose ultimate origin is in the land itself.

For example, explaining why he is staying on his farm after the region has been evacuated by the French army, a *pied-noir* farmer admits he knows he will not succeed in defending his farm, but he prefers to "croak" on his land rather than abandon it. This is a position he knows will be generally misunderstood in Paris and by the French in general. He claims, however, that it will be understood (although not necessarily accepted) by other Algerians, especially Arabs. And because of this "understanding," he projects a different outcome to the conflict than the victory of either side: "We were made to understand each other. As stupid and brutal as we are, but with the same blood of men. We'll kill each other a little more, cut off each other's balls and torture each other a bit. And then we'll begin again living together as men. The land [*le pays*] wants that" (181, trans. mod. [168–169]). And it is clear that for the farmer, only Algerians, both French and Arab, understand they are of the same human species and that what the "land wants" is that they continue to live together "as men," that is, as human beings who understand and accept the limits of what men can and should do. The problem also is how to know what the land wants and how to reconcile what it wants—whatever that might be—with what men want and to which they have the fundamental right: freedom and justice. And even more, how to reconcile the farmer's right to continue to farm the land that is legally his under French law but that had originally been taken from Arab farmers. What the farmer says the land wants and what different Algerians themselves want most often constitute diametrically opposed desires.

A little more torture along with from time to time a few castrations and murders would seem to constitute the basis for the form of "living-together" that the farmer claims has always characterized the history of the different peoples inhabiting Algeria, a history that began well before the arrival of the French. And "what the land wants," he claims, the land will eventually get. Alternating between murder, torture, castration, and peacefully living together, what the land really wants seems to be more of the same history: that of a divided community built on relations of both extreme violence and unlimited hospitality. A community of brothers who are also enemies and in constant combat, but who remain "equals" in dignity and grandeur, even if it is precisely social, political, and economic equality and respect that colonialism denies to those who are not allowed either to be French or even to affirm that they are Algerian. What the land seems to want is the continuation of a history that is shown in the novel to be rapidly coming to an end.[13]

But the words of a fictional *pied-noir* farmer should not be taken as directly expressing Camus' own thoughts or political beliefs. They are not his own words but those of a fictional character in a novel, and they in fact give the opposite but potentially as dangerous a justification for violence as Fanon and Sartre. They also represent the opposite position from the one Camus took in numerous essays, since they serve to explain away the violence of the war and seem to ignore the responsibility of both the colonial system in general and French, Berber, and Arab Algerians in particular for it. The farmer who refuses to leave his land and yet has no hope of actually succeeding in defending it accepts the increased violence of the war as if it were not just a violent reaction to the inequalities and injustices of the French colonial system itself, but more the repetition of an original, precolonial violence, that of the struggle of all inhabitants with a land that "refused to be occupied and took its revenge on whatever it found" (190 [176]). The revenge of the land against its inhabitants is thus presented by

him as being directed not just at its most recent conquerors and exploiters, the French colonizers, but also at its previous Spanish and Ottoman
conquerors, and even its Arab and Berber inhabitants as well, against all
those who at any time attempted to conquer, occupy, cultivate, and possess
the land and make it exclusively their own. But even if this personification
of the land does not legitimize a total war against oppressors, it also does
not justify the colonialists' occupation and exploitation of the land and its
inhabitants either.

But the struggle against an unforgiving, hostile land is one thing, and
the history of the violence of different peoples against each other is entirely
another. If the FLN and their supporters have an interest in presenting all
violence as originating in the colonial system, *pieds-noirs* on the contrary
have an interest either in ascribing it to revolutionary fanatics or criminals
(the FLN were typically called "bandits" by the *pieds-noirs*) or in situating the violence between colonizer and colonized, even the crimes committed during the war by both sides, within a longer cycle of violence. To
inscribe colonial violence within a history of long, even infinite duration
means that the first scene of violence—whether of conquest, settlement,
revolt, or war—is never really the first, for there always exists a prior scene
of violence against which to react and that can then be used to justify one's
own violent actions.

As the old *pied-noir* doctor from Jacques Cormery's native village admits, "we shut them up in caves with their whole brood. . . . They cut the
balls off the first Berbers, who themselves . . . and so on all the way back to
the first criminal—you know, his name was Cain—and since then it's been
war; men are abominable, especially under a ferocious sun" (191 [177]).[14]
The problem is thus never really the first violence or the origin of violence,
since the *first* crime and the *first* victim of violence are mythical and outside of history. This means that no subsequent injustice or murder can be
considered original, nor can it be justified on the basis of a prior injustice
or murder. For there is always another injustice, another murder, another
violence, prior to the previous one, a prior victim before the murderer and
a prior murderer before the victim. This abyssal history of violence exoner-
ates no one but also makes no one and no one act entirely responsible for
inaugurating the cycle.

This history thus makes it impossible to refer to a prior act of violence
as the justification for the present or next act of violence. Rather than be an

excuse for the continuation of violence, the reference to the mythical origin of violence should rather be seen as placing the responsibility for each terrorist act primarily on the shoulders of those who plan it, commit it, or justify it. In such a scenario, innocence can never be legitimately claimed for one's own terrorist acts because of the guilt of others for prior terrorist acts.

The extension of the history of colonialism into the entire geographical history of the land and even into religious mythology and the biblical story of Cain and Abel thus does not have the effect of denying, mitigating, or legitimizing the horrible violence, crimes, and terrorism of the war itself. Or the responsibility of specific groups, political parties, and individuals for particular injustices, crimes, and terrorist acts. On the contrary, it highlights that responsibility all the more by refusing either side the right to first martyrdom, the "privilege" of first victimhood, and thus any justification for the violence and terror it inflicts on innocent civilians. If there is no Algerian Adam, there is also no original sin. The only way the cycle of terrorism can be broken is if both sides recognize that there is in fact no unique origin of violence, no first murder, and no first murderer, and therefore no first or pure victim. The cycle of terror and violence can be stopped, but not by more terrorism nor more counterterrorism, both of which only perpetuate it. The victory of one side at any one moment in such a cycle of violence and terrorism would not necessarily indicate then that the cycle of violence and terrorism had effectively ended. In fact, it would indicate that it had not.

Terrorism takes its victims among the innocent, and that is what Camus was unable to accept and felt should not be accepted by anyone. In a scene from *The First Man* that brings the war once again close to Jacques Cormery's family, his mother is petrified by a terrorist bomb that explodes in the street below her apartment:

> The explosion resounded at the very moment Lucie Cormery came back into the room. It sounded very close, enormous, as if it would never stop reverberating. It seemed that they had long since stopped hearing it, but the bulb in the dining-room light was still shaking behind its glass shell. His mother had recoiled to the back of the room, pale, her dark eyes full of a fear she could not control, and she was unsteady on her feet. "It's here. It's here," she kept saying.
>
> (74 [73–74])

Choosing to defend his mother before (not instead of) justice meant defending her against the possibility of being blown up inside her own apartment or in the street below. It meant recognizing her fears and anguish, and the fears and anguish of others like her, as legitimate; it meant that it was necessary to find other ways of achieving justice than the killing of her and other civilians as the means to an allegedly redemptive end—even an independent Algeria and the birth of new men.

As we have seen, after 1958 Camus refused to speak publicly or publish further essays on Algeria because of what he claimed were the potential consequences of political discourse in a generalized context of terror:

> Terrorism as it is practiced in Algeria greatly influenced my attitude. . . . In my case, if I am aware that in criticizing the course of the rebellion, I risk giving a good conscience to those who for the longest time and in the most brazen way are most responsible for the Algerian drama, I never cease fearing that by pointing out the long series of French mistakes, I may, without running any risk myself, provide an alibi for the insane criminal who may throw his bomb into an innocent crowd that includes my family.
>
> (preface to "Algerian Reports," 113, trans. mod. [*Essais*, 892])

This statement reflects Camus' total lack of confidence in politics to bring about a just resolution to the war and marks his retreat from public political involvement in Algeria. But as his autobiographical novel demonstrates, he never actually stopped writing about Algeria. He simply wrote in a fictional rather than political mode, a fiction that was also his autobiography and the story of the end of "his tribe," the story of the last first man.

The End

Camus' novel of the life of a first man and an anonymous people of first men was never completed. Even had he not died in an automobile accident at the age of forty-six, it could be argued that the novel never could have been—never should have been—completed. For as Camus suggests in one of the entries in the "Notes and Sketches" that are included at the end of the novel, it is a novel that logically needs to remain unfinished, since its project—to "snatch this poor family from the fate of the poor, which is to disappear from history without a trace. The Speechless Ones" (300, trans. mod. [293])—could not in any case be successfully realized and completed without giving the anonymous "poor family" a name, a history, a legacy, and thus "saving it," but, at the same time, ending its anonymity and transforming it into the opposite of what it was: a family without (a) history. Such a history could not be written without deforming or destroying the family's true dignity and value, its deep anonymous links to the land and to the other anonymous, speechless men and women of Algeria. The novel thus could not have succeeded except by failing; it could not leave a written chronology of this imaginary family and the fictional people to which the family belongs without making them less anonymous and giving them an identity, a history, a future, by making them *a people*. Without placing them at a distance from and even opposing them to the fiction of an Algeria of anonymous first men.

In the notes included in *The First Man*, however, Camus sketches out an incomplete conclusion of sorts for the unfinished life of the first man, as well as expresses the impossible, contradictory autobiographical project of the novel as a whole. The "conclusion" has the form of an impossible utopian wish or plea, perhaps even a prayer, but one that can never be answered or fulfilled. It is not clear to whom the plea is addressed, but it is made through and in terms of his mother, who of course was absolutely powerless to grant such a demand and who would never even be able to read or understand it:

> Give back the land, the land that belongs to no one. Give back the land that is to be neither sold nor bought. . . . And he cried out, looking at his mother and then the others: "Give back the land. Give all the land to the poor, to those who have nothing and who are so poor that they never even wanted to have and to possess, to those in this land like her [his mother], the immense herd of the wretched, most of them Arab and a few French, who live and survive here through stubbornness and endurance, with the only pride that is worth anything in the world, that of the poor, give them the land as one gives what is sacred to those who are sacred, and then I, poor once more and definitively, cast into the worst of exiles at the very end of the

earth, I will smile and die content, knowing that under the sun of my birth are at last reunited the land I loved so much and she and those others whom I revered." (Then shall the great anonymity become fruitful and envelop me also—I shall return to this land.)

(318–319, trans. mod. [320–321])[15]

This impossible, hopeless wish or plea is rooted in despair. The end is near, and it is clearly too late for such wishes to be fulfilled—or even still made. And in colonial Algeria, it was perhaps always too late, no matter when such pleas for justice were made, always too late for them to be responded to and acted on. And who or what could ever have responded to such a plea in the first place?

Buried in the notes of an unfinished novel and without a clear place in that novel, this plea constitutes what could be called the last words of the first man. But they are also the last words of an imaginary community of Algerians, of a people who existed not in reality but in Camus' fictions and in his deepest aspirations for Algeria and Algerians. Camus' last gift, his last testimony to his "true country" and the Algerians he imagined inhabiting the "land of his flesh," thus tells the impossible story of a people emerging out of, living in, and then once again destined to return to anonymity and to be forgotten. Words that lead to silence. The end of the first man, and of the novel *The First Man* as a whole, narrates in this way the end of colonialism in Algeria and tells the story of a people without a story or with one destined to be immediately forgotten in history. Whatever else he previously wished for Algeria, whatever he struggled for but failed to achieve, by the time he wrote these lines Camus himself could do no more than express his own desire for this anonymous end for himself and for the fiction of an Algerian people, "the immense herd of the wretched, most of them Arab and a few French," he felt he belonged to and to whom he hoped until the end of his own life he could help bring justice.

I have always been and still am a proponent of a just Algeria, where the two populations can live in peace and equality. I have said and repeated that it is necessary to render justice to the Algerian people and grant them a fully democratic regime. . . . I have always condemned terror. I must also condemn a terrorism that is practiced blindly, in the streets of Algiers for example, and that one day could strike my mother or my family. I believe in justice, but I will defend my mother before justice.

—Albert Camus, *Le Monde* (December 14, 1957)

I approve of nothing that has been occurring: the crimes, torture, massacres, assassinations, executions, the destitution, fear, shame, death. It is on all this that we are getting ready to build.

—Mouloud Feraoun, *Journal* (February 9, 1958)

Terrorism and Torture: From Algeria to Iraq

In the spring of 2003, it was reported that Gillo Pontecorvo's 1965 film, "The Battle of Algiers," was being shown to the American military intelligence officers who would be involved in planning and carrying out the interrogation of suspects and other counterterrorist activities in Iraq. One can only speculate as to what lessons those watching the film were expected to learn, but the Pentagon announcement claimed that the film showed how the French plan for Algeria had succeeded "tactically" but failed "strategically."[1] It would be interesting to know specifically why Pentagon strategists thought that France's overall strategy had failed, even though the French counterterrorist tactics in general and the systematic torture and summary executions of suspects in particular were successful in the short term and resulted in the elimination of the FLN terrorist network in Algiers and a victory for the French army in the Battle of Algiers. Why did they feel France lost the war in spite of their victory in this crucial battle against terrorism?

For those responsible for the Pentagon announcement, it would seem as if the "successful tactics" of the French against terrorism, which in fact solidified opposition in both Algeria and France to continued French control of Algeria, had no role in their ultimate defeat and no effect on the French soldiers participating in the torture and executions, not to mention the horrible suffering of the Algerian people. But, at the very least, by deciding to show "The Battle of Algiers" to Pentagon strategists, the very people responsible for planning and implementing America's counterterrorist war explicitly linked the French counterterrorist actions taken against FLN terrorists in Algeria and American counterterrorist tactics in the United States' "global war on terrorism."

It is unfortunate that, after seeing the film, Pentagon strategists did not also read Camus' essays on Algeria, especially those that denounce the criminal nature of both terrorist and counterterrorist activities. Reading the essays in which Camus repeatedly denounces the use of violence and terror against civilians and his remarkable short story, "The Renegade," in which he depicts the escalating cycle of terrorism/counterterrorism as an absolute form of madness, one is led to question all justifications for both terrorism and *wars* on terrorism" that use and justify the use of torture and other extreme counterterrorist tactics to combat terrorism. Camus' criticism of the crimes committed by both sides during the Algerian War was not intended to support or advance the cause of either, however, but rather first and foremost to save innocent civilian lives. Saving lives, he repeatedly argued, had to be given priority over any cause, even over the cause of justice itself. This meant that no armed struggle for independence and no promise of justice for the future could ever justify the murder of civilians or the use of torture in the present. Given that the armed struggle for Algerian independence used terrorism against innocent French Algerians to advance its cause and the French army tortured and executed Arab, Berber, and even French suspects to defend *Algérie française*, Camus refused to take either side.

For Camus, the question was never *whether* to oppose colonial injustices in Algeria, but *how best to do it*; never whether to work for the demise of the colonial system that produced, institutionalized, and thus "legitimized" discrimination and oppression, but how to do it without inflicting further injustices on the Algerian people. In the pursuit of any just cause, but particularly in the struggle for justice, he insisted that the means used could never be separated from or at odds with the end being pursued, since the means used to eliminate injustice would ultimately determine whether the cause being pursued was indeed just. Not only, then, would the victory of the French in Algeria and thus the continuation of colonial rule be unjust and unacceptable, but independence achieved through terrorism would be as well.

As *The Rebel* and other political essays written during the cold war clearly indicate, Camus was a relentless opponent of ideology in general, whether of the revolutionary Left, the extreme nationalist Right, or even the democratic Center, and thus his opposition to third-world nationalist revolutionary ideology, especially as concerns his "true country" Algeria, should have surprised no one. But as I have argued in various chapters, only if one accepts that there were in fact only two diametrically opposed positions on Algeria to choose between once the war began—a third-world, revolutionary, anticolonialist position and a reactionary, procolonialist position—is it possible to characterize his attacks on the FLN's terrorist tactics as constituting in themselves a defense of the colonial status quo in Algeria and therefore a justification for the continuation of *Algérie française* and the perpetuation of colonial injustices. Camus himself simply refused to accept that stark ideological oppositions ever determined all alternatives, whether during the Resistance to the Nazi occupation of France, the cold war, or the Algerian War. His way was always the search for a "third way," a way that promised no political redemption, no definitive, total cure for the different varieties of the plague of oppression, but that accepted the limitations of politics, of what could and should be done in pursuit not just of freedom but of justice as well.

In a series of essays Camus wrote in 1946 entitled "Neither Victims nor Executioners"[2] and as he would also do at greater length five years later in *The Rebel*, Camus attacked not only the ideologies of the extreme Left and Right, but those of the political Center as well—not only communism and fascism, but also what could be called the ideology of imperialist democracy. As we have seen, he referred to the postwar period as an "age of terror," given that the contending ideologies allowed for no middle ground, no room for dissent, and no alternatives to the "Truth" each proposed and claimed to defend. In an age of terror, you are either with us or against us, friend or foe, a believer or an infidel, either on the side of Good or the side of Evil. Ideologies, for Camus, because they demand blind faith in an absolute Truth, thus inevitably provoke religious wars or political crusades of one type or another, in which the end being pursued justifies the use of whatever means are deemed necessary to achieve it.

Ideological conflict has of course not disappeared today, after the break-up of the Soviet Union, the destruction of the Berlin Wall, and the disappearance of the Iron Curtain once separating the communist "East" from the democratic "West." Although the victory of one side over the other in the cold war (and even the "end of history") has been triumphantly declared, ideological terror and counterterrorist "wars on terror" have certainly not come to an end. The world remains divided among violently opposed ideologies, which although they may differ from those of the cold war era, continue nevertheless to demand faith in a dominant Idea, to silence dissent, and to support increasingly violent "holy wars," with each of the opposing sides seeing itself as engaged in war against "evil." In a war conceived in such terms, it is difficult if not impossible to restrict the means used, since all means must by definition be "good" if they serve "the Good." This is precisely the logic of "political realism" that Camus deplored and repeatedly attacked.

During the cold war, Camus argued that it was just as necessary to continue to struggle against the reign of ideological terror after the defeat of Nazi Germany as it was before and during World War II. For him, independent political leaders, journalists, and intellectuals had the obligation to analyze critically and speak out against the dogmatism and terror not of one of the ideologies engaged in deadly combat, but of both or all of them. The choice of the "lesser evil" in the name of either an abstract ideal or simple political efficacy in his mind could not fail to perpetuate further injustices. The climate of terror itself had to be destroyed, as did the dogmatism of all sides in the ideological struggle; unacceptable alternatives had to be refused, even if they appeared to serve a good or, at least, a better cause than that of the other side. Limits, especially in the pursuit of justice, had to be acknowledged and respected.

As alternatives to ideological terror that would not themselves be counterterrorist forms of terror, Camus, however, had very little to propose: critical reflection, dissent, and dialogue as forms of resistance and rebellion. If no existing state of injustice, no matter how severe, justifies the use of terrorism, torture, or murder to bring about justice, if true justice cannot be rooted in a system that privileges some at the expense of or to the exclusion of others, and if justice for one people can never depend on the oppression of another, then actions taken in the name of justice for one people but that result in the segregation, oppression, exploitation, degradation, or destruction of another people are in fact the antitheses of justice. Having no faith in ideology and only disgust for all forms of terrorism, what has recently been called Camus' "rebellious politics"[3] consist rather of critical reflection, active dissent and resistance, and finally dialogue as the only means that can be used in the unending struggle for justice that have a chance of not perpetuating further injustices and crimes.

In a scene from *The First Man* that was discussed in chapter 7, Jacques Cormery, Camus' fictional double, responds to the anger of a French Algerian who has just witnessed the explosion of a terrorist bomb in the streets of Algiers. The worker, seeing the number of dead and wounded who had been attacked while waiting at a bus stop, directs his despair and hatred at an innocent Arab who happens to be at the wrong place at the wrong time: "Filthy race [*sale race*]," the French worker screams. "You're all in it together, all you fucking sons-of-bitches [*bande d'enculés*]. . . . We should kill them all."[4] Cormery's (Camus') response is to save the innocent Arab from the crowd's desire for revenge and quietly to urge the worker to "think it over [*réfléchis*]." The worker shrugs his shoulders and refuses, telling Jacques that he should first "go over there and see what you say after you've seen the mess." The last words of the scene speak of the "cries of anger or suffering, you could not tell which," (76 [88]) coming from the victims in the café, to which there is no response.

Words and reflection can never measure up to the anger of witnesses to the suffering of innocent victims of terrorism—or counterterrorism. And yet, since each side justifies its actions as necessary reactions to the injustices and crimes of the other side, producing a potentially infinite cycle of unrestrained violence, Camus refused to abandon "reflection." "Think it over"—before, during, and after acting as well—not instead of acting, but in order to act differently, more humanely, and in the long run more effectively. And think not exclusively about ends, but first and foremost about means, about how not to be in the place of either victim or executioner. Thinking it over will never be enough to eliminate the plague of terror completely, but it could lead to containing it and in this way succeed in eventually breaking the terrorist cycle, which counterterrorist tactics only exacerbate. And is there really any other acceptable, any other just alternative?

In the face of the loss of innocent lives and the suffering and anger terrorism causes and is meant to cause, "to think" does not seem like much at all. To refuse to act in anger and out of a desire for revenge and, above all, to refuse to indict a people or "race" (or religion) for the acts of criminals or

political extremists—whether they be isolated groups, a network of terrorists, or soldiers obeying orders from military or political leaders, and even
whether the acts are committed to advance a legitimate cause, the freedom
of an oppressed people, for example—is clearly no match for the violence
itself. And it is true that Camus' writings were unable to bring about any
change in the terrorist tactics of either side in the face of the fears, hatred,
and continually escalating violence of the Algerian War. The Algerian
pied-noir community for the most part considered him a traitor, Parisian
intellectuals on the Left opposed him or simply ignored what he had to say,
and members of the FLN either severely criticized him or at best expressed
regrets that he refused to actively support them and the cause of Algerian
independence. In spite of his *political* failure to positively affect the outcome
of the Algerian War, this entire book has attempted to think about the elements in Camus' work that are the most critically successful and that we
could most profit from thinking about again today—especially given that
religious/ideological divisions have made it once again increasingly difficult
to think at all.

I do not believe it would be an exaggeration to claim that today we are
once again living in an "age of terror," which in its general ideological con-
figuration could be compared to the climate described by Camus during
both the cold war and the Algerian War. In this age, we are once again
being given the choice of being "for" or "against"; the voices of moderation,
voices that include both sides in their dissent and all sides in their concern
for justice, voices that refuse to accept that the lives of innocent civilians
should be sacrificed for any cause, are once again being ignored, rejected,
or treated as traitorous. If this is the case, it is all the more reason to listen
to a voice like Camus' again, not because he was always right or had all or
even necessarily the best answers for ending the injustices of colonialism or
other forms of political oppression—he was not and never claimed to be a
sophisticated political theorist—but rather because he steadfastly refused to
accept the unacceptable, even in the name of justice.

Instead of showing the film "The Battle of Algiers" so that Pentagon officials could learn about how France succeeded "tactically" but failed "strategically" in Algeria, it would have been better for all of us, but especially
for the civilians who have died or been horribly maimed in "the war on
terrorism," if the Pentagon, the president, and all the president's men had
studied the effects on both the Algerian and French participants in France's

"dirty war" in Algeria and thought about the long-term consequences of France's allegedly "successful" counterterrorist tactics. It would have been even better if those involved in the counterterrorist "war on terrorism" had read and discussed the work of Albert Camus, if they had taken seriously his denunciation of both terrorism and torture and had been sensitive to the anguish his later work expresses, if they had "thought about it" more and differently than their subsequent actions revealed that they did. If they had listened to rather than ignored or suppressed dissident voices within and outside the administration. If they had understood and accepted that no end justifies the use of criminal means, no matter how atrocious the acts committed by the "terrorists" on the other side. If they were incapable of this kind of critical reflection, or, more likely, if they refused even to consider it, then oppositional politicians, the press, the intellectual community, and citizens of this country and other countries who were still capable of "thinking" needed to have done more to oppose the means being used to counter terrorism, and opposed it sooner and more effectively. That little if any of this happened does not prevent us from doing now what was not done before. Camus' writings on Algeria, both his political essays and his fictions, dramatically show how terror is a trap for both sides in any conflict and why justice demands the recognition of limits and a respect for human lives that must come *before* the pursuit of any cause. Even *before* the cause of freedom, even *before* justice itself. For to defend life before justice as a general principle is in fact to defend justice itself.

Notes

Preface. A Voice from the Past

1. Albert Camus, *The First Man*, trans. David Hapgood (New York: Vintage Books, 1995), vii [*Le premier homme* (Paris: Gallimard, 1994)]. Here and throughout this book, the first reference given will be to the English translation of the French text being cited, with the reference to the original French edition given in brackets. When an English translation of a text does not exist, the translation from the French is my own. Catherine Camus, whose comments appear only in the American edition of the novel and who describes herself as "neither a writer, nor an academic, nor even an expert on Camus," but "just his daughter," gives the following explanation for the thirty-four-year delay in publishing her father's last work: "In denouncing totalitarianism, and in advocating a multicultural Algeria where both communities would enjoy the same rights, Camus antagonized both the right and the left. At the time of his death he was very much isolated and subject to attacks from all sides designed to destroy the man and the artist so that his ideas would have no impact. . . . In these circumstances, to have published an unfinished manuscript . . . might well have given ammunition to those who were saying Camus was through as a writer. His friends and my mother decided not to run that risk. . . . Between 1980 and 1985 voices began to be heard saying that perhaps Camus had not been so wrong, and little by little the old disputes died down" (vi–vii).

2. "'You have to choose sides,' cry those gorged on hatred. Yes! I have chosen. I have chosen my land [*mon pays*], I have chosen the Algeria of justice, where French

and Arabs associate with each other freely." Albert Camus, "Trêve pour les civils" Truce for Civilians], in *Essais* (Paris: Gallimard, Bibliothèque de la Pléiade, 1965), 984. This article originally appeared in the journal *L'Express* on January 10, 1956, and was part of a series entitled "L'Algérie déchirée" [Algeria Torn Apart].

Introduction. "The Algerian" in Camus

1. This quotation is taken from a statement given by Mohamed Dib at the Centre Culturel Algérien in Paris on March 17, 1995. Cited in Olivier Todd, *Albert Camus: A Life*, trans. Benjamin Ivry (New York: Alfred A. Knopf, 1998), 765 [*Albert Camus: une vie* (Paris: Gallimard, 1996), 420].

2. In my opinion, the most complete intellectual biographies of Albert Camus are Herbert Lottman, *Albert Camus: A Biography* (Garden City, N.Y.: Doubleday, 1979); Olivier Todd, *Albert Camus: A Life*; and Patrick McCarthy, *Camus: A Critical Study of His Life and Work* (London: Hamish Hamilton, 1982).

3. For an analysis of the "colonial relation" that in the colonies determines both colonizers and colonized, see Albert Memmi, *The Colonizer and the Colonized*, trans. Howard Greenfeld (Boston: Beacon Press, 1965) [*Portrait du colonisé, précédé par portrait du colonisateur* (Paris: Gallimard, 1957)].

4. In Albert Camus, *The First Man*, trans. David Hapgood (New York: Vintage Books, 1995) [*Le premier homme* (Paris: Gallimard, 1994)], Camus distinguishes nevertheless between the poverty of a family such as his own and complete destitution in the following description of a street in the neighborhood of his fictional double, Jacques Cormery: the "street, which led to the market, was dotted with garbage cans that famished Arabs or Moors, or sometimes an old Spanish tramp, had pried open at dawn to see if there was still something to be retrieved from what poor and thrifty families had so disdained they would throw it away" (139 [132]). Camus' view of the multicultural Algeria experienced by the poor is perhaps best represented by the neighborhood in which Jacques' kindly schoolteacher lives: "M. Bernard was facing Jacques in his small apartment in the winding streets of the Rovigo, almost at the foot of the Casbah, a district that overlooked the city and the sea, occupied by small shopkeepers of all races and all religions, where the homes smelled at once of spices and of poverty" (137 [129]).

5. Camus makes this statement in an essay entitled "A Short Guide for Cities Without a Past," which he published in 1947, in his collection of lyrical essays, *Summer* [*L'été*], in *Lyrical and Critical Essays*, ed. Philip Thody, trans. Ellen Conroy Kennedy (New York: Vintage Books, 1968), 147 [*Essais* (Paris: Gallimard, Bibliothèque de la Pléiade, 1965), 850].

6. It could be argued that all Algerians, for vastly different reasons and with radically different consequences, suffered from what Jacques Derrida has termed, in describing his own case as a French-Algerian Jew, a "disorder of identity [*un trouble de l'identité*]." See Jacques Derrida, *Monolingualism of the Other; or, The Prosthesis of Origin*, trans. Patrick Mensah (Palo Alto, Calif.: Stanford University Press, 1998), 14 [*Le monolinguisme de l'autre ou la prothèse d'origine* (Paris: Galilée, 1996), 32].

7. The idea of "uprootedness" is of course central to the writings of the turn-of-the century extremist nationalist Maurice Barrès. The title of his best-known novel, *Les déracinés* (1897; Paris: Gallimard, 1988), designates those who are French in name only and who share none of the authentically rooted cultural values that for him constitute the essence of "Frenchness"—all cosmopolitans, "Orientals," and especially Jews.

8. In his chapter on "The Colonizer Who Accepts [Himself] ["Le colonisateur qui s'accepte"] in *The Colonizer and the Colonized*, Albert Memmi analyzes the fervent, exaggerated patriotism of the colonialist, the way he constantly evokes "the qualities of his native land—extolling them, exaggerating them—stressing its special traditions, its cultural originality" (58 [82]), as a justification for his own privileged status in the colonies. But the nationalism of the *colon* is selective, since he "directs his attention essentially to that aspect of his native country which tolerates his colonialist existence" and rejects all democratic reforms that "would challenge his way of life" and treats them as "a matter of life or death, a questioning of the sense of his life" (62, translation completed [85]).

9. Olivier Todd quotes the testimony of one of Camus' closest Algerian friends, Charles Poncet, who, in "Dans le sillage de Camus," an unpublished essay, states that it was only when German troops marched down the Champs-Elysées in June 1940 that "Camus, the Algerian, the man from Algiers, felt 'truly French.'" Olivier Todd, *Albert Camus: A Life*, 113 [253].

10. Camus himself ironically encouraged such thinking by making provocative statements that challenged the self-righteous conformity of many on the Left, such as the one he made in his response to Francis Jeanson's harsh critique of *The Rebel* [*L'homme révolté*] in Jean-Paul Sartre's journal *Les Temps Modernes*: "If the truth appeared to me to be on the Right, I would be there" (in a letter addressed to Sartre as "Monsieur le Directeur" dated June 30, 1952, originally published in *Les Temps Modernes*, no. 82 [1952] and republished in Camus' *Essais*, 754). It should be noted that the statement is made in the conditional mode and that, for Camus, "the truth" never appeared on the Right, where, whatever his shortcomings might have been, he never went.

11. Camus, *The First Man*, 317 [318].

12. Jean-Paul Sartre, "An Explication of the Stranger," trans. Annette Michel-

son, in *Camus: A Collection of Critical Essays*, ed. Germaine Brée (Englewood Cliffs, N.J.: Prentice-Hall, 1962), 108 ["Explication de *L'etranger*," *Situations I* (Paris: Gallimard, 1947), 99].

13. See the chapters in both Lottman and Todd on the Sartre-Camus antagonism. See also Germaine Brée, *Camus and Sartre: Crisis and Commitment* (New York: Delacorte Press, 1972), which staunchly defends Camus; and Ronald Aronson, who in *Camus and Sartre: The Story of a Friendship and the Quarrel That Ended It* (Chicago: University of Chicago Press, 2004) gives a more balanced account of their political differences but is ultimately, I think, more sympathetic to Sartre than to Camus.

14. Conor Cruise O'Brien, *Albert Camus: Of Europe and Africa* (New York: The Viking Press, 1970).

15. Michael Walzer, "Albert Camus's Algerian War," in *The Company of Critics: Social Criticism and Political Commitment in the Twentieth Century* (New York: Basic Books, 2002), 137.

16. Edward W. Said, "Camus and the French Imperial Experience," in *Culture and Imperialism* (New York: Alfred A. Knopf, 1993), 174.

17. Tony Judt, *The Burden of Responsibility: Blum, Camus, Aron, and the French Twentieth Century* (Chicago: University of Chicago Press, 1998), 20. On the same page, Judt defines irresponsibility as "the propensity in various spheres of public life to neglect or abandon intellectual, moral, or political responsibility."

18. O'Brien is especially critical of Germaine Brée, the leading Camus critic of the 1950s and 1960s, who, he claims, "probably has done more than anyone else to shape ideas about Camus prevalent among English-speaking people," and he mocks her assertions that the "working-class population of Belcourt," the poor section of Algiers where Camus' family lived, was "impervious to the racial barriers that exist in more prosperous middle-class milieux" or that "the Berber and Arab never seemed 'strangers' to Camus" (O'Brien, *Albert Camus*, 5–6). See Germaine Brée, *Camus* (New Brunswick, N.J.: Rutgers University Press, 1961), 13. It is true that Camus believed that there was less racism and fewer racial barriers among the different groups of the Algerian poor than among wealthy Algerians, mainly because the former lived in ethnically mixed neighborhoods and in much closer contact with Arabs, and each suffered from the same economic exploitation. O'Brien is dismissive of this idea: "A working-class population 'impervious' to racial barriers would be an unusual phenomenon. A population which could attain this condition when the barriers were not only 'of race' but also of religion, language, and culture, all reinforcing 'race' . . . would be unique" (O'Brien, *Albert Camus*, 6). Camus in fact did believe that Algerians were unique—at least potentially so. O'Brien is certainly right to question Brée's sweeping claim that Camus' position on the Algerian War "seems

now to have prevailed among Algerians whether of European or Arabic extraction" but is perhaps a bit too harsh in characterizing her evaluation from the perspective of independent Algeria as "a little comic. In 1959, when the statement was first written, it was just wrong" (O'Brien, *Albert Camus*, 7, referencing Brée, *Camus*, 5). Brée answers O'Brien in her later book, *Camus and Sartre: Crisis and Commitment*, in which, criticizing O'Brien's book, she asserts that there is no excuse "for the lack of serious documentation, the faulty quotations, erroneous statements, and arbitrary inferences that seriously mar an essay in which the author is anxious only to bring his interpretation into line with his own rather schematic view of Western guilt" (151).

19. Edward Said, for example, compares what he claims are Camus' limitations, which he qualifies as "unacceptably paralyzing," unfavorably to "the decolonizing literature of the time, whether French or Arab—Germaine Tillion, Kateb Yacine, Fanon, or Genet" ("Camus and the French Imperial Experience," 185). And even though it is certainly true that Camus, unlike Sartre, would have vigorously opposed the revolutionary zeal of Fanon and Genet and considered their glorification of violence and indifference to its victims to be criminal, his relationship with Kateb Yacine was far more complicated than such a list suggests, even if it is certainly true that they disagreed politically, especially after Kateb supported the FLN. But Camus was in fact very close to Germaine Tillion and repeatedly praises her analyses of the devastation of the Kabyle region and her courageous efforts to bring about an end to the use of terrorism and torture in the war very shortly after his own efforts to produce a civilian truce had failed. If Tillion is considered to have written "decolonizing literature," then Camus could or should be considered to have done the same. See Germaine Tillion, *L'Algérie en 1957* (Paris: Minuit, 1957); and especially *Les ennemis complémentaires* (Paris: Editions de Minuit, 1960). Nowhere is she closer to Camus than in statements such as the following, the first one appearing in a chapter entitled "The Link Between France and Algeria Is Not a Political Fiction": "France and Algeria are indeed linked today through a double exodus that binds them beyond their will: the ancient exodus of 'colons' who came from Europe to which the modern exodus of Muslim workers to mainland France responds" (*L'Algérie en 1957*, 84). In *Les ennemis complémentaires*, a title that Camus himself could have used, Tillion states, "French and Algerian—it is not possible to conceive of two populations whose mutual dependence is more certain. We've 'got' them and they've 'got' us" (11).

20. For a more complete and judicious political interpretation of Camus' political trajectory, see Jeanyves Guérin, *Albert Camus: portrait de l'artiste en citoyen* (Paris: Éditions François Bourin, 1993); as well as the collection of essays he edited entitled *Camus et la politique: actes du colloque de Nanterre 5–7 juin 1985* (Paris: Éditions l'Harmattan, 1986). The most interesting study in English of Camus' political per-

spective in my mind is Jeffrey C. Isaac's *Arendt, Camus, and Modern Rebellion* (New Haven, Conn.: Yale University Press, 1992). See especially chapter 6, "Swimming Against the Tide," in which Isaac gives a thorough and, I feel, judicious assessment of Camus' Algerian politics and compares his position on Algeria with Arendt's on Israel.

1. The Place of the Other

1. Albert Memmi, *The Colonizer and the Colonized*, trans. Howard Greenfeld (Boston: Beacon Press, 1965) [*Portrait du colonisé, précédé par portrait du colonisateur* (Paris: Gallimard, 1957)] describes in great detail the colonialists' mythical and stereotypically racist portrait of the colonized, which he argues is made up of images that serve as "excuses without which the presence and conduct of a colonizer . . . would seem shocking" (79 [101]). Images of the colonized's "often-cited laziness," for "nothing could better justify the colonizer's privileged position than his industry, and nothing could better justify the colonized's destitution than his indolence" (79 [101]); of the colonized as a "weakling" (*débile*), since "this deficiency requires protection (81–82 [103]); of the colonized as "a wicked, backward person with evil, thievish, somewhat sadistic instincts," which justifies the colonizer's "police and his legitimate severity" (82 [104]); of "the colonized's lack of desires, his ineptitude for comfort, science, progress, his astonishing familiarity with poverty," which explains why colonizers need to accept the destitution of the colonized and why the colonized should not be pushed into "the disadvantages of civilization" (82 [104]); and finally of the colonized's "notorious ingratitude," which calls attention to "everything the colonized owe the colonizers, that all improvements the colonizer has made have been wasted, and that it is fruitless to try to improve the state of the colonized" (82, trans. modified [104]).

2. Conor Cruise O'Brien, *Albert Camus: Of Europe and Africa* (New York: The Viking Press, 1970) argues that "despite [Camus'] revulsion from the methods of the repression, his position was necessarily one of support for repression, since he constantly opposed negotiation with the actual leaders of the rebellion, the FLN. . . . The rejection of negotiation is basic and necessarily implies support for the substance, if not for the details of the methods, of the French government's policy of pacification. . . . The regime of 'free association' which he foresaw required French military victory over the insurgents" (90–91). As we will see in subsequent chapters, O'Brien's analysis constitutes a simplification and serious distortion of Camus' actual position, and his generalizations are often hastily made and lacking in convincing supporting evidence.

3. Pierre Nora, *Les Français d'Algérie* (Paris: René Julliard, 1961).

4. For example, Nora interprets the warm greetings he received from *pieds-noirs* in the following way: "They are ready to smother you in their arms; cordiality in all circumstances, aggressive hospitality, and the outspokenness that you are invited to share are neither Mediterranean specialties, nor borrowings from Islam, as they would have you believe. They are the first philters of an Algerian nationalism. If you give into its warm greetings even just a little, you are immediately incorporated into it, initiated at little cost, devoured, and soon digested" (*Les Français d'Algérie*, 44). A very different picture of what could be found under the surface of colonialism is presented by the *pied-noir* writer Jean Pélégri, in *Ma mère l'Algérie* (Arles: Actes Sud, 1990): "It was not difficult to foresee that one day, at the moment when metropolitan France was washing its hands of it, *pieds-noirs* would be made scapegoats and held responsible for everything. But I certainly knew . . . that if they most often manifested an unjust or racist behavior as concerns political rights . . . they were also often, in private, open, warm, brotherly, and that they had constituted a multicultural and often baroque community, in which could be found all the faults but also all the qualities of Mediterranean peoples: the sense of hospitality, the joy of living, the need to dramatize daily life. . . . I also knew that under the apparent and official history of Algeria, a history of colonial injustice and inequality, another history was unfolding, that of the daily relations between the *pieds-noirs* and the Algerians, and this history was just as real as the official one but underground. A history that in spite of the colonial system was made up of meetings, consultations, exchanges, and sometimes tenderness. This was my people." (71–72). This was Camus' Algerian people as well.

5. This section heading is intended to recall René Girard's seminal essay on Camus, "Camus's Stranger Retried," in *"To Double-Business Bound": Essays on Literature, Mimesis, and Anthropology* (Baltimore, Md.: Johns Hopkins University Press, 1978; originally published in *PMLA* 79 [December 1964]). Girard's own retrial of the novel is not concerned, as I am here, with the question of colonialism, however, but rather with setting the record straight as concerns its "Romantic" characteristics and the way in which Meursault emerges from his trial as a hero, with the society that condemns him to death for his crimes in the position of the guilty party. Girard criticizes the opposition he argues the novel establishes between the Self (authenticity) and Others (inauthenticity), which he claims is "the final democratization of the Romantic myth, the universal symbol of the separated ego in a world where almost everyone feels like an 'outsider'" (22). Girard's argument is that "the outsider is really inside, but he is not aware of it," which he claims is what Camus reveals in *The Fall*, trans. Justin O'Brien (New York: The Modern Library, 1958), 34.

6. "The colonial relationship which I had tried to define chained the colonizer

and the colonized into an implacable dependence, molded their respective characters and dictated their conduct." Memmi, 1965 preface to *The Colonizer and the Colonized*, ix [13–14].

7. Meursault first describes the murder "as it was occurring" and later acknowledges his responsibility for the death of the Arab several times more in the novel, once immediately after he is arrested: "On the day of my arrest they put me in a room where there were already several other prisoners, mostly Arabs. They laughed when they saw me. Then they asked me what I'd done. I said that I'd killed an Arab, and they became silent." Albert Camus, *The Stranger*, trans. Stuart Gilbert (New York: Vintage Books, 1954), 89, trans. modified [*Théâtre, récits, nouvelles* (Paris: Gallimard, Bibliothèque de la Pléiade, 1962), 1177]. I have frequently modified this translation to have it conform more closely to the French text. Patrick McCarthy is one of the very few critics who have commented on the importance of this scene in terms of how it reflects the change in Meursault's place in colonial society after he is arrested: "This is a key paragraph because it reveals the identification between Meursault and the Arab. In a colonial society the prisons will be populated chiefly by the colonized, who will not recognize themselves as criminals of specific crimes but will consider it normal to be in prison. So they welcome Meursault as one of them, even when he tells them he has killed an Arab, they do not ask for explanations because they do not believe in the pseudo-logic of the French state. In this they are different from the judges and akin to Meursault. By sleeping in the same way as they do, Meursault becomes, albeit briefly, an Arab. Thus the *pied-noir*'s quest for authenticity is realized, but in a paradoxical manner. A prisoner of the state, he shares the condition of the colonized." Patrick McCarthy, *The Stranger* (Cambridge: Cambridge University Press, 1988), 58. I would take exception with McCarthy's analysis only concerning the brevity of Meursault becoming an Arab, or rather, occupying the place of the Arab in colonial society. As will become clear later in the chapter, in my analysis, when Meursault "becomes . . . an Arab" and shares "the condition of the colonized," it is a definitive change of condition for which he pays with his life.

8. Albert Camus, "Preface to *The Stranger*," in *Lyrical and Critical Essays*, ed. Philip Thody, trans. Ellen Conroy Kennedy (New York: Vintage Books, 1968), 335–337 [*Essais* (Paris: Gallimard, Bibliothèque de la Pléiade, 1965), 1928].

9. Roland Barthes was perhaps the first critic to question whether Meursault is really condemned by society for not conforming to its practices or overtly challenging them, that is, for being a rebel. Barthes claims rather that it is Meursault's "opaqueness" that troubles society the most, because it cannot support his foreign and yet at the same time familiar look: "Meursault rebel, society would have fought him; Meursault opaque, that is the world put into question, and society can only

reject him with its most intense horror as an object soiled by its own alterity." In "*L'etranger*, roman solaire," originally published in the *Bulletin du Club du Meilleur Livre*, no. 12 (April 1954); republished in Roland Barthes, *Oeuvres complètes*, vol. 1, *1942–1965* (Paris: Seuil, 1993), 398.

10. In June 1947, Camus wrote in his notebooks "that it is impossible to say whether a person is absolutely guilty and consequently impossible to proclaim total punishment." Albert Camus, *Carnets II: janvier 1942–mars 1951* (Paris: Gallimard, 1965), 200. In 1957, in "Reflections on the Guillotine," he challenges the right of society to impose the ultimate punishment on anyone: "Capital punishment is not simply death. It is just as different, in essence, from the privation of life as the concentration camp is from prison. It is a murder, to be sure, and one that arithmetically pays for the murder committed. But it adds to death a rule, a public premeditation, an organization, in short, which is in itself a source of moral sufferings more terrible than death. Hence there is no equivalence. . . . Capital punishment . . . is the most premeditated of murders, to which no criminal's deed, however calculated it may be, can be compared." Albert Camus, "Reflections on the Guillotine," in *Resistance, Rebellion, and Death*, trans. Justin O'Brien (New York: Knopf, 1961), 199 [*Essais*, 1039]. He also argues that "every society has the criminals it deserves" (206 [1044]). See chapter 4 for a more developed analysis of Camus' position on capital punishment and its relation to his perspective on the terrorism and torture used by the opposing sides during the Algerian War.

11. Given what he characterizes as the multiple but inescapable roles of the sun in the novel, Barthes considers *The Stranger* to be a modern tragedy: "The mixture of the sun and of nothingness sustains each word of the novel: Meursault battles not only against an idea of the world but also against a fatality—the Sun. . . . Because the Sun is everything here: warmth, drowsiness, celebration, sadness, power, madness, cause, and illumination. And it is this ambiguity between the Sun-Warmth and the Sun-Lucidity that makes *The Stranger* a tragedy." Barthes, *Oeuvres complètes*, 400.

12. The following is the description of the murder in the novel in Meursault's words: "The whole beach, pulsing with heat, was pressing on my back. . . . The heat of the sun was beginning to scorch my cheeks, and I felt beads of sweat gathering in my eyebrows. It was the same sun as when I buried my mother, and just as then, my forehead really hurt and all my veins seemed to be bursting through the skin. Because of this burning sensation that I couldn't stand any longer, I took a step forward. I knew that was stupid, that I couldn't get rid of the sun by moving just one step. But I took that step, just one step forward. And then the Arab drew his knife and held it up in the sunlight for me to see. The light shot out onto the steel, and it was as if a long shining blade had penetrated my forehead. . . . I felt only the

cymbals of the sun on my forehead and, less distinctly, the sharp blade of light flashing from the knife still in front of me. This blazing sword ravaged my eyelashes and gouged my suffering eyes. . . . It seemed to me as if the sky had opened up from end to end to let fire rain down. My entire being tightened and I closed my hand on the revolver. The trigger gave" (75–76, trans. mod. [1168]). In this description, it is the sun, not Meursault, that is the agent of death.

13. Numerous critics, including O'Brien, have argued that Meursault's entire trial is a gross distortion of colonial justice, since they claim that a French citizen in colonial Algeria would never have been accused and convicted of a capital offense for killing an Arab. The irony, of course, is that Meursault is not in fact convicted for that crime. In his courageous study of the use of torture during the Algerian War, which includes a discussion of the colonial legal system, Pierre Vidal-Naquet, however, disagrees that a *pied-noir* would not have been brought to justice for killing an Arab: "From a juridical point of view, nothing distinguishes the public prosecutor of the appeals court in Algiers . . . from his counterpart in Riom or Aix-en-Provence, and in his celebrated novel *The Stranger*, Albert Camus . . . with definite verisimilitude was able to imagine the death sentence and execution of a European for the murder of a Muslim." Pierre Vidal-Naquet, *La torture dans la république* (Paris: Editions de Minuit, 1972), 22.

14. In his notebooks, Camus makes the following statement about the novel: "You are never condemned for the crime you think you will be." Albert Camus, *Carnets II, janvier 42 à mars 51* (Paris: Gallimard, 1964), 29–30. Meursault's most serious crime in the eyes of the court and society, the one for which he is ultimately convicted, is the crime of not crying at his mother's funeral, which for the prosecutor makes him a man who "morally killed his mother" (128 [1197]). When Meursault's defense lawyer asks if Meursault is "on trial for having buried his mother or for killing a man," the prosecutor replies, "speaking with great vehemence, 'I accuse the prisoner of burying his mother with a criminal's heart'" (122, trans. mod. [1194]). The prosecutor also claims that Meursault's crime is worse than the next crime on the docket, a parricide: "the horror of that crime paled beside the loathing inspired by my callousness" (138 [1197]). Because of what he *is*, Meursault is thus guilty of a more monstrous crime than even what the prosecutor calls the unimaginable crime of parricide.

15. Assimilation and full French citizenship was possible for a very limited number of assimilated Muslims, but only if they renounced their religious affiliation. The same situation existed for Algerian Jews until 1870, when the Crémieux Decree granted French citizenship to all the Jews of Algeria. For an analysis of Vichy policy toward Jews, see Michael R. Marrus and Robert O. Paxton, *Vichy France and the Jews* (New York: Schocken Books, 1983); and Richard Weisberg, *Vichy Law and*

the Holocaust in France (New York: New York University Press, 1996). In terms of the role played by religion in Vichy anti-Semitic laws and the contradictory logic of assimilation in general, see David Carroll, "What It Meant to Be a 'Jew' in Vichy France: Xavier Vallat, State Anti-Semitism, and the Question of Assimilation," *SubStance* 27, no. 3 (1998).

16. The woman is described in the novel only as "a Moor." Even though her name is not revealed in the novel, Meursault acknowledges that Raymond revealed it to him: "The moment [Raymond] mentioned the woman's name, I realized she was a Moor" (40–41 [1148]). In fact, she is the sister of the man Meursault eventually kills. It should be noted again that the murder is itself not either the first or the last violent act in a series of violent acts. The first aggression is committed by Meursault's friend, Raymond, a French pimp who viciously beats his Arab mistress, with Meursault refusing to intervene; the last act in the series will be committed by the State, with the execution of Meursault. Between Raymond's aggression and Meursault's execution, a fight occurs on the beach between Meursault's French friends and the group of anonymous Arabs that includes Raymond's mistress's brother, during which Raymond is stabbed. The murder of the Arab, who is unnamed but identified nonetheless by his relation to the victim of Raymond's assault, should thus be situated within the entire series of violent acts and not treated as if it were a completely isolated occurrence or as if it were the first time Meursault had any involvement in or responsibility for the escalating violence between the two groups, who recognize each other and are in constant and violent contact with each other.

17. I borrow the term from Etienne Balibar: "I apply the term 'fictive ethnicity' to the community instituted by the nation-state. This is an intentionally complex expression in which the term fiction . . . should not be taken in the sense of a pure and simple illusion without historical effects, but must, on the contrary, be understood by analogy with the *person ficta* of the juridical tradition in the sense of an institutional effect, a 'fabrication.' No nation possesses an ethnic base naturally, but as social formations are nationalized, the populations included within them, divided up among them or dominated by them are ethnicized—that is, represented in the past or in the future *as if* they formed a natural community." Etienne Balibar, "The Nation Form: History and Ideology," in *Race, Nation, Class: Ambiguous Identities*, by Etienne Balibar and Immanuel Wallerstein, trans. Chris Turner (New York and London: Verso, 1991), 96 [*Race, nation, classe: les identités ambigues* (Paris: La Découverte, 1997), 130]. Balibar argues that the two principal and often competing means for producing ethnicity are language and race, the latter being what he calls a "second-degree fiction" that "also derives its effectiveness from everyday practices, relations which immediately structure the 'life' of individuals" (99 [135–36]).

18. "I do not need to know why Dreyfus betrayed. Psychologically speaking, it is

enough for me to know that he is capable of betrayal to know that he betrayed. The gap is filled in. That Dreyfus is capable of betrayal, I conclude from his race." Maurice Barrès, *Scènes et doctrines du nationalisme* (Paris: Editions du Trident, 1987), 111–112.

19. Michel Ansky, *Les juifs d'Algérie: du décret crémieux à la libération* (Paris: Editions du Centre de Documentation Juive Contemporaine, 1950), 88.

2. Colonial Borders

1. Carlier's essay is included in the collection edited by Mohammed Harbi and Benjamin Stora, *La guerre d'Algérie: 1954–2004, la fin de l'amnésie* (Paris: Robert Laffont, 2004), and is a subtle analysis of colonialist violence that could be contrasted with both Franz Fanon's and Jean-Paul Sartre's mystifications of revolutionary third-world violence, which are discussed below, in chapter 5.

2. Balibar's essay was first delivered as a talk at a colloquium entitled "Algérie-France: regards croisés" at the Collège International de Philosophie (with the collaboration of the University of Oran and La Maison des Écrivains), May 18–20, 1995. It was published in Etienne Balibar, *Droit de cité: culture et politique en démocratie* (Paris: Editions de l'Aube, 1998), 73–88.

3. See especially Benjamin Stora, *La gangrène et l'oubli: la mémoire de la guerre d'Algérie* (Paris: Editions de la Découverte, 1991). Stora argues that "an entire system of subtle lies and repressions organizes 'Algerian memory.' And this denial continues to eat away like a cancer, like gangrene, at the very foundations of French society. . . . For the French, a 'war without a name'; for the Algerians, a 'revolution without a face'" (7–8).

4. Edward Said, *Culture and Imperialism* (New York: Alfred A. Knopf, 1993), xx, my emphasis. The emphasis is meant to indicate my own reservations concerning the absolute nature of the break between colonialist and postcolonialist eras and thus over whether the postcolonial era is really *the first time* that the history of cultures can or should be studied as hybrid rather than monolithic.

5. *The Fall*, of course, takes place in Amsterdam, a cold, rainy, and culturally overloaded "hell," a city with mass extermination as part of its recent history, one that represents the diametric opposite of the sun-drenched and culturally deficient Algerian cities of Camus' other works. In the novel, Jean-Baptiste Clamence describes Amsterdam in the following way: "Holland is a dream, monsieur, a dream of gold and smoke. . . . We are at the heart of things here. Have you noticed that Amsterdam's concentric canals resemble the circles of hell? The middle-class hell, of

course, peopled with bad dreams. When one comes from the outside, as one gradually goes through those circles, life—and hence its crimes—becomes denser, darker. Here, we are in the last circle." Albert Camus, *The Fall*, trans. Justin O'Brien (New York: The Modern Library, 1958), 13–14 [*Théâtre, récits, nouvelles* (Paris: Gallimard, Bibliothèque de la Pléiade, 1962), 1482–1483]. Later, he describes the city as "a soggy hell, indeed! Everything horizontal, no relief; space is colorless, and life dead. Is it not universal obliteration, everlasting nothingness made visible?" (72 [1512]).

6. René Lespès, *Oran: etude de géographie et d'histoire urbaine* (Paris: Librairie Félix Alcan, 1938), published as part of the "1830–1930 Collection du Centenaire de l'Algérie."

7. The category itself of "Native" (*Indigène*) until 1870 included both Muslims and Jews. In 1872, however, out of a total population of 41,130, Lespès lists 35,834 inhabitants of Oran as being "Europeans," with only 5,296 considered "Natives," a decrease of 3,500 from 1866. Lespès explains this change by saying that the number of Europeans was, as he puts it, "in reality 30,534 without Israelites" (103). This is because the Jewish population of the city had moved from the category of "Natives" to that of "Europeans" when in 1870, with the Décret Crémieux, Algerian Jews were granted citizenship and thus full "European status." But a decree can always be undone, and the Jews of Algeria, who at the start of World War II had been citizens since 1870, would also be the only segment of the population to lose their status as French citizens (and thus as "Europeans"), when the Décret was rescinded by the Maréchal Pétain on October 7, 1940.

8. In 1901, for example, the Muslim population was still only 12 percent of the total population of Oran, while in Algiers it was 21.8 percent. In 1926, the number of Muslims in Oran increased to 17.1 percent; in 1931, to 20 percent; and in 1936, to 23.7 percent of the total population.

9. The term "internal exclusion" (*exclusion intérieure*) is used by Etienne Balibar in reference to the heritage of colonialism. See especially his essay "Racism and Nationalism," in *Race, Nation, Class: Ambiguous Identities*, by Etienne Balibar and Immanuel Wallerstein, trans. Chris Turner (New York and London: Verso, 1991) [*Race, nation, classe: les identités ambigues* (Paris: La Découverte, 1997)]: "We must, however, observe that the *exteriority* of the 'native' populations in colonization, or rather the representation of that state as *racial* exteriority . . . is by no means a given state of affairs. It was in fact produced and reproduced within the very space constituted by conquest and colonization . . . and therefore on the basis of a certain *interiority*. Otherwise one could not explain the ambivalence of the dual movement of assimilation and exclusion of the 'natives' nor the way in which the subhuman nature attributed to the colonized comes to determine the self-image developed within the colonized nations in the period when the world was being divided up. The heritage

of colonialism is, in reality, a fluctuating combination of continued exteriorization and 'internal exclusion'" (42–43 [61–62]). See also Suzanne Gearhart's analysis of the implications of Balibar's use of this term in "Inclusions: Psychoanalysis, Transnationalism, and Minority Cultures," in *Minor Transnationalism*, ed. Françoise Lionnet and Shu-mei Shih (Durham, N.C.: Duke University Press, 2005), 27–40.

10. Albert Memmi points out that "within the colonial framework, assimilation has turned out to be impossible." First, because "the candidate for assimilation almost always comes to tire of the exorbitant price which he must pay and which he never finishes owing." Albert Memmi, *The Colonizer and the Colonized*, trans. Howard Greenfeld (Boston: Beacon Press, 1965), 123 [*Portrait du colonisé, précédé par portrait du colonisateur* (Paris: Gallimard, 1957), 140]. And second, because "even if he agrees to everything, he would not be saved. In order to be assimilated, it is not enough to leave one's group, but one must enter another; now he meets with the colonizer's rejection" (124 [140]). Memmi concludes that "assimilation and colonization are contradictory" (127 [143]). The problem of assimilation will be discussed at greater length in chapter 6.

11. Conor Cruise O'Brien, *Albert Camus: Of Europe and Africa* (New York: The Viking Press, 1970), chap. 2.

12. In equally inflammatory language, Césaire claims that the "very Christian bourgeois of the twentieth century" has "a Hitler inside him, that Hitler *inhabits* him, that Hitler is his *demon* [*un Hitler qui s'ignore, qu'Hitler l'habite, qu'Hitler est son* démon]." Césaire further asserts that the crime for which the white European cannot pardon Hitler is "not crime in itself, the crime against man, it is not the humiliation of man as such, it is the crime against the white man, the humiliation of the white man, and the fact that he applied to Europe colonialist procedures which until then had been reserved exclusively for the Arabs of Algeria, the coolies of India, and the blacks of Africa." Aimé Césaire, *Discourse on Colonialism*, trans. John Pinkham (New York: Monthly Review Press, 1972), 14 [*Discours sur le colonialisme* (Paris: Présence Africaine, 1955), 12].

13. See chapter 6 for a more developed analysis of Camus' editorials on Algeria for *Combat*, all of which are included in *Camus at* Combat: *Writing 1944–1947*, ed. Jacqueline Lévi-Valensi, trans. Arthur Goldhammer (Princeton, N.J.: Princeton University Press, 2006) [*Camus à* Combat: *éditoriaux et articles d'Albert Camus 1944–1947* (Paris: Gallimard, 2002)]. At the time of the massacre of Arab Algerians in Sétif by French Algerians, the Communist newspaper *L'Humanité* called the demonstrations against colonial rule reactionary riots and "the provocation of Hitlerian agents." Quoted in Olivier Todd, *Albert Camus: une vie* (Paris: Gallimard, 1996), 378, but not included in the abridged translation of his work, *Albert Camus: A Life*, trans. Benjamin Ivry (New York: Alfred A. Knopf, 1998).

14. In *The Rebel* as well, Camus claims that the "crimes of the Hitler regime, among them the massacre of the Jews, are without precedent in history, because history gives no other example of a doctrine of such total destruction being able to seize the levers of command of a civilized nation." Albert Camus, *The Rebel*, trans. Anthony Bower (New York: Vintage Books, 1956), 184 [*L'homme révolté*, in *Essais* (Paris: Gallimard, Bibliothèque de la Pléiade, 1965), 590]. After discussing the Nazi destruction of the rebellious town of Lidice and the execution of all its male inhabitants, Camus adds the following in a footnote: "It is striking to note that atrocities reminiscent of these excesses were committed in colonies (India, 1857; Algeria, 1945; etc.) by European nations that in reality obeyed the same irrational prejudices of racial superiority" (185 [590]).

15. The events of the war that touched the citizens of Oran most directly were undoubtedly the British destruction of the French fleet in the port of Mers-el-Kebir, located on the outskirts of Oran, and the abolition of the Décret Crémieux by the Vichy government, which retracted the citizenship of all Algerian Jews.

16. Barthes' article, "'La peste': annales d'une épidémie ou roman de la solitude," was originally published in February 1955 and has been reprinted in Roland Barthes, *Oeuvres complètes*, vol. 1, *1942–1965* (Paris: Editions du Seuil, 1993), 452–456.

17. In his response to Camus' objections to his critique, it might be surprising to those familiar only with Barthes' later work that he acknowledges that his own position on realism is the opposite of Camus': "As for me, I believe in it [historical realism]; or at least . . . I believe in a literal form of art where plagues are nothing other than plagues, and where the Resistance is all of the Resistance. . . . You ask me in name of what I find the morality of *The Plague* insufficient. I make no secret of it; it is in the name of historical materialism" (*Oeuvres complètes*, 479).

18. See again chapter 6 for a discussion of these editorials.

19. Camus dramatizes the limits of legitimate resistance and whether the murder of innocents can ever be justified in his play "The Just" ["Les justes"], in the contrast between the positions of two terrorists, Stepan and Kaliayev, who are planning to assassinate the Russian Grand Duke Sergei Alexandrovitch. Kaliayev describes his commitment to the revolution in the following terms: "Revolution—yes! . . . but revolution for the sake of life—to give life a chance. . . . We are killing to build a world where there'll be no more killing at all. We must accept our role as criminals, until finally everyone on earth is innocent." Albert Camus, "The Just," in *Caligula and Other Plays*, trans. Henry Jones (New York: Penguin Books, 1984), 174–175 [*Théâtre, récits, nouvelles*, 322]. Kaliayev initially does not carry out the plan to throw a bomb into the carriage of the Grand Duke because the Duke's young niece and nephew are accompanying him. Dora defends his decision by saying that "killing the Grand Duke's niece and nephew won't prevent a single child from starving. Even in de-

struction, there is an order, there are limits" (186–187, trans. mod. [338]). For Stepan, commitment to the revolution must be total, which means being willing to sacrifice innocent children to the cause of the revolution: "There are no limits! The truth is that you don't believe in the revolution. No, you don't believe in it. If you believed in it totally, completely, if you were sure that by our sacrifices and our triumphs we will succeed in building a new Russia, freed of tyranny, a land of freedom that will gradually spread over the entire world . . . how could the death of two children be given any weight? You'd feel justified in doing everything, completely everything" (187, trans. mod. [338]).

20. One of the articles Camus wrote on Algeria for *Combat* in 1945 is entitled "It Is Justice That Will Save Algeria from Hatred." *Camus at* Combat (May 23, 1945), 214–217 [528–532]. After acknowledging that "democratic elements were in the minority" in Algeria and that "the Vichy regime found its warmest supporters in Algeria" (215 [528]), Camus refers to the recent massacres of Arab civilians by the police and *pieds-noirs* vigilantes and asserts that "despite the repressive actions we have just taken in North Africa, I am convinced that the era of Western imperialism is over" (216 [531]). When he wrote this in 1945, Camus was either overly optimistic, prescient, or both.

21. Albert Camus, "The Minotaur, or Stopping at Oran," in *Lyrical and Critical Essays*, ed. Philip Thody, trans. Ellen Conroy Kennedy (New York: Vintage Books, 1968), 116 [*Essais*, 818].

22. The description of the disposal and destruction of the dead bodies in *The Plague* is the element of the novel that most directly evokes the details of the horror of the war and specifically the Nazi "final solution": "The first step was to bury the dead by night, which obviously permitted a more summary procedure. The bodies could be piled on top of each other in larger and larger numbers in the ambulances. . . . The bodies were hastily dumped into pits and had hardly settled into place when the spadefuls of quicklime began to sear their faces and the earth covered them over anonymously in holes that were dug increasingly deeper. Shortly afterwards, however, it became necessary to look elsewhere to find still more space. By a special urgency measure the denizens of grants in perpetuity were evicted from their graves and their exhumed remains dispatched to the crematory ovens. And soon the plague victims also had to be taken to the crematorium. . . . Near dawn, at least during the first few days, a thick, nauseating cloud hung low upon the eastern districts of the town. . . . An elaborate system of vents for diverting the smoke had to be installed to appease [the inhabitants]. Thereafter only when a strong wind was blowing did a faint odor coming from the east remind them that they were living under a new order and that the flames of the plague were taking their toll each night." Albert Camus, *The Plague*, trans. Stuart Gilbert (New York: Vintage Books,

1948), 177–179, trans. mod. [*Théâtre, récits, nouvelles,* 1363–1364]. See Shoshana Felman, "Camus' *The Plague,* or a Monument to Witnessing," in *Testimony: Crises of Witnessing in Literature, Psychoanalysis, and History,* by Shoshana Felman and Dori Laub (New York: Routledge, 1992), 93–119. Felman argues that the novel is an allegory not of political plagues but of the limits of historical discourse and thus the impossibility of representing the plague (for her, the Holocaust) as such: "The allegory seems to name the *vanishing of the event* as part of *its actual historical occurrence.* The literality of history includes something which, from inside the event, makes its literality vanish. Camus' testimony is not simply to the literality of history, but to its *unreality,* to the historical vanishing point of its unbelievability.... The Plague (the Holocaust) is disbelieved because it does not enter, and cannot be framed by, any existing frame of reference (be it of knowledge or belief)" (103).

3. Exile

1. "The Rolling Stone" ["La pierre qui pousse"] and "The Artist at Work" ["Jonas ou l'artiste au travail"] are the exceptions, for the former takes place in Brazil and the latter is set in Paris and recounts the double exile of an artist unsuccessfully trying to balance the demands of his personal and public lives, of his society and his art. Jonas' last painting testifies to his divided state: "the canvass completely blank, at the center of which Jonas had simply written in very small letters a word that could be made out, but without any certainty as to whether it should be read 'solitary' or 'solidary.'" Albert Camus, *Exile and the Kingdom,* trans. Justin O'Brien (New York: Vintage Books, 1957), 158 [*Théâtre, récits, nouvelles* (Paris: Gallimard, Bibliothèque de la Pléiade, 1962), 1654]. *The Fall* was also originally intended to be a short story in the collection.

2. The narrator of the story, speaking from or through the perspective of Janine, conveys her reservations by describing the bus as being "full of Arabs pretending to sleep, shrouded in their burnooses.... Their silence and impassivity began to weigh upon Janine; it seemed to her as if she had been traveling for days with that mute escort. And yet the bus had left only at dawn" (5 [1560]).

3. In his portrait of "the colonizer who accepts [himself]," a good model for which could be found in Camus' portrait of Marcel, Albert Memmi argues that "accepting the reality of being a colonizer means agreeing to be a nonlegitimate, privileged person, that is, a usurper [*s'accepter comme colonisateur, ce serait essentiellement s'accepter comme privilégié non légitime, c'est-à-dire comme usurpateur*].... How can usurpation try to pass for legitimacy? One attempt can be made by demonstrating

the usurper's eminent merits, so eminent that they deserve compensation. Another is to harp on the usurped's demerits, so deep that they cannot help leading to misfortune." Albert Memmi, *The Colonizer and the Colonized*, trans. Howard Greenfeld (Boston: Beacon Press, 1965), 52–53 [*Portrait du colonisé, précédé par portrait du colonisateur* (Paris: Gallimard, 1957), 76–77].

4. In his preface to *Algerian Reports*, Camus warns against "condemning the French of Algeria as a group" and gives what he calls the history of the men of his family: "Being poor and free of hatred, [they] never exploited or oppressed anyone. But three quarters of the French resemble them." Albert Camus, *Resistance, Rebellion, and Death*, trans. Justin O'Brien (New York: Knopf, 1961), 119 [*Essais* (Paris: Gallimard, Bibliothèque de la Pléiade, 1965), 897]. However, in *The First Man*, trans. David Hapgood (New York: Vintage Books, 1995) [*Le premier homme* (Paris: Gallimard, 1994)], Camus also acknowledges that "in this country of immigration, of quick fortunes and spectacular collapses, the boundaries between classes were less clear-cut than between races" (203 [186]). He also qualifies somewhat the attitude of the poor working-class French Algerians toward other ethnic groups, especially in terms of their struggle to stay employed: "Unemployment, for which there was no insurance at all, was the calamity they most dreaded. That is why these workers . . . who in their daily lives were the most tolerant of men, were always xenophobes on labor issues, accusing in turn the Italians, the Spaniards, the Jews, and the Arabs, and finally the whole world of stealing their work. . . . It was not for the mastery of the earth or the privileges of wealth and leisure that these unexpected nationalists were contending against other nationalities; it was for the privilege of servitude" (257 [236–237]).

5. "But [Janine] liked his courage in facing up to life, which he shared with all the French of this country" (6 [1560]).

6. It is suggested that Marcel's openly expressed racism is another source of conflict in the couple, since Janine responds to his racist remark by telling him to stop.

7. Janine's reaction to her husband's racism highlights once again her increasing distance from him and manifests an irony of which Marcel is not capable: "Janine was not thinking of anything, or perhaps of that victory of the cooks over the prophets" (15 [1565]). When Marcel also quibbles over the price a young Arab demands for carrying his trunk and expresses his belief in what is described as "the vague principle that they always asked for twice as much in the hope of settling for a quarter of the amount." Janine is described as being "ill at ease" after hearing him say this (16 [1566]).

8. Edward Said was certainly right to insist on the crucial importance of the descriptions of the Algerian landscape in Camus' fictions and the way these descriptions raise fundamental political issues related to colonialism, even if I would argue

that the question of how these descriptions relate to colonialism is much more complex than Said acknowledges in statements such as the following: "What I want to do is see Camus's fiction as an element in France's methodically constructed political geography of Algeria . . . the better to see it as providing an arresting account of the political and interpretative contest to represent, inhabit, and possess the territory itself. . . . Camus's writing is informed by an extraordinarily belated, in some ways incapacitated colonial sensibility, which enacts an imperial gesture within and by means of form, the realistic novel, well past its greatest achievements in Europe." Edward Said, "Camus and the French Imperial Experience," in *Culture and Imperialism* (New York: Alfred A. Knopf, 1993), 176. Said further asserts that Camus' "novels and short stories narrate the victory won over a pacified, decimated Muslim population whose rights to the land have been severely curtailed. In thus confirming and consolidating French priority, Camus neither disputes nor dissents from the campaign for sovereignty waged against Algerian Muslims for over a hundred years" (180–181). It should already be clear that one of the purposes of the present analysis is to show how Camus in fact most definitely did "dispute and dissent from the campaign for sovereignty" in Algeria, in both his political essays and fictions— and nowhere more dramatically than in "The Adulterous Woman." The effectiveness of his dissent can certainly be debated, but not its existence. Said is thus wrong about both the realist form and the political implications of Camus' story.

9. "It is accurate to say, therefore, that Camus' narratives lay severe and ontologically prior claims to Algeria's geography" (Said, *Culture and Imperialism*, 183).

10. Camus uses practically the same language in *The First Man* to describe the feelings of the young Jacques Cormery, in a very different setting, when he spends the day hunting with his uncle Ernest and his friends: "Staggering under the sun, his master, and so, for hours without end on a land without boundaries, his head lost in the unremitting light and the immense space of the sky, Jacques felt himself to be the richest of children" (111 [106]).

11. This double, contradictory title was carefully chosen, for before deciding on it Camus considered and then rejected a number of other titles, such as "In the Snow," "The High Plateau and the Condemned Man," "The Law," and "Cain." To complicate things further, as Derrida points out, "'Hostis,' in Latin *means guest but also enemy*." Jacques Derrida, *De l'hospitalité* (Paris: Calmann-Lévy, 1997), 12.

12. In *De l'hospitalité*, Derrida speaks of what he calls "absolute hospitality," a hospitality that is not governed or limited by the rules or conventions of "conditional hospitality" but rather offered without conditions and with no expectation of reciprocity. Absolute hospitality is not the hospitality offered to "the foreigner" with a name and identity papers but rather to what Derrida calls "the absolute other": "The difference . . . between the foreigner and the absolute other is that the latter

might not have either a name or a family name; the absolute hospitality I would like to offer him assumes a break with hospitality in its conventional sense, with conditional hospitality, with the law or pact of hospitality. . . . Absolute hospitality demands that I open my home and that I give not only to the foreigner (endowed with a family name, a social status, etc.) but to the unknown, anonymous, absolute other, that I give him (a) place [*je lui donne lieu*], that I let him come in, that I let him arrive and have a place in the place that I offer him, without demanding from him either reciprocity . . . or his name" (29).

13. In his notes for the Pléiade edition of Camus' literary texts, Roger Quilliot reveals the external source for the opening scene of the story. He quotes El Aziz Kessous, Camus' friend from the time they were in the Algerian Communist Party together, who indicates that in a much-publicized incident in the 1930s a Muslim union member underwent similar inhumane treatment at the hands of a French gendarme. The incident was widely reported in the leftist press and much discussed, especially by those affiliated with the Communist Party in Algeria. Recruiting cards were even printed by the Communist Party, showing a Muslim attached by rope to a man on horseback. Because Camus, "at that time about twenty years old, was already an activist in the political party that he would soon abandon," Kessous claims that he "must have seen this document that was widely circulated in the groups he frequented" and taken by everyone as an "image of inhumanity" (*Théâtre, récits, nouvelles,* 2049).

14. Being French gives him an economic superiority, for example, for no matter how modestly he lives, Daru is rich compared to the starving Algerian families to whom he gives food during the drought: "Faced with such poverty, he who lived almost like a monk in his remote schoolhouse, nonetheless satisfied with the little he had and with the rough life, had felt like a lord with his white-washed walls, his narrow couch, his unpainted shelves, his well, and his weekly provision of water and food" (88 [1612]).

15. Among the first eight victims of the initial insurrection organized by the FLN on November 1, 1954, was a twenty-three-year-old schoolteacher named Guy Monnerot, who had volunteered to teach in Algeria. His wife was seriously wounded but survived the attack.

4. Justice or Death?

1. After he has been sentenced to death, Meursault thinks constantly about public executions and remembers a story his mother repeatedly told him about his father.

"I blame myself for not having given more attention to accounts of public executions. One should always take an interest in such matters. You never know what can happen. . . . During these moments, I remembered a story Mother used to tell me about my father. I never knew him. The only precise thing I knew about this man was what Mother had told me: he had gone to see a murderer executed. The idea of going made him sick. But he did it anyway and, after coming home, he vomited a good part of the morning. Because of that my father disgusted me a bit. But now I understood; it was such a natural reaction." Albert Camus, *The Stranger*, trans. Stuart Gilbert (New York: Vintage Books, 1954), 136, 138, trans. mod. [*Théâtre, récits, nouvelles* (Paris: Gallimard, Bibliothèque de la Pléiade, 1962), 1202–1203]. In *The First Man*, Jacques Cormery questions his mother about his father but learns almost nothing from her, not "even this detail that had made such an impression on him as a child, had pursued him throughout his life and even into his dreams . . . even that he had learned from his grandmother." Albert Camus, *The First Man*, trans. David Hapgood (New York: Vintage Books, 1995), 81 [*Le premier homme* (Paris: Gallimard, 1994), 79–80]. The story is told in more detail in his autobiographical novel, which also emphasizes the disturbing effect of the story on Jacques: "On the night he heard the story, Jacques himself, when he was lying huddled in on the side of the bed to avoid touching his brother, with whom he slept, choked back his nausea and his horror as he relived the details he had heard and those he imagined. And throughout his life those images had followed him even into his sleep when now and then, but regularly, a recurrent nightmare would haunt him, taking many forms, but always having the one theme: they were coming to take him, Jacques, to be executed" (82 [80–81]).

2. Albert Camus, "Reflections on the Guillotine," in *Resistance, Rebellion, and Death*, trans. Justin O'Brien (New York: Knopf, 1961), 199 [*Essais* (Paris: Gallimard, Bibliothèque de la Pléiade, 1965), 1039].

3. In *The Plague*, a similar story is told from a slightly different perspective. One of the main characters involved in fighting the epidemic, Tarrou, who early in the novel admits that he "is horrified by death sentences" (Albert Camus, *The Plague*, trans. Stuart Gilbert [New York: Vintage Books, 1948], 125, trans. mod. [*Théâtre, récits, nouvelles*, 1321]), later explains why. He tells the story of his own father, who, as a prosecuting attorney, was frequently involved in capital cases and on one occasion invited his son, aged seventeen, to hear him plead such a case: "I realized he was demanding the death of this man in the name of society and demanding even that his head be cut off. Not exactly in those words, I admit. 'This head must fall,' was the formula. But the difference in the end was slight. And the result was the same, since he obtained the head he asked for. Only of course it wasn't he who did the actual job. . . . Nevertheless, he had to, as is the custom, be present at what's po-

litely termed the prisoner's last moments, but what would be better called the most abject of assassinations" (248, trans. mod. [1422]).

4. Mohammed Harbri, in his groundbreaking work *Le F.L.N.: mirage et réalité* (Paris: Editions J.A., 1980), describes the project of the FLN in the following terms: "One obsession drove the founders of the FLN: . . . independence could be won only through war. . . . They condemned pell-mell Ferhat Abbas, the Oulémas, and the Algerian Communist Party, and later the centrists, not because they were hostile to independence but because they believed in achieving it by successive steps. . . . Motivated by a messianic vision of an equalitarian society, they had an absolute faith in ideas" (117).

5. The French *Milice* was a paramilitary organization created in 1943 by Vichy Secretary of State Joseph Darnand to support German actions taken against the French Resistance and aid in the arrest and deportation of Jews.

6. Unsigned editorial, "Outlaws" (*Combat*, underground, no. 56, April 1944), in *Camus at* Combat: *Writing 1944–1947*, ed. Jacqueline Lévi-Valensi, trans. Arthur Goldhammer (Princeton, N.J.: Princeton University Press, 2006), 4 [*Camus à* Combat: *éditoriaux et articles d'Albert Camus 1944–1947* (Paris: Gallimard, 2002), 128]. Lévi-Valensi acknowledges in a note that not all scholars agree that Camus was the author of this article, but she herself is convinced that it should nevertheless be attributed to him because of "the mix of irony and seriousness is frequent in Camus's writing" and because the attack on "outlaws" is similar to another article he wrote and signed (3 [126]).

7. Albert Camus, untitled editorial (*Combat*, November 2, 1944), in *Camus at* Combat, 97 [303]. As Herbert Lottman points out, when Pétain was eventually brought to trial after the war, *Combat*, like Camus, had changed positions and opposed the death penalty for him in the following terms: "First of all because one must resolve oneself to say what is true, that any death sentence is a denial of morality, and then because, in this particular case, it would give this vain old man the reputation of a martyr, according him a new status in the minds even of his enemies." *Combat* (August 2, 1945), cited in Herbert Lottman, *Albert Camus: A Biography* (Garden City, N.Y.: Doubleday, 1979), 349.

8. Camus insists that only the families of the victims have the right to speak of pardon: "I see for our country two ways unto death (and there are ways of surviving that are no better than death): the way of hatred and the way of pardon. One seems to me as disastrous as the other. I have no taste for hatred. . . . But pardon seems no better to me, and in today's circumstance it would look like an insult. In any case, I am convinced that it is not up to us. If death sentences horrify me, that is my business. I shall join M. Mauriac in granting open pardons when Vélin's parents and Leynaud's wife tell me that I can. But not before. Never before." Albert

Camus, "Justice and Charity" (*Combat*, January 11, 1945) in *Camus at* Combat, 169 [440–441]. François Mauriac was the well-known conservative Catholic novelist and fellow member of the French Resistance who wrote for *Le Figaro* and with whom Camus had an extended polemical exchange over the death penalty. Vélin (André Bollier) was *Combat*'s printer, who committed suicide rather than be captured by the Gestapo. René Leynaud was a poet and close friend of Camus and an early contributor to *Combat*; he was captured by the French *Milice* and executed by the Germans in June 1944, immediately before the liberation of Paris. Camus published a moving tribute to him in *Combat* on October 27, 1944 (90–92 [290–294]).

9. In a letter Camus sent on January 27, 1945, to the novelist Marcel Aymé, who had written to Camus to ask him to sign a petition to de Gaulle to spare Brasillach's life, Camus reluctantly agreed to sign the petition for the following reason: "I have always been horrified by the death penalty, and I have judged that as an individual the very least I could do is not participate in it, even by abstention. . . . This is a scruple that I suppose would make the friends of Brasillach laugh. And as for him, if his life is spared and if an amnesty frees him as it probably will in one or two years, I would like him to be told the following as concerns my letter: it is not for him that I join my signature with yours, it is not for the writer, whom I consider to be worth nothing, nor for the individual, for whom I have the strongest contempt." Cited in Olivier Todd, *Albert Camus: une vie* (Paris: Gallimard, 1996), 374. Only a part of the above quotation is given in the English translation, *Albert Camus: A Life*, trans. Benjamin Ivry (New York: Alfred A. Knopf, 1998), 200.

10. During a discussion with students a day after having received the Nobel Prize, Camus was repeatedly interrupted by an Algerian student who questioned his commitment to democracy and justice in Algeria. In reply, Camus made the following controversial and oft-misunderstood remark: "I have always supported a just Algeria, where the two populations must live in peace and equality. I have said and repeated that we have to bring justice to the Algerian people and grant them a fully democratic regime. . . . I have always condemned terror. I must also condemn a terrorism that is practiced blindly, in the streets of Algiers, for example, and which one day could strike my mother or my family. I believe in justice, but I will defend my mother before justice" (*Le Monde*, December 14, 1957; *Essais*, 1881–1882). If Camus had said "innocent civilians" in general rather than his own mother, perhaps he could have avoided the confusion to which his statement gave rise and given his political opponents one less weapon to use against him. In any case, he was astounded by the hostile reaction to his words.

11. The character from *The Plague* who expresses ideas closest to the ideas Camus expresses in this essay is Tarrou, who describes how he became a political activist in order to oppose the society in which he lived, which he claims was based on

the death sentence. He soon discovered that his own revolutionary political movement (clearly the Communist Party) also had to "pronounce death sentences. But I was told that these few deaths were inevitable for the building up of a new world in which murder would cease to be. . . . Until the day when I was present at an execution—it was in Hungary—and exactly the same vertigo that had taken over the child I had once been obscured the eyes of the man I was. . . . I've never been able to sleep well since then. The bad taste remained in my mouth. . . . And thus I came to understand at least that I had had the plague all those long years in which, however, I'd believed with all my soul that I was fighting it. I learned that I had indirectly contributed to the deaths of thousands of people; that I'd even brought about their deaths by approving of acts and principles which could only lead to death. . . . So that is why I resolved to reject anything which, directly or indirectly, for good reasons or bad, has anyone killed or justifies that anyone be killed" (250–254, trans. mod. [1423–1425]).

12. Albert Camus, *The Rebel*, trans. Anthony Bower (New York: Vintage Books, 1956), 4, trans. mod. [*L'homme révolté*, in *Essais*, 414].

13. Jean-Paul Sartre considered Camus' critique of Marxism to be hopelessly idealistic and ultimately irrelevant, the musings of a "*belle âme*" who had retreated from politics and was criticizing history "from above." In his response to Camus' reply to Francis Jeanson's attack on *The Rebel* in *Les Temps Modernes*, Sartre derisively asks if "the Republic of Beautiful Souls [*belles âmes*] had chosen [Camus] to be their principal prosecutor." Jean-Paul Sartre, "Réponse à Albert Camus," *Les Temps Modernes*, no. 82 (August 1952), reprinted in *Situations IV* (Paris: Gallimard, 1964), 97. After acknowledging that because Camus "had hundreds of times denounced and combated with all his force the tyranny of Franco and the colonial politics of our government," he had acquired what Sartre calls "the relative right to speak of Soviet concentration camps" (106); he nevertheless attacks Camus for being "hostile to history" (113) and for considering it "the madness of others": "You didn't dream of 'making History,' as Marx said, but in keeping it from being made" (116). For a presentation of the Camus-Sartre polemical exchange and break, see Lottman, *Albert Camus: A Biography*, 495–507; Olivier Todd, *Albert Camus: A Life*, 305–310 [555–572]; and Ronald Aronson, *Camus and Sartre: The Story of a Friendship and the Quarrel That Ended It* (Chicago: University of Chicago Press, 2004), 131–154.

5. Terror

1. When I read a draft of a much shorter version of this chapter at a colloquium on Camus at Cornell University, I prefaced the paper by reading the following state-

ment made by Hanna Nasir, then president of Birzeit University, after a terrorist attack on Hebrew University: "There is no way that one can consider justifying the latest attack on the Hebrew University campus. More precisely, it is unacceptable to justify such attacks. Targeting the lives of innocent civilians, whether they are enemies, or from a different religion, or from a different race, is intolerable from a moral and religious point of view.... We should in no way respond to our oppressor's barbaric attacks with similar actions.... The most apt definition of terrorism refers to acts that involve the killing of innocent civilians; there is a wide gap between resistance and terrorism, and one should not be confused with the other. What is worrisome is that we may, due to the great pain we are facing from the occupation, begin to justify terrorist acts. We all live the tragedy and devastation of this occupation.... Despite all of this, we should not allow ourselves to kill our occupier's innocent civilians, even when they kill our own.... What concerns me most, is that in our just struggle towards liberation and freedom, we should never turn a deaf ear to our conscience nor should we ever lose our internal integrity or our own humanity." This statement originally appeared on August 10, 2002, in the Arabic-language Palestinian daily *Al Ayyam*, published in Ramallah by the Palestinian Authority.

2. Albert Camus, "Preface to Algerian Reports," in *Resistance, Rebellion, and Death*, trans. Justin O'Brien (New York: Knopf, 1961), 111 [*Essais* (Paris: Gallimard, Bibliothèque de la Pléiade, 1965), 891].

3. Jeffrey Isaac argues in a similar vein that Camus "defended a vision of coexistence informed by a universalist conception of the human right to be free from torture, persecution, and murder, and of the political right to citizenship in autonomous political communities.... As a *pied noir* who honestly acknowledged his hybrid identity and refused to adopt a mythic, hyperinflated identity as a 'true' Frenchman, Camus seemed genuinely caught in the middle; and as a writer he sought, without denying his irreducibly *pied noir* attachments, to occupy the no-man's land between the antagonists, the ground of minimal common humanity that might support dialogue and mutual recognition." Jeffrey C. Isaac, *Arendt, Camus, and Modern Rebellion* (New Haven, Conn.: Yale University Press, 1992), 194–195.

4. Albert Memmi, *The Colonizer and the Colonized*, trans. Howard Greenfeld (Boston: Beacon Press, 1965), 39, 43 [*Portrait du colonisé, précédé par portrait du colonisateur* (Paris: Gallimard, 1957), 65, 68–69]. In his 1965 preface to *The Colonizer and the Colonized*, Memmi further explains that his "model for the colonizer of good will was taken in particular from a group of philosophy professors in Tunis who were my colleagues and friends. Their generosity was unquestionable; so, unfortunately, was their impotence, their inability to make themselves heard by anyone else in the colony. However, it was among these men that I felt the most comfortable" (xv [19]). Memmi considered Camus also to be in this category.

5. In *Peregrinations: Law, Form, Event* (New York: Columbia University Press, 1988), Jean-François Lyotard describes the heated debates that occurred during the Algerian War among the members of Socialisme ou Barbarie, the radical Marxist group to which he belonged at the time, over whether they should support the FLN in its armed struggle. Even though they were militant anticolonialists, the FLN also presented problems, "given their radical critique of Soviet-style bureaucracies" and their "refutation of political and trade unionist organizations . . . for being impediments obstructing the free development of popular struggles. . . . During those years I came to the conclusion that the only position that had a chance of being correct was hopelessly contradictory. Yes, the Algerians have the right, even the duty, to become free and be recognized as a free community with its own name and equal to others—so we must accept their struggle. Nevertheless, that struggle has no chance of instituting any of the principles of worker democracy, and it will not fail to produce a new class society under the control of bureaucratic military leadership—so why should we give our support to the coming of power of new exploiters?" (26–27). Lyotard makes similar comments in "The Name of Algeria," in *Political Writings*, trans. Bill Readings and Kevin Paul (Minneapolis: University of Minnesota Press, 1993), 168 [*La guerre des Algériens: écrits 1956–1963*, ed. Mohammed Ramdani (Paris: Galilée, 1989), 36]. Camus' criticism of the FLN was in certain respects similar to the radical syndicalist position of Socialisme ou Barbarie, but unlike those on the radical Left like Lyotard who chose to support the armed struggle of the Algerian people for independence in spite of the FLN, Camus denounced the FLN's use of terrorism both because of its human costs and because he also considered the terrorist means being used to achieve independence to be a sign of the kind of society Algeria would become with the victory of the FLN. Perhaps the greatest difference in their positions is that Lyotard, while supporting the struggle for independence, describes a *political* opposition to the FLN based on class analysis; Camus, while he would have agreed that colonial "injustices were so flagrant" that they had to be immediately resolved, remained skeptical of all revolutionary promises of independence and opposed on *moral* grounds the terrorist means being used to achieve a form of independence that would bring to power the "new exploiters" responsible for them.

6. On February 18, 1957, Mouloud Feraoun, who was executed at the end of the war by the OAS, the reactionary French-Algerian secret army, after meeting in Algiers with Emmanuel Roblès, a close friend of Camus' who had recently spoken with him in Paris, wrote in his journal that Camus "believes that the FLN is fascist and that the possibility of the future of his country being in the hands of the FLN was strictly speaking unthinkable." Mouloud Feraoun, *Journal 1955–1962* (Paris: Seuil, 1962), 204. Roblès, who was editor of the "Collection Meditéranée" in which

Feraoun's journal was published, added the following note to Feraoun's comment: "Camus's opinion was more nuanced. He thought that a fascist tendency within the Front risked taking it over."

7. Olivier Todd, for example, claims that "on August 8, 1945, Camus was one of the few French editorial writers to express his horror after America dropped the atomic bomb on Hiroshima." Olivier Todd, *Albert Camus: A Life*, trans. Benjamin Ivry (New York: Alfred A. Knopf, 1998), 204 [*Albert Camus: une vie* (Paris: Gallimard, 1996), 381]. Camus' editorial in fact denounces both the savagery of the action and the way it was presented in the media: "The world is what it is, which isn't much. This is what everyone has known since yesterday, thanks to the formidable concert that the radio, newspapers, and news agencies have unleashed on the subject of the atomic bomb. . . . American, British, and French newspapers have poured forth a steady stream of elegant dissertations concerning the future, the past, the inventors, the cost, the peaceful uses and military implications, the political consequences, and even the independent character of the atomic bomb. We can sum it all up in a sentence: the civilization of the machine has just achieved its ultimate degree of savagery. A choice is going to have to be made in the fairly near future between collective suicide and the intelligent utilization of scientific discoveries. In the meantime, one has the right to think that there is something indecent about celebrating in this way a discovery that has been put to its first use by the most formidable destructive rage that man has exhibited for centuries. In a world that has torn itself apart with every conceivable instrument of violence and shown itself incapable of exerting any control while remaining indifferent to justice or even mere human happiness, the fact that science has dedicated itself to organized murder will surprise no one, except perhaps an unrepentant idealist." Albert Camus, *Combat* (August 8, 1945), in *Camus at* Combat: *Writing 1944–1947*, ed. Jacqueline Lévi-Valensi, trans. Arthur Goldhammer (Princeton, N.J.: Princeton University Press, 2006), 236 [*Camus à* Combat: *éditoriaux et articles d'Albert Camus 1944–1947* (Paris: Gallimard, 2002), 569–570].

8. Ronald Aronson, *Camus and Sartre: The Story of a Friendship and the Quarrel That Ended It* (Chicago: University of Chicago Press, 2004), 214. Aronson uses this phrase to characterize the Lauriol Plan for dividing Algeria into different areas controlled by different populations, for which Camus in one of his last essays on Algeria offers support. Aronson describes the plan as a "neocolonial scheme" and argues that "in this way Camus claimed to serve justice as well as his own people, while actually serving neither. It was, of course, impossible to end colonialism *and* leave existing French rights intact, a fact that Camus never faced" (214). Even though I do not agree that Camus "never faced" this fact, it is true that the Lauriol Plan did not adequately face it. Jeffrey Isaac, on the other hand, even though he

acknowledges that "the Lauriol Plan was doomed to failure by the furious pace of events" and that "Camus's position was quixotic, pleading for morality at a time when war was the spirit of the day" (Isaac, *Arendt, Camus, and Modern Rebellion*, 204), defends Camus' interest in the Lauriol Plan. For no matter how quixotic, Isaac nevertheless presents the Lauriol Plan's (and Camus') intentions in a generally positive light: "The Lauriol's repudiation of the principle of unitary sovereignty, and its acknowledgment of multiple layers of genuine authority and political membership resonates with the localism and anarchism that was at the heart of Camus's political vision. Yet given the balance of forces in Algeria, France, and the world, the kind of creative, conciliatory politics of peace and justice envisioned by Camus had little chance of political success" (204).

9. In *Le temps qui reste: essai d'autobiographie professionnelle* (Paris: Stock, 1973), Jean Daniel includes a previously unpublished interview with Jean-Paul Sartre that took place on January 13, 1958. In the interview, Sartre argues that "it is necessary to dissimulate" when doing politics, for "otherwise, one is a 'beautiful soul,'" which is, of course, the term he and others at *Les Temps Modernes* frequently used to describe Camus. Sartre acknowledges that for him involvement in politics in general and being a political journalist in particular meant having "to keep certain things silent." The example he gives is the FLN massacre of villagers at Melouza, an atrocity that Sartre claims was a serious political mistake to denounce, because in denouncing it or other crimes committed by the FLN, he claims that he, Daniel, and others had "served the enemy," that is, colonialist France (251). When Daniel strenuously objects and insists that because of such atrocities those who support Algerian independence on the contrary are obliged to question the FLN, Sartre rejects all such criticism: "Whatever else the FLN is, it exists, it is the Algerian revolution. You have to take it as it is" (252). Near the end of the interview, however, Sartre laments that even he, one of its strongest supporters, had lost all contact with the FLN militants he once knew and even with Frantz Fanon: "It's awful, there's no longer any contact. They have all disappeared, just like at certain moments the Communists. That Fanon, who used to come to see me all the time, doesn't even write me any more. They are all in the machine. It grinds them up" (255). Camus, unlike Sartre, could never support a machine that "grinds people up."

10. Frantz Fanon, *The Wretched of the Earth*, trans. Constance Farrington (New York: Grove Press, 1963), 36 [*Les damnés de la terre* (Paris: François Maspero, 1970), 6].

11. By defining the violence produced by the colonialist system as a form of terror, Fanon can thus treat the violence used by the colonized against the colonial system as a form of counterterror. This does not mean, however, that Fanon thinks that the results of violence are the same on both sides, since each side has completely

different resources: "From the moment the native [*le colonisé*] has chosen the methods of counter-violence, the police reprisals automatically call forth reprisals on the side of the nationalist. However, the results are not equivalent, for machine-gunning from airplanes and bombardments from the fleet go far beyond in horror and magnitude any answer the natives can make" (89 [48]).

12. Fanon describes other beneficial "cleansing" effects of violence as well: "The colonized's violence unifies the people.... Violence is in practice totalizing and national. It follows that it entails within itself the liquidation of regionalism and of tribalism.... At the level of individuals, violence is a cleansing force. It frees the colonized from his inferiority complex and from his despair and inaction; it makes him fearless and restores his self-respect" (94, trans. mod. [51–52]). Violence is also claimed to be the ultimate weapon against dictators or any other form of a "living god": "When the people have taken violent part in the national liberation, they will allow no one to set themselves up as 'liberators.' They show themselves to be jealous of the results of their action and take good care not to place their future, their destiny, or the fate of their country in the hands of a living god. Yesterday they were completely irresponsible; today they mean to understand everything and make all decisions. Illuminated by violence, the consciousness of the people rebels against any pacification. From now on the demagogues, the opportunists, and the magicians have a difficult task.... The attempt at mystification becomes, in the long run, practically impossible" (94–95 [52]). Fanon, of course, died soon after writing these words and thus did not see the results of Algerian independence and the military coup d'état.

13. After hearing on the radio that Algerian rebels had massacred a number of small farmers, Mouloud Feraoun takes the opposite position from Fanon on the allegedly salutary effects of violence and its essential role in the birth of "new men": "They [the farmers] were machine-gunned, their farms were burned, because they were the enemy, and for nothing else.... These people who coldly kill innocents, are they liberators? If yes, do they have the slightest idea that their 'violence' will call forth the other 'violence,' legitimize it, hasten its horrible appearance.... Are they knowingly preparing to massacre 'their brothers?' In admitting even that they are bloodthirsty brutes—which doesn't excuse them but rather pleads against them, against us, against the ideal they claim to defend—they should think about sparing us, thus about not provoking repression. Unless liberation means something for them very different from what we understand by the term. We once believed they wanted to liberate the country with its inhabitants. For the moment they are in the process of doing away with its inhabitants. Perhaps they estimate that this entire generation of cowards that proliferates in Algeria first has to disappear and that a truly free Algeria must be repopulated with new men who have not experienced

the yoke of the secular occupier. Logically such a point of view is defensible. Too logically, alas. And one thing leading to another, suspicions to shady compromises, and shady compromises to betrayals, we will all end up by being declared guilty and executed on the spot." Mouloud Feraoun, *Journal 1955–1962* (entry of March 9, 1956) (Paris: Seuil, 1962), 91. At the very end of the war, Feraoun was "executed on the spot" not by FLN liberators but by members of the reactionary terrorist French secret army, the OAS.

14. Albert Memmi characterizes Fanon's portrait of the colonized in the following way: "Like many other defenders of the colonized, he had in him a certain dose of revolutionary romanticism. The Colonizer was the complete bastard; the colonized, the integrally good man. As for most social romantics, the victim remains intact and proud within the oppression that he endures while suffering but without being harmed. And the day that oppression ceases, the new man has to immediately appear. But, and I say this without any pleasure, what decolonization precisely shows us is that this is not true." Albert Memmi, "Note on Frantz Fanon and the Notion of Inadequacy," in *Dominated Man: Notes Toward a Portrait* (New York: Orion Press, 1968), 87 [*L'homme dominé* (Paris: Gallimard, 1968), 66].

15. Frantz Fanon, *Studies in a Dying Colonialism*, trans. Haakon Chevalier (London: Earthscan Publications, 1965), 24 [*Sociologie d'une revolution* (Paris: François Maspero, 1972), 6–7; originally published in 1959 as *L'an V de la révolution algérienne*]. Fanon claims that the FLN, "at the time when the people were undergoing the most massive assaults of colonialism, did not hesitate to prohibit certain forms of action and constantly to remind the fighting units of the international laws of war" (24 [6]). This is undoubtedly true, but overall neither side respected the "international laws of war," which would in principle mean that the actions of neither side can be defended.

16. This is close to the dilemma faced by the terrorists in Camus' play *The Just*: whether to bomb the carriage of the Archduke, knowing that innocent children are in the carriage with him. Camus is, of course, on the side of those who do not just hesitate for a moment but actually refuse to kill innocents in all situations.

17. Jean-Paul Sartre, *Colonialism and Neocolonialism*, trans. Azzedine Haddour, Steve Brewer, and Terry McWilliams (New York: Routledge, 2001), 139 [in Frantz Fanon, *Les damnés de la terre* (Paris: La Découverte, 2002), 20].

18. In her preface for the 2002 re-edition of Fanon's text, Alice Cherki argues that Sartre's preface "distorts the preoccupations and tone of Fanon. . . . Above all his preface radicalizes the analysis of Fanon on violence. In effect, Sartre justifies violence, while Fanon analyzes it and does not promote it as an end in itself but sees it as a necessary step. For this reason Sartre's preface at times has the appearances of an incitement to criminality" (11). The issue may not be whether either promotes vi-

olence as an end in itself, but rather that both see violence as redemptive, the means to "salvation" in the form of the birth of "new men."

19. In "On Violence," Hannah Arendt harshly criticizes what she calls the "irresponsible grandiose statements" of Fanon and Sartre: "Sartre with his great felicity with words has given expression to the new faith. 'Violence,' he now believes, on the strength of Fanon's book, 'like Achilles' lance, can heal all the wounds it has inflicted.' If this were true, revenge would be the cure-all for most of our ills. This myth is more abstract, farther removed from reality, than Sorel's myth of a general strike ever was. It is on a par with Fanon's worst rhetorical excesses.... No history and no theory is needed to refute this statement; the most superficial observer of the processes that go on in the human body knows its untruth." Hannah Arendt, *Crises of the Republic* (New York: Harcourt Brace Jovanovich, 1972), 122. See Jeffrey Isaac's discussion of Arendt's essay in chapter 6 of his *Arendt, Camus, and Modern Rebellion*, "Swimming Against the Tide." Isaac argues that Arendt "reject[s] the effort to ideologize this reality [that of the Third World], to offer a grand historical scheme in terms of which all postcolonial struggles make sense and all political agents can be deemed progressive or reactionary. Like any grand ideology, Third Worldism grossly oversimplifies political reality, and it offers its proponents a false comfort about their own righteousness. The connection between such righteousness and an authoritarian attitude toward dissent and disagreement is not fortuitous" (192).

20. This testimony was originally published in *Les Temps Modernes* (May–June 1958) and later in Vidal-Naquet, *Les crimes de l'arméé française: Algérie 1954–1962* (Paris: Maspero, 1975).

21. All references will be to Albert Camus, *Exile and the Kingdom*, trans. Justin O'Brien (New York: Vintage Books, 1957) [*Théâtre, récits, nouvelles* (Paris: Gallimard, Bibliothèque de la Pléiade, 1962)]. The complete title of the story, which is not given in English, is "The Renegade or a Confused Mind" ["Le renégat ou un esprit confus"].

22. Edward W. Said, "Camus and the French Imperial Experience," in *Culture and Imperialism* (New York: Alfred A. Knopf, 1993), 178.

23. The following is from *The Unnamable*: "This voice that speaks, knowing that it lies, indifferent to what it says, too old perhaps and too abased ever to succeed in saying the words that would be its last, knowing itself useless and its uselessness in vain ... is it one? ... It issues from me, it fills me, it clamors against my walls, it is not mine, I can't stop it, I can't prevent it, from tearing me, racking me, assailing me. It is not mine, I have none, I have no voice and must speak, that is all I know." Samuel Beckett, *The Unnamable*, in *Three Novels by Samuel Beckett* (New York: Grove Press, 1955), 307.

24. Hannah Arendt defines "ideology" in the following terms: "It is the logic of an idea. Its subject matter is history, to which the 'idea' is applied. . . . The ideology treats the course of events as though it followed the same 'law' as the logical explanation of its 'idea.'" Hannah Arendt, *The Origins of Totalitarianism* (New York: Harcourt Brace Jovanovich, 1973), 469. Arendt calls the totalitarian application of ideology "the tyranny of logicality" (473).

25. The original French is *"sale Europe,"* which in the English translation becomes "lousy Europe" (36 [1580]). Here as elsewhere, I have modified the translation in order to retain the violence of the language of the story, which the English translation tends to mitigate.

6. Anguish

1. Alice L. Conklin, *A Mission to Civilize* (Stanford, Calif.: Stanford University Press, 1997), 1–2. "They were continually undertaking—or claiming to undertake, as the case may be—civilizing measures on behalf of their subjects that appeared to make democracy and colonialism compatible. However misguided, self-deluding, or underfunded—indeed because they were all these things—these claims merit our attention. As an enduring tension of French republicanism, the civilizing ideal in whose name the nation of the 'rights of man' deprived so many people of their freedom deserves to be better understood" (10). But Conklin also questions "why it took a country with as strong a republican tradition as France so long to see the discrepancy between ideal and reality, between ends and means. Racist assumptions about Africans, the spoils the empire yielded, and the prestige it bestowed upon *la grand nation* are only half the answer. Equally to blame was a civilizing ideology that was never *only* racist in content. . . . If the empire endured as long as it did, it was in part because French racism often worked hand-in-hand with more progressive values" (256).

2. Conklin convincingly argues that the "mission" to civilize and liberate grew out of the logic of the French Revolution itself: "While the savagery of most New World inhabitants was attributed to environmental factors, the barbarism of Asians and Arabs was defined in terms of oriental despotism and ignorance. To civilize them would thus mean not only mastering nature and encouraging commercial exchange but also liberating them from political tyranny and superstition. In the end, however, these differences in no way altered the general conclusions of the French. By the time of the French Revolution, it was simply taken for granted that the entire non-Western world was in need of French civilization. . . . Such a reworking and

expansion of the definition of France's responsibilities as a colonizer was in the logic of the Revolution, which saw itself as remaking French society and, in the process, receiving a mandate to transform all humankind. . . . The French had a special obligation to be generous toward those different from themselves and even to make them French." Conklin, *A Mission to Civilize*, 16, 18.

3. See once again Albert Memmi, *The Colonizer and the Colonized*, trans. Howard Greenfeld (Boston: Beacon Press, 1965), 91 [*Portrait du colonisé, précédé par portrait du colonisateur* (Paris: Gallimard, 1957), 112]: "Colonization creates the colonized just as we have seen that it creates the colonizer [*la colonisation fabrique les colonisés, comme nous avons vu qu'elle fabriquait les colonisateurs*]."

4. Albert Camus, *Chroniques algériennes: actuelles III* (Paris: Gallimard, 1958), reprinted in Albert Camus, *Essais* (Paris: Gallimard, Bibliothèque de la Pléiade, 1965), 909.

5. In "The Guest/Host," a drought and famine of the same type and magnitude are described: "It would be hard to forget the destitution, the army of ragged ghosts wandering in the sun, the plateaus burned to a cinder month after month, the earth shriveled up little by little, literally scorched, every stone busting into dust under one's foot. The sheep then died by thousands and even a few men, here and there, without it always being noticed." Albert Camus, *Exile and the Kingdom*, trans. Justin O'Brien (New York: Vintage Books, 1957), 87–88 [*Théâtre, récits, nouvelles* (Paris: Gallimard, Bibliothèque de la Pléiade, 1962), 1612].

6. In 1937, Camus drafted a "Manifesto of Intellectuals of Algeria in Favor of the Violette Project" on behalf of his fellow members of the "Maison de la Culture." The Blum-Violette Project would have given the right to vote to approximately sixty thousand Muslim Algerians, but because of the political influence of rich colonialists, even though it was cosponsored by Léon Blum, the project never came to a vote. The manifesto reads: "Considering that culture cannot live where dignity dies and that civilization cannot prosper under laws that crush it; that one cannot speak of culture, for example, in a country where 900,000 inhabitants are deprived of schools and civilization, and when it is a question of a people diminished by an unprecedented form of destitution and harassed by laws of exception and inhuman codes; Considering as well that the only way of restoring their dignity to the Muslim masses is to allow them to express themselves; . . . Considering finally that far from harming the interests of France this project serves them in the most positive way to the extent that it displays to the Arab people the face of humanity that should be that of France; . . . For all these reasons and for the good of culture and the popular masses to which the future of Muslim culture is closely connected, the following have decided to appeal to intellectuals of this country to indicate with their signature their support for the Violette Project, considered as a step in the

integral parliamentary emancipation of Muslims, and to declare with all their force and conscience that a project they consider a small part of the work of civilization and humanity should be that of the new France." The manifesto was originally published in *Jeune Méditerranée*, the monthly bulletin of the "Maison de la Culture" of Algiers, no. 2 (May 1937); reprinted in *Essais*, 1328–1329. Camus would remain faithful to the principles proclaimed in this manifesto for his entire life.

7. In the section of his essay "Algeria 1958" entitled "The New Algeria," Camus explains why he supports the Lauriol Plan for an Algeria federated with France, which is, he claims, similar to but more original than the Swiss model: "Algeria . . . offers the very rare example of different populations overlapping in the same territory. Hence it is essential to associate without fusing together (since federation is to begin with the union of differences), not different territories, but communities with different personalities." Albert Camus, *Resistance, Rebellion, and Death*, trans. Justin O'Brien (New York: Knopf, 1961), 149 [*Essais*, 1016]. Camus also acknowledges that the recognition of the relative autonomy of different Algerian communities that the Lauriol Plan would guarantee would necessitate a radical change in the French Constitution, something he feels is long overdue: "Contrary to all our practices, contrary above all to the deep-rooted prejudices inherited from the French Revolution, we should thus have sanctioned within the republic two equal but distinct categories of citizens. From one point of view this would mark a sort of revolution against the regime of centralization and abstract individualism resulting from 1789, which in so many ways, now deserves to be called the '*Ancien Régime*'" (151 [1018]).

8. Nowhere are the basic inequalities that result from exploitation and segregation and function as impediments to assimilation more evident, Camus claims, than in education: "The people of Kabylia will have more schools the day the artificial barrier that separates European education and indigenous education will have been eliminated, the day when finally, on the benches of the same school, two peoples capable of understanding each other will finally begin to understand each other. . . . If assimilation is truly desired, if it is desired that this so worthy people become French, it is necessary not to start out by separating them from the French. If I have understood correctly, that is all they are asking for. . . . It is up to us to tear down the walls separating us from each other" (*Essais*, 923). Without the destruction of the colonialist walls separating the different populations of Algeria in the schools, assimilation would remain only a broken promise. Camus insists that this does not have to be the case.

9. Ferhat Abbas wrote in a similar vein about the advantages of French schools for those Arabs and Berbers fortunate enough to have access to them and how a vast improvement in education could have produced a very different path toward independence: "School was our chance. It alone was emancipatory. . . . School was

also a remedy. It can attenuate the violence of antagonisms and heal wounds. It is at the doors of the school where the reconciliation of the races is forged, prejudices fall, hatreds are extinguished, and friendships formed. . . . What would have happened to Algeria if the schooling of the 'natives' . . . had been generalized? How would Algeria evolved if, by example, we had been able to be mayors, judges, prefects, high-ranking bureaucrats, superior officers, without having been obliged to renounce our religion? I say simply that the Algerian War would not have occurred. It is probable that Algeria would have become, one day or another, an independent country. But without bloodshed, without the death of hundreds, thousands of innocents, without racial hatred. It would have detached itself from metropolitan France just as a ripe fruit detaches itself from a tree: naturally." Ferhat Abbas, *Le jeune algérien (1930) suivi de rapport au Maréchal Pétain* (Paris: Editions Garnier Frères, 1981), 20–21.

10. Albert Camus, "Crisis in Algeria" (May 13–14, 1945), in *Camus at* Combat: *Writing 1944–1947*, ed. Jacqueline Lévi-Valensi, trans. Arthur Goldhammer (Princeton, N.J.: Princeton University Press, 2006), 200 [*Camus à* Combat: *éditoriaux et articles d'Albert Camus 1944–1947* (Paris: Gallimard, 2002), 500].

11. Historians agree that the figure of 1,500 Algerian deaths given by the French administration is much too low, while the figure of 40,000 deaths given by the FLN is most likely inflated. Most place the number of deaths resulting from the French retaliation to be between 6,000 and 10,000, but some still argue the true figure could be even higher.

12. For example, Mohammed Harbi argues that the chief lesson drawn by Algerians from the massacre of May 1945 was that "the idea of a multiracial society had not withstood the test. The gulf between the Algerian people and the European minority was growing so large as to be impossible." Mohammed Harbi, *Le FLN: mirage et réalité* (Paris: Éditions Jeune Afrique, 1980), 30.

13. In a postindependence work, Abbas continues to expresses ideas very close to Camus' and acknowledges that the means of achieving independence in Algeria could have been very different: " Throughout the entire century of colonization men rallied to protest the condition of the colonized and to demand their emancipation in the name of the lessons they had received from France. This is to say that the history of the last half-century could have been written differently. 'Revolution by law' was not a utopia. . . . In opposing every political change, the *colon* made it impossible." Ferhat Abbas, *Autopsie d'une guerre: l'aurore* (Paris: Garnier Frères, 1980), 14. In another chapter, he comments on the departure of the *pied-noir* community after independence: "No one, neither Camus, nor members of the Church, nor liberals, nor resistance fighters thought for one instant that Algeria was going to lose its French inhabitants. This exodus resulted from a spiral of reactive violence provoked by the French of Algeria themselves. Fascists, stray soldiers, congenital

racists, and 'Arab Eaters' all joined together to ruin the last chances for European populations in a new Algeria" (126).

14. Jeanyves Guérin argues that Camus, at least until after he had come to Algiers in 1956 to support his friends in their attempt to bring about a civilian truce, had not realized how little support there was for moderate solutions to the war or that his friends in the Truce Party "represented scarcely more than themselves. Camus clearly overestimated their number and influence. From Paris, he did not see (or did not want to see) that the war had pushed the poor whites over to the extremist side. His friends were off on their own and, like him, condemned to ineffectiveness. A few men of good will cannot influence the course of history." Jeanyves Guérin, *Albert Camus: portrait de l'artiste en citoyen* (Paris: Éditions François Bourin, 1993), 241.

15. See Paul-F. Smuts, ed., *Albert Camus éditorialiste à L'Express (mai 1955–février 1956)* (Paris: Gallimard, 1987). When asked by Jean Daniel why he had decided to return to journalism, Camus gave three reasons: "The first is that I am isolated in my era. I am also, as you know, in solidarity with it—and closely. The second is that journalism has always appeared to me as the most agreeable form of political involvement, on the condition of always saying everything. The third finally is that I want to bring Pierre Mendès-France back into power. We will be going through a very difficult period, and I have subjective reasons for wanting him. . . . When I went to see Mendès-France in 1945 at the Ministry of the Economy, he seemed to me when I met him for the first time to be a genuine statesman." Quoted in *Essais*, 1840.

16. "La Table Ronde," *Essais*, 971. This essay first appeared as an editorial in *L'Express* on October 13, 1955. Camus had made similar remarks in his open letter to Aziz Kessous, a friend who was a socialist and had been a member of Fehrat Abbas's Party of the Manifesto. His "Letter to an Algerian Militant" appeared in the first issue of Kessous's short-lived journal *Communauté algérienne* (October 1, 1955). In this essay, Camus evokes their friendship as a counterforce to the violence of the war and the sign that not all French and Arabs in Algeria were intent on "inflicting the greatest possible pain on each other, inexpiably" (*Resistance, Rebellion, and Death*, 127 [963]). In opposition to a tragedy that would end in total destruction, Camus projects a different destiny for the majority of the Algerians who he claims are like Kessous and himself: "You and I, who are so much alike—having the same background [the same culture—*de même culture*], sharing the same hope, having felt like brothers for so long now, united in our love for our land [*notre terre*]—know that we are not enemies and that we could live happily together on this soil [*cette terre*] that belongs to us. For it is ours, and I can no more imagine it without you and your brothers than you can probably separate it from me and those who resemble

me. You have said it very well, better than I can say: we are condemned to live together" (127 [963]).

17. Camus' notion of an "Algerian family" was very close to that of Germaine Tillion, who wrote two important studies of colonial Algeria that described the horrible conditions under which the colonized lived. Camus was influenced by her work and agreed with her description of what could be called the "family traits" of all Algerians in her study of the effects of colonialism: "'*Colons*' and 'natives' resemble each other like brothers—a sense of honor, physical courage, fidelity to their word and friends, generosity, tenacity—but also by their faults—a taste for violence, an unrestrained passion for competition, vanity, susceptibility, jealousy." Germaine Tillion, *L'Algérie en 1957* (Paris: Minuit, 1957), 17. Tillion states that it was colonialism itself that produced this "dysfunctional family" and that was the "epidemic" responsible for the destitution of the colonized. She adds, in a chapter entitled "The Link Between France and Algeria Is Not a Political Fiction," that it was not politicians or bureaucrats but rather "hundreds of thousands of people from each of the two countries, who, without intending it, without knowing it, wove together the millions of threads of the warp and woof [of the fabric connecting them] across the Mediterranean. This explains the gravity and irreversible character of the relations that commit us to each other, *on one side and the other*, beyond our own will" (90).

18. Jean Daniel, a fellow *pied-noir* and friend of Camus until their divergent politics separated them in the last years of Camus' life, describes his own trajectory in the following way: "Shortly before November 1, 1954, if I no longer believed in assimilation, I still felt—and the friends of Ferhat Abbas thought it as well!—that a Franco-Algerian federation still had some chances. After the launching of the insurrection, I understood that everything was lost if we didn't deal with the rebels as soon as possible." Jean Daniel, *Le temps qui reste: essai d'autobiographie professionnelle* (Paris: Stock, 1973), 76. In retrospect, he considers Camus, who "had the despondency of a prophet," to have been "the most lucid among us": "He declared that he knew his people, the French of Algeria with whom he would express his solidarity until the end, and that power would from then on no longer be in Paris but Algiers. He predicted the regroupings of liberals around the extremists, racist attacks, counterterrorism, and secession. He had seen in Algiers, at the moment when he proposed a truce for civilians, which the FLN had not rejected but which [General Governor of Algeria] Jacques Soustelle had sabotaged, the exasperation of passions and the insanity of mediocrities. In his mind, there was not much that could any longer be done. . . . We all tended to think, I did as well, that he was exaggerating, that his predictions were apocalyptic, and that he had found a reason to withdraw from a struggle that was literally making him sick. The future would prove that politically he was right" (78).

19. The English translation of the text in *Resistance, Rebellion, and Death* errone-ously gives the date as February 1956.

20. Mohamed Lebjaoui, who was a member of the first National Council of the Algerian Revolution and former chief of the Federation of France of the FLN, was also a friend of Camus' and a member of the group that proposed the civilian truce. Neither Camus nor his other French-Algerian friends knew that Lebjaoui and the other Arab-Algerian supporters of the movement were at that time already mem-bers of the FLN. Lebjaoui insists, however, that the FLN's commitment to the "Ap-peal for a Civilian Truce" was genuine: "This decision was taken by the national leadership after a long and serious discussion. In accepting to support the movement for a civilian truce, the leadership envisioned a gathering of European liberals in the hope of winning them gradually over to the idea of direct negotiations with the Front.... Our agreement in principle with a civilian truce was not a maneuver." Mohamed Lebjaoui, *Vérités sur la révolution algérienne* (Paris: Gallimard, 1970), 47.

21. Lebjaoui describes the group responsible for the "Appeal for a Civilian Truce," which started as a theater discussion group, in the following way: "There was at that time a group of remarkable men from all points of view, but very dis-tanced from political problems.... We began to get together and to talk. These discussions, as passionate, as concrete as they were, appear with the passing of time to be strangely unreal. The war had started, a ruthless war. Each day more men fell. But young Frenchmen and young Muslims, pretending to ignore all that, could still meet with each other to discuss the theater.... On our side there was Boualem Moussaoui (a future ambassador in Paris), Amar Ouzegane, Mouloud Amarane, myself, and several others. We were all militants who were already associated with the FLN. Not one of our French friends knew that—nor for an instant could they have imagined that such a thing could ever be possible." Lebjaoui, *Vérités sur la révolution algérienne*, 38–39.

22. Amar Ouzegane, another participant in the movement who was at the same time a member of the FLN, describes the meeting and Camus' speech in the fol-lowing emotional terms: "Our famous compatriot, sickened by the massacre of ci-vilian populations, volunteered to come to Algiers to make an appeal for a civilian truce and for the respect of children, women, and the old.... The generous idea of the future Nobel Prize recipient was identical to the sentiment expressed to us by Sheik Larbi Tebessi, who was shocked by the horrors perpetuated at Tébessa by the Foreign Legion against women and children.... This psychological encounter between two great Algerians, different by origin, language, culture, social milieu, faith, and ideals, is more than symbolic. It is the same cry of suffering and hope of two sons around the same mother, martyred Algeria." Amar Ouzegane, *Le meil-leur combat* (Paris: René Julliard, 1962), 231.

23. In an entry in his notebooks months after the appeal and dated October 1, 1956, Camus notes his visit with Germaine Tillion and describes her recent meeting with two leaders of the FLN in Algiers, whom she found out only afterward were Yassef Saadi and Ali la Pointe: "At that moment the one who seemed to be the leader said: 'You take us for assassins.' So Germaine Tillion replied: 'But you are assassins' (it was soon after the attack on the Casino of the cliff). Then the other, a terrible reaction: tears in his eyes. Then: 'Those bombs, I would like to see them at the bottom of the ocean.' 'That depends entirely on you,' said G. T. They then speak of torture. . . . They succeed in reaching an agreement. Suppression of terrorism against civilians against the suppression of executions. Approximately what I had proposed (but what followed, alas . . .)" Albert Camus, *Carnets III: mars 1951– décembre 1959* (Paris: Gallimard, 1989), 213.

24. As does Assia Djebar, in *Le blanc de l'Algérie* (Paris: Albin Michel, 1995), where she movingly describes Camus' appeal in the following terms: "Pale and tense, but determined, Albert Camus reads the text of a talk calling for a truce. With him on the podium, Ferhat Abbas, the moderate nationalist leader (who will join the FLN several months later) listens to the writer. Nationalist Muslims and French liberals mingle and fraternize with each other. This scene from the past will later seem to be from another age. Nevertheless, this dialogue which tried to continue could have led to an Algeria which, like its neighbors, would have come to independence without paying such a bloody price. All Franco-Algerian relations were not broken all at once: in short, a solution 'à la Mandela' of South Africa today could have materialized. Instead, it is the law of arms . . . that will settle things. That will settle things on a heap of civilian dead. A independent and sovereign state is constituted in 1962, bled dry" (127).

7. Last Words

1. In his 1958 preface to the republication of his first published work, *The Wrong Side and the Right Side* [*L'envers et l'endroit*], which contains lyrical essays originally written in 1935 and 1936 when he was twenty-two years old, Camus claims that "the final and most revolting injustice is consummated when poverty is wed to life without hope or the sky I found on reaching adulthood in the appalling slums of our [metropolitan] cities; everything must be done so that men can escape from the double humiliation of poverty [*la misère*] and ugliness." Albert Camus, *Lyrical and Critical Essays*, ed. Philip Thody, trans. Ellen Conroy Kennedy (New York: Vintage Books, 1968), 8 [*Essais* (Paris: Gallimard, Bibliothèque de la Pléiade, 1965), 7]. The

absence of natural beauty transforms a geographic space of destitution—unacceptable in itself—into a space of absolute injustice, one to which even the "extreme Arab poverty [of his native Algeria] cannot be compared" (8 [7]). Beauty in itself of course does not diminish destitution and injustice, but its absence in the cold, dreary, working-class suburbs of northern France, what he calls an "injustice of climate," raises them to another level. Camus describes his own childhood as being "halfway between poverty and the sun. Poverty kept me from thinking all was well under the sun and in history; the sun taught me that history was not everything. . . . It was not poverty that got in my way: in Africa, the sun and the sea cost nothing. The obstacle lay rather in prejudices or stupidity" (7 [6]).

2. Albert Camus, *Exile and the Kingdom*, trans. Justin O'Brien (New York: Vintage Books, 1957), 98 [*Théâtre, récits, nouvelles* (Paris: Gallimard, Bibliothèque de la Pléiade, 1962), 91].

3. As we have seen, during his trial, Meursault claims that it "because of the sun" that he killed his victim, which provokes laughter in the courtroom. Albert Camus, *The Stranger*, trans. Stuart Gilbert (New York: Vintage Books, 1954), 130 [*Théâtre, récits, nouvelles* (Paris: Gallimard, Bibliothèque de la Pléiade, 1962), 1166]. His reason for returning to the spot where the initial confrontation between the Arabs and the French had taken place was not to seek revenge for his friend having been knifed, since for him, "the incident was closed" (74 [1167]). It was rather to flee the sun: "The small black lump of rock came into view far down the beach. It was rimmed by a dazzling sheen of light and feathery spray, but I was thinking of the cold, clear stream behind it, and wanting to hear again the murmur of its water, wanting to flee the sun . . . and to find again shade and rest" (73, trans. mod. [1167]).

4. See especially "The New Mediterranean Culture," a talk Camus gave on February 8, 1937, for the inauguration of the "Maison de la Culture" in Algiers. In the talk, he first rejects all notions of a Mediterranean nationalism and the Roman roots of Mediterranean identity and then praises its living, culturally hybrid nature: "The Mediterranean lies elsewhere. It is the very denial of Rome and Latin genius. It is living and wants nothing to do with abstractions. . . . The Mediterranean, an international basin traversed by every current, is perhaps the only land linked to great ideas from the East. . . . The most basic aspect of Mediterranean genius springs perhaps from this historically and geographically unique encounter between East and West." Camus, *Lyrical and Critical Essays*, 193–194 [*Essais*, 1324–1325].

5. In Memmi's 1965 preface to *The Colonizer and the Colonized*, he refers to himself as "a sort of *métis* of colonization." Albert Memmi, *The Colonizer and the Colonized*, trans. Howard Greenfeld (Boston: Beacon Press, 1965), xvi [*Portrait du colonisé, précédé par portrait du colonisateur* (Paris: Gallimard, 1957), 29]. In his preface to

Memmi's early autobiographical novel, *La statue de sel*, Camus insists on Memmi's ambiguous identity: "Here is a French writer from Tunisia who is neither French nor Tunisian. He's scarcely Jewish, because in a sense he doesn't want to be. The curious subject of the book . . . is the impossibility for a Tunisian Jew of French culture to be anything precise at all." Albert Camus, in Albert Memmi, *La statue de sel* (Paris: Gallimard, 1966), 10. In a similar vein, Jacques Derrida describes his own "identity problems" in the following way: "To be Franco-Machrebian, one 'like myself,' is not . . . to have a surfeit or richness of identities, attributes, or names. In the first place, it would rather betray a *disorder of identity* [trouble de l'identité]." Jacques Derrida, *Monolingualism of the Other; or, The Prosthesis of Origin*, trans. Patrick Mensah (Palo Alto, Calif.: Stanford University Press, 1998), 14 [*Le monolinguisme de l'autre ou la prothèse d'origine* (Paris: Galilée, 1996), 32].

6. Comery, without the first "r," is in fact the family name of Camus' paternal grandmother, who was born in Algeria in 1852. All references to *The First Man* in this chapter are to Albert Camus, *The First Man*, trans. David Hapgood (New York: Vintage Books, 1995) [*Le premier homme* (Paris: Gallimard, 1994)].

7. The "first men" of Camus' Algeria are of course explicitly *men*, and women, outside of Jacques Cormery's mother and grandmother, have little if any role to play in the novel. At the same time, it could be argued that the real subject of the novel is not the son, but his silent, illiterate mother. It is in fact to Camus' own illiterate mother that the novel is dedicated or addressed: "Intercessor: Widow Camus. To you who will never be able to read this book" (3, [11]). In the novel, through an uncorrected slip of the pen, Camus' mother is directly identified with the fictional Jacques Cormery's mother. To receive her war widow's pension each quarter, Jacques' mother must each time sign her name to a form: "After the first time when she had problems, a neighbor (?) had taught her to copy a sample of the signature 'Widow Camus', and she managed to do this more or less well, but anyway it was always accepted" (206 [189]).

8. Nowhere in his work is Camus closer to the turn-of-the-century Catholic poet Charles Péguy, who like Camus' own father died at the beginning of World War I, than in his presentation of what could be called the civic virtues of poverty and anonymity. Péguy, for example, describes the authenticity and "spirituality" of the poor (but for him, exclusively Catholic) French in the following way: "Being poor and French, Catholic and peasant, [the most authentic Frenchman] has no family papers. . . . Nothing that left any trace in the papers of *notaires*. They never possessed anything. . . . [The poor Catholic] sees nothing but an immense mass and a vast race, and immediately after, immediately behind, he distinguishes nothing else. . . . He plunges with pride into this anonymity. The anonymous is his patrimony. Anonymity is his immense patrimony. The more communal the land is, the more he

wants to grow out of the land." Charles Péguy, "Note conjointe sur M. Descartes et la philosophie cartésienne," in *Oeuvres en prose complètes* (Paris: Gallimard, Bibliothèque de la Pléiade, 1992), 3:1298–1299. Unlike Péguy, of course, Camus' defense of the virtues of poverty is secular and has nothing to do with Catholicism.

9. If the colonized (both Arab and Berber) are referred as "the Arabs," Jacques Cormery's mother and his entire family refer to the citizens of mainland France in the same general terms as "the French." When Jacques tells his mother that his father's grave in France, which she has never visited, is well kept and has flowers on it, she responds by saying, "Yes. The French are good people" (73 [73]), as if she herself were not French.

10. Omar Carlier, after arguing that no people is by nature more violent than another, for, as he puts it, "there is no violence gene," explains atrocities similar to the scene that appears in Camus' novel in the following way: "To cut the sex of the enemy and put it in his mouth is to humiliate and defy the dead and to pursue him after death, to condemn him not to arrive intact in the afterlife, and even worse, to have him make the journey in a ignominious state. This anthropological form of violence returned during the war of Independence, and the FLN had trouble eliminating it, even against its own men." Omar Carlier, "Violences," in *La guerre d'Algérie: 1954–2004, la fin de l'amnésie*, edited by Mohammed Harbi and Benjamin Stora (Paris: Robert Laffont, 2004), 347, 377.

11. "And those who still heroically think that a brother should die rather than principles, I shall limit myself to admiring them from afar. I am not of their race." Albert Camus, "Preface," in *Resistance, Rebellion, and Death*, trans. Justin O'Brien (New York: Knopf, 1961), trans. mod., 113 [*Essais* (Paris: Gallimard, Bibliothèque de la Pléiade, 1965), 892–893].

12. I therefore agree with Jeffrey Isaac's criticism of Michael Walzer's assertion that because of his "connectedness" with the *pied-noir* community, Camus valued French lives more than Arab lives: "I think that Walzer is wrong when he writes, for example, that 'Camus would not have said . . . that French lives and Arab lives were of equal importance in his eyes. French lives, even *pied noir* lives, on the wrong side of history, meant more to him—just as Arab lives meant more to the intellectuals of the FLN' [Michael Walzer, *The Company of Critics: Social Criticism and Political Commitment in the Twentieth Century* (New York: Basic Books, 1988), 146]. . . . Certainly as a *pied noir* his own community and its culture mattered more to him than the community and culture of the Arabs. But it does not follow that French-Algerian lives mattered more, that he was any less pained by the suffering of Arab children than he was by the suffering of French children." Jeffrey C. Isaac, *Arendt, Camus, and Modern Rebellion* (New Haven, Conn.: Yale University Press, 1992), 194–195. There is ample evidence in his writings that this is the case, that Camus

was not just "pained" by the suffering of both Arab and French children and other innocent civilians but made saving innocent lives the first principle of his perspective on politics, that which had to come first, before everything else. If different value were to be given to different lives, then terrorism could in fact be justified.

13. In "Algeria 1958," Camus lists what he considers to be legitimate in Arab demands and the injustices he claims "every Frenchman" knows the Arabs are right to point out and reject: "(1) Colonialism and its abuses, which are well-established. (2) The perennial lie of constantly proposed but never realized assimilation. . . . (3) The obvious injustice of the agrarian allocation and of the distribution of income (sub-proletariat). . . . (4) The psychological suffering; the often scornful or indifferent manner of many French, and the development among the Arabs (as a result of a series of stupid measures being taken) of the complex of humiliation that is at the center of the present drama." Camus, *Resistance, Rebellion, and Death*, 144, trans. mod. [*Essais*, 1011–1012].

14. "Cain" was one of the titles Camus considered for his short story "The Guest/ Host," and the "abominable" and mad actions of men under "a ferocious sun" of course evoke the madness and devotion to violence of "The Renegade." In the "Notes and Sketches" Camus made for *The First Man* can be found the following entry: "Chapter *going backwards*: Hostages Kabyle village. Emasculated soldiers— raids, etc., back step by step to the first shot fired during colonization. But why stop there? Cain killed Abel" (304, trans. mod. [300]).

15. In the French text, the quotation marks appear at the beginning but not at the end of the wish or plea expressed by Jacques (by all first men?), and even if it is simply an uncorrected mistake or an editorial oversight, it seems fitting that the quotation itself should remain open, unfinished, unending.

Conclusion. Terrorism and Torture

1. David Ignatius in his editorial in the *Washington Post* quotes from the flier that the Pentagon sent out announcing the showing of film, which, as he phrases it, "puts it in eerie perspective": "How to win a battle against terrorism and lose the war of ideas. . . . Children shoot soldiers at point blank range. Women plant bombs in cafes. Soon the entire Arab population builds to a mad fervor. Sound familiar? The French have a plan. It succeeds tactically, but fails strategically. To understand why, come to a rare showing of this film." David Ignatius, "Think Strategy, Not Numbers," *The Washington Post* (August 26, 2003). Ignatius in this article avoids any mention of the French systematic use of torture (which was at the heart of the "tac-

tics" that supposedly succeeded so brilliantly) and claims that the fact that the Pentagon's special operations chiefs arranged the showing of the film is "a hopeful sign that the military is thinking creatively and unconventionally about Iraq." "Thinking creatively" and justly would seem to be exactly what the military and political leaders were not doing. The use of torture can never be considered "creative."

2. Albert Camus, "Neither Victims nor Executioners," (*Combat*, November 19–30, 1946), in *Camus at* Combat: *Writing 1944–1947*, ed. Jacqueline Lévi-Valensi, trans. Arthur Goldhammer (Princeton, N.J.: Princeton University Press, 2006) [*Camus à* Combat: *éditoriaux et articles d'Albert Camus 1944–1947* (Paris: Gallimard, 2002)].

3. This is the term Jeffrey Isaac uses in his book to describe the politics of both Arendt and Camus. For example, he states in his introduction that his "aim is not to present these thinkers as saints or authorities, only as exemplary theorists and political actors, who point the way toward a rebellious politics that is alive to many of the concerns of postmodern writing and yet is self-assuredly normative and humanistic." Jeffrey C. Isaac, *Arendt, Camus, and Modern Rebellion* (New Haven, Conn.: Yale University Press, 1992), 12.

4. Albert Camus, *The First Man*, trans. David Hapgood (New York: Vintage Books, 1995), 75 [*Le premier homme* (Paris: Gallimard, 1994), 87].

Abbas, Ferhat, 142–44, 152, 208n. 4,
220–21n. 9, 221–22n. 13, 222–23n.
16, 223n. 18, 225n. 24

Algerian War, xii–xiii, 4, 6, 9, 12–14,
22, 25, 55, 57, 63, 83, 90, 104, 120,
129, 133–34, 139, 143, 145, 221n. 5,
221n. 9; Camus' condemnation of
tactics of both sides, 85–86, 89–90,
97–98, 108–13, 180–81, 184, 190–91n.
18, 195n. 10; comparison with war
in Iraq, xii–xiii, 179–80, 229–30n. 1;
relation of *The Plague* to, 55–57

Algérie française, 8, 108, 147, 180–81

Ali la Pointe, 225n. 23

allegory, in *The Plague*, 45, 50–59, 86,
202–3n. 22

anguish: of Algerians during war,
148–53, 175, 185; of condemned
criminal, 88, 105

Arabs, xi, xiii, 46, 49–52, 68, 72, 78–80,
104, 106, 108–9, 133, 136–38, 141–45,
151, 155, 162, 167, 172–73, 191n. 19,
194n. 7, 195n. 12, 196n. 13, 204n. 4,
220n. 9, 224n. 20, 226n. 3, 228n. 9;
absence or anonymity of in Camus'
fictions, 20–21, 25–37, 49–50, 52,
58, 74–78, 81, 162, 197n. 16; colonialist myths of, 62, 65–67, 218n. 2;
colonialists' hatred and oppression
of, 22–25, 65, 67, 76–78, 169, 183,
190–91n. 18, 200nn. 12–13, 202n.
20, 203n. 2, 204n. 7, 221–22n. 13;
as colonized French subjects or
nationals in Algeria, 1–6, 37, 47, 74,
162; living conditions of in Algeria,
2–6, 64, 102–12, 176–77, 188n. 4,
225–26n. 1, 229n. 13; overlapping
of condition and fate of French
Algerians with, 31–33, 35–37, 74, 76,
79, 82–83, 145–48, 162, 171, 187–88n.
2, 190–91n. 18, 194n. 7, 222–23n. 16;
recognition of, as a people, 139–40,
219n. 6; as soldiers in French army,
138, 164; as victims of violence,

Arabs (*continued*)
107–12, 114–21, 139, 169–70, 180,
228–29n. 12, 229–30n. 1
Arendt, Hannah, 192n. 20, 217n. 19,
218n. 24, 230n. 3
Aronson, Ronald, 113, 190n. 13, 210n.
13, 213n. 8
assimilation, 4, 33, 47–49, 196–97n. 15,
210n. 10; myth, promise, and failure
of, 131–43; Camus' idea of, 135–43,
220n. 8, 229n. 13

Balibar, Etienne, 39–42, 197n. 17, 198n.
2, 199–200n. 9
Barrès, Maurice, 36, 189n. 7,
197–98n. 18
Barthes, Roland, 54–55, 194–95n. 9,
195n. 11, 201n. 17
Battle of Algiers, 63, 113–14, 153,
179–80, 184
Beckett, Samuel, 123, 217n. 23
Berbers, 1–6, 22, 49, 55, 58, 64, 68,
82, 102, 104, 107, 109, 111–12, 118,
120, 136–37, 141–42, 145, 151, 162,
172–73, 180, 190n. 18, 220n. 9,
228n. 9
borders, colonial, 39–46, 53–54, 69, 71;
cultural, 39–48; of Oran, 48, 59
Brasillach, Robert, 97, 209n. 9
Brée, Germaine, 190n. 13,
190–91n. 18

Cain, 173–74, 205n. 11, 229n. 14
Camus, Albert: the absurd, 7, 9–11,
32, 37; agnosticism, religious and
political, 8, 91, 103; Algeria as true
country of, 3, 8, 15, 155–59, 164,
177; anonymity, problem of, 20–33,
75–78, 82, 161–66, 175–77, 197n.
16, 227n. 8; anticommunism, 8, 86,
102–3; capital punishment, argument against, 28–29, 37, 85–93, 95,
97, 102–4, 195n. 10, 208n. 7, 209nn.
8–9; death penalty as legal or justified murder, 29–30, 86–91, 100–104,
107–11, 113, 195n. 10, 201n. 19,
215–16n. 13; editorialist at *L'Express*,
144–46, 187–88n. 2, 222nn. 15–16;
portraits of colonizers in fictions, 22,
65–67, 122, 192n. 1, 203–4n. 3, 211n.
4; postcolonial critique of, xii–xiii,
12–15, 20–21, 25, 43, 45, 49–58, 61,
64–66, 97, 110, 117, 144
Camus, Albert, works: "The Adulterous Woman" ("La femme adultère"),
63–72, 80, 156, 205n. 8; "Appeal
for a Civilian Truce," 144–47,
224nn. 21–22; *Algerian Reports*
(*Chroniques algériennes*), 63, 108–12,
158, 167, 175, 204n. 4; "Destitution
of Kabylia" ("Misère de la Kabylie"), 134–38, 220n. 8; *Exile and the
Kingdom* (*L'exil et le royaume*), 14,
63–83, 122–29, 203nn. 1–2, 204nn.
5–7, 217n. 21, 219n. 5; *The Fall* (*La
Chute*), 7, 123, 198–99n. 5, 203n. 1;
The First Man (*Le premier homme*),
xiii, 14, 16, 86, 158–77, 183, 187n.
1, 188n. 4, 204n. 4, 205n. 10, 207n.
1, 227n. 6, 229n. 14; "The Guest"
("L'hôte"), 20, 63, 73–83, 156, 162,
219n. 5, 229n. 14; "The Just" ("Les
justes"), 201n. 19, 216n. 16; "Manifesto of Intellectuals of Algeria
in Favor of the Violette Project,"
219–20n. 6; *The Myth of Sisyphus* (*Le
mythe de Sisyphe*), 9–10; "Neither
Victims nor Executioners" ("Ni
victimes ni bourreaux"), 98–100, 121,
146, 181; "The New Mediterranean

Culture," 226n. 4; *The Plague* (*La peste*), 49–60, 86, 201n. 17, 202–3n. 22, 207n. 3, 209–10n. 11; *The Rebel* (*L'homme révolté*), 57, 168, 181, 189n. 10, 201n. 14, 210n. 13; "Reflections on the Guillotine" ("Réflexions sur la guillotine"), 29–30, 86–90, 195n. 10; "The Renegade" ("Le renégat ou un esprit confus"), 63, 122–29, 156, 167, 180, 217n. 21, 218n. 25, 229n. 14; *The Stranger* (*L'étranger*), 7, 9–11, 14, 20, 22, 24–37, 45, 74–75, 81–82, 86, 92, 162, 194nn. 7–9, 195nn. 11–12, 196nn. 13–14, 207n. 1, 226n. 3;

Camus, Catherine (Camus' daughter), 187n. 1

Camus, Catherine Hélène Sintès (Camus' mother), 2, 87–88, 97, 104–5, 162, 175–77, 209n. 10, 227n. 7

Camus, Lucien (Camus' father), 1–2, 86–89, 92, 95, 97–98, 103, 161, 163–68, 170, 227n. 8

Carlier, Omar, 56, 198n. 1, 228n. 10

Césaire, Aimé, 52, 200n. 12

Cherki, Alice, 216–17n. 18

civilizing mission (*mission civilisatrice*) of French colonialism, 24, 47, 131–32, 135

collaboration (with Nazi Germany), 10–11, 92, 95

colonialism, xii–xiii, 1–2, 4, 6–9, 12–15, 19–22, 24–26, 29, 33, 35, 37, 40–64, 70–76, 78–80, 82, 89, 97, 108–10, 112–13, 115–17, 119, 120–21, 131–42, 146–47, 156–57, 171–74, 177, 181, 184, 189n. 8, 192n. 1, 193n. 5, 198nn. 1, 4, 199–200n. 9, 200n. 12, 204–5n. 8, 213n. 8, 214nn. 9, 11, 216n. 15, 218n. 1, 220n. 8, 223n. 17; Camus' criticism of, 18, 69–72, 108–10, 112–13,

135–44, 151–53, 175–77, 184, 229n. 13; colonialist apology for, 45–49; demise of, 9, 133–35; effects of, xii, 20, 39–45, 133–34, 223n. 17; hospitality as antithesis of, 73–81; as plague, 55–61; similarities with Nazism, 51–53, 200n. 12

colonized (the), 1–2, 4, 18–20, 64, 66, 69–70, 132–34, 140–42, 162, 167–71, 188n. 3, 216n. 14, 219n. 3, 221–22n. 13, 228n. 9; colonizers' domination and hatred of, 23–26; destitution of, 134–37; humiliation of, 109, 155, 192n. 1, 193–94n. 6, 199–200n. 9, 203–4n. 3; invisibility or absence of, 46–52; Meursault in the place of, 31–32, 37, 194n. 7; reversal of position of, 76–82; violence and, 115–20, 141, 173, 214–15n. 11, 215n. 12, 223n. 17

colonizers (colonialists, *colons*), xii–xiii, 1, 8, 12–15, 20–25, 64–68, 70–71, 78, 115, 120, 133, 135, 137, 141, 147, 162, 170, 173, 189n. 8, 191n. 19, 192n. 1, 218–19n. 2, 219n. 6, 223n. 17; Camus' portraits of, 65–72; as *colons*, 24, 64, 78, 106, 132, 135, 141, 147, 162, 170, 191n. 19, 223n. 17; liberal or leftist, 109, 133, 229n. 4; Meursault as embodiment of, 25–26; myth of first to arrive in Algeria, 160–61; relation to colonized, 1–2, 19–20, 25–26, 76, 78–79, 82, 133, 137, 173, 188n. 3, 189n. 8, 192n. 1, 193–94n. 6, 200n. 10, 203–4n. 3, 219n. 3

Combat, 5, 7, 52–54, 92–103, 138–43, 146, 200n. 13, 202n. 20, 208nn. 6–8, 213n. 7, 221n. 10, 230nn. 1–2

Conklin, Alice, 132, 218n. 1, 218–19n. 2

counterterrorism (counterterrorist), xii,
    6, 102–4, 107–8, 111, 113–14, 116,
    144, 169–71, 174, 179–80, 182–85,
    214n. 11, 223n. 18
Crémieux Decree, 37, 196n. 15, 199n. 7,
    201n. 15

Daniel, Jean, 11, 214n. 9, 222n. 15,
    223n. 18
democracy (democratic), 85, 89, 92, 97,
    109, 132–33, 182, 212n. 5; critique
    of imperialist forms of, 91, 103–4,
    142–43, 181, 202n. 20; desire for in
    Algeria, xi–xii, 4–6; 15, 21, 117, 135,
    140–43, 180, 209n. 10; perversion of
    in colonies, 4, 108, 133, 136–43, 189n.
    8, 202n. 20, 209n. 10, 218n. 1
Derrida, Jacques, 38, 73, 189n. 6,
    205nn. 11–12, 227n. 5
Dib, Mohamed, 188n. 1
Djebar, Assia, 225n. 24

education, colonized deprived of,
    219–20n. 6, 220n. 8, 220–21n. 9
ends and means, 56–57, 89–91, 97, 101,
    104, 107–8, 116–19, 132, 139–42, 149,
    152, 165–71, 175, 180–85, 212n. 5,
    216–17n. 18, 218n. 1, 221n. 13
ethnicity, 71, 151, 158, 160; fictive, 35,
    197n. 17
exclusion, interior (internal), 42, 47–48,
    199–200n. 9
exile, 4, 64–71, 74, 80–82, 157, 176,
    203n. 1

Fanon, Frantz, 114–19, 121–22, 170–72,
    191n. 19, 198n. 1, 214n. 9, n. 11,
    215nn. 12–13, 216nn. 14–15, 18,
    217n. 19

Feraoun, Mouloud, 106, 178, 212–13n. 6,
    215–16n. 13
FLN (Front de Libération Nationale),
    xii–xiii, 4–5, 117–20, 139, 144–49,
    152–53, 184, 191n. 19, 208n. 4,
    212nn. 5–6, 216nn. 13, 15, 221nn.
    11–12, 224nn. 20–22, 225nn. 23–24,
    228n. 12; Camus' opposition to, xii,
    8, 13–15, 55–56, 107–14, 152, 170,
    181, 192n. 2, 223n. 18; support for
    in France, 8, 21, 109–11, 114–21, 143–
    46, 170–71, 223n. 18; use of terror-
    ism, 4, 8, 15, 63, 97, 109–14, 170–73,
    179–81, 206n. 15, 214n. 9, 216n. 15,
    225n. 13, 228n. 10
freedom, xi, 5, 10–11, 32, 51, 63–64,
    67–73, 75, 80–82, 97, 99, 105, 108–9,
    113, 116, 118, 127, 137–38, 140–42,
    156, 172, 181, 184–85, 202n. 19,
    211n. 1, 218n. 1
French Algeria (French Algerians), xi,
    1–6, 8–9, 23–25, 47, 51, 66, 70, 72, 74,
    82, 104, 111, 118, 140, 142, 145–46,
    151, 159–60, 162, 164, 169–70, 180,
    200n. 13, 204n. 4
French subjects (nationals), 1, 4, 6, 33, 74

de Gaulle, Charles, 4, 209n. 9
Gearhart, Suzanne, 200n. 9
Girard, René, 193n. 5
Guérin, Jeanyves, 144, 191n. 20,
    222n. 14

Harbi, Mohammed, 221n. 12
hospitality, 22, 68; absolute or pure form
    of, 70, 75–77, 80–83, 172, 205–6n. 12;
    in "The Guest" ("L'Hôte"), 73–83;
    paradoxes of in a colonial context, 73–
    76, 79; trait of *pieds-noirs*, 22, 193n. 4

host, 73–83, 205n. 11

L'Humanité, 200n. 13

hybridity, cultural, 4, 8, 16, 42, 44–47, 157, 198n. 4, 211n. 3, 226n. 4

ideology, 7–8, 21, 65, 122–23, 128, 132–33, 136, 149, 218n. 24, 218n. 1; Camus' critique of, 99–102, 151, 181–82

Ignatius, David, 229–30n. 1

injustice, 74, 90, 99–100, 104, 108, 151, 173–74, 182–83; of capital punishment, 37, 88; colonialist form of, xii–xiii, 7, 9, 14–15, 21, 28–29, 49–52, 55, 57–58, 64, 75, 77–80, 85, 109, 112, 120, 132–34, 138–40, 142–43, 145, 151–52, 155–56, 167, 172–74, 180–84, 193n. 4, 196n. 13, 212n. 5, 225–26n. 1, 229n. 1; of Nazi Germany and Vichy France, 92, 96

Iraq, war in, 179, 229–30n. 1

Isaac, Jeffrey C., 191–92n. 20, 211n. 3, 213–14n. 8, 217n. 19, 228n. 12, 230n. 3

Jeanson, Francis, 189n. 10, 210n. 13

Jews, Algerian, 3, 37, 58, 147, 196n. 15, 199n. 7, 201n. 15, 204n. 4; persecution of 51, 92, 98, 189n. 7, 210n. 14, 208n. 5

Judt, Tony, 12–13, 190n. 17

justice, 5, 7, 13–15, 29, 31, 104, 108, 127, 167, 175, 180–85; for Arab and Berber Algerians, xi, xiii–xiv, 5–9, 11, 13–16, 29, 31–32, 36–37, 49–51, 82–83, 85–91, 108, 120, 136, 138, 140, 142, 149–50, 167–68, 170–72, 175, 177–78, 180–85, 187n. 2, 196n. 13, 202n. 20, 209n. 10, 213–14n. 8; and

capital punishment (murder), 85–98, 103, 120, 182, 213n. 7; and ideology, 99–103, 129, 182; and purge trials, 92–98, 104, 208–9n. 8; in *The Stranger*, 28–37

Kabyle (Kabylie), 134–38, 191n. 19, 220n. 8, 229n. 14

Kessous, Aziz, 206n. 13, 222–23n. 16

Lauriol Plan, 213–14n. 8, 220n. 7

Lebjaoui, Mohamed, 224nn. 20–21

Lespès, René, 45–49, 199n. 7

Lévi-Valensi, Jacqueline, 200n. 13, 208n. 6, 213n. 7, 221n. 10, 230n. 2

Lottman, Herbert, 188n. 2, 190n. 13, 208n. 7, 210n. 13

Lyotard, Jean-François, 212n. 5

Marrus, Michael R., 196n. 15

Mauriac, François, 96, 208–9n. 8

McCarthy, Patrick, 188n. 2, 194n. 7

Mediterranean, 3, 9–10, 45, 156, 158, 193n. 4, 223n. 17, 226n. 4

Memmi, Albert, 19, 22, 26, 40, 65, 109, 133, 137, 188n. 3, 189n. 8, 192n. 1, 193–94n. 6, 200n. 10, 203–4n. 3, 211n. 4, 216n. 14, 219n. 3, 226–27n. 5

Mendès-France, Pierre, 145, 147, 222n. 15

Mitterand, François, 4, 208–9n. 8

multicultural, xi–xii, 4–5, 16, 117, 136, 152, 158, 187n. 1, 188n. 4, 193n. 4

natives (indigènes), in Algeria, 3–4, 24, 46–48, 115, 140–41, 160, 162, 164, 199nn. 7–9, 215n. 11, 221n. 9, 223n. 17

Nazi Germany (Nazi), 5, 7, 50–54, 58, 92, 95, 97–99, 135, 181–82, 201n. 14, 202n. 22

new men, birth or creation of, 108, 111, 116, 151, 171, 175, 215n. 13, 217n. 18

Nora, Pierre, 21–26, 193n. 4

O'Brien, Conor Cruise, 11–13, 20–21, 25–26, 29, 43, 49–55, 190–91n. 18, 192n. 2, 196n. 13

Occupation, the German, 10, 50–51, 54, 60, 181

Oran, 201n. 15; Camus' depiction of in *The Plague*, 45, 49–60; colonialist depiction of, 45–49, 199nn. 7–8

Ouzegane, Amir, 224nn. 21–22

Paxton, Robert O., 196n. 15

Péguy, Charles, 227–28n. 8

Pélégri, Jean, 193n. 4

Pétain, Philippe (Maréchal), 37, 94, 199n. 7, 208n. 7

pieds-noirs, xi, 11–12, 26, 39, 67, 111, 137, 162, 169–73, 196n. 13, 221n. 13, 223n. 18, 228n. 12; differences with French of continent, 3–5, 23–25, 171, 193n. 4, 194n. 7; divided identity of, 2–5, 22–25, 211n. 3; liberal minority of, 144, 146; and racism, 6, 22–25, 67, 111, 169, 202n. 20

politics, limits of, xiv, 15, 56, 85–86, 110, 117, 120, 150, 165–69, 171, 182, 185, 201–2n. 19

Poncet, Charles, 189n. 9

Pontecorvo, Gillo ("The Battle of Algiers"), 179–80, 184

postcolonial (postcolonialism), xi–xiv, 11, 15, 20, 39–45, 63, 81, 135, 198n. 4, 217n. 19

purge trials, 92–98, 104

race, 7, 35–36, 52, 151, 166–70, 183, 188n. 4, 190n. 18, 197n. 17, 198n. 18, 199n. 9, 204n. 4, 211n. 1, 221n. 9, 227n. 8, 228n. 11

racism, 6–7, 23, 53, 65, 67, 132, 190n. 18, 199n. 9, 204nn. 6–7, 218n. 1

realism, literary-historical, 13, 50, 64, 69, 201n. 17, 204–5n. 8; political, 15, 102–3, 110, 113, 144, 182

Rebatet, Lucien, 97

resistance, 5–7, 45, 50–57, 60–61, 63, 86, 92, 98, 102, 104, 106, 138, 141, 170, 181–83, 201n. 17, n. 19, 208n. 5, 209n. 8, 211n. 1, 221n. 13

Resistance, French, 5–7, 45, 51, 55, 104, 208n. 5, 209n. 8

revolution (revolutionary), 85–86, 89–92, 110, 132, 150, 157, 168, 173, 181, 210n. 11, 218n. 2, 220n. 7, 221n. 13; faith in and redemptive characteristics of, 57, 102–4, 119, 122, 201–2n. 19, 212n. 5, 216n. 14; as justification for violence, 115–16, 119–22, 191n. 19, 198n. 1, 210n. 11; represented by FLN, 6, 8, 113, 115–16, 118–19, 198n. 3, 212n. 5, 214n. 9, 224n. 20

Saadi, Yassef, 225n. 23

Said, Edward, 12–13, 41–44, 68, 122, 124, 128, 191n. 19, 198n. 4, 204–5n. 8, 205n. 9

salvation, 56–57, 116, 119, 129, 156, 217n. 18

Sartre, Jean-Paul, 9–11, 103, 110, 113–15, 119–22, 170–72, 189n. 10, 190n. 13, 191n. 19, 198n. 1, 210n. 13, 214n. 9, 216n. 18, 217n. 19

Sétif, massacre at, 52, 58, 139–40, 143, 200n. 13, 220nn. 11–12

Soustelle, Jacques, 223n. 18
Stora, Benjamin, 198n. 3

terror, 57, ideological climate and
    destructive effects of, 98–101, 104,
    125, 129, 181–85; of Nazi Germany,
    52–53, 99, 182; use in Algeria, 53,
    57–58, 90–91, 104, 106, 110, 116–20,
    146, 150–51, 169, 174–75, 180–85,
    209n. 10; revolutionary use of, 90–91,
    168–69
terrorism (terrorist), xii–xiii, 41, 52,
    97, 195n. 10, 201n. 19, 210–11n. 1,
    215–16n. 13, 216n. 16, 228–29n. 12;
    Camus' condemnation of, xiii, 15, 85,
    89, 97, 102–21, 129, 146–53, 167–75,
    180–85, 191n. 19, 209n. 10, 225n. 23;
    FLN use of, xii, 4–8, 57, 63, 107–21,
    144, 148–53, 169–75, 178–83, 212n. 5,
    225n. 23; global war on, xii, 179–80,
    182–83, 185, 229–30n. 1; revolution-
    ary justification for, 110–11, 114–21,
    170–71
Tillion, Germaine, 191n. 19, 223n. 17,
    225n. 23
Todd, Olivier, 188nn. 1–2, 189n. 9,
    190n. 13, 200n. 13, 209n. 9, 210n. 13,
    213n. 7
torture, 125, 171–72, 182; French use
    of in Algerian War, 4–5, 15, 63, 89,
    98, 107–8, 110–14, 119, 125, 148, 150,
    152–53, 179–82, 185, 191n. 19, 195n.
    10, 196n. 13, 225n. 23, 229–30n. 1;
    Nazi use of, 92–95, 172

Vichy France, 6, 10, 28, 35, 37, 92–98,
    196–97n. 15, 201n. 15, 202n. 20,
    208n. 5

Vidal-Naquet, Pierre, 196n. 13,
    217n. 20
violence: against civilians, 83, 108–21,
    146, 149–50, 169, 180, 221n. 13; of
    colonialist system and colonialists,
    26, 53, 75, 82–83, 115–21, 140–42,
    164–65, 167, 169–73, 197n. 16, 198n.
    1, 214–15n. 11, 221n. 13, 223n. 17,
    228n. 10; as counterviolence, 78,
    108–121, 141–42, 171, 173, 214–15n.
    11; cycle of, 82–83, 109–12, 121,
    124–29, 170, 172–74, 183; defense
    and mystification of, 110–11, 114–21,
    191n. 19, 215n. 12, 216–17n. 18, 217n.
    19; Fanon on, 113–19, 121, 170–71,
    214–15n. 11, 215nn. 12–13, 216–17n.
    18, 217n. 19; of ideology and absolute
    faith, 125–29, 156, myth of origin
    of, 171–74; in "The Renegade,"
    122–29, 156, 170, 229n. 14; Sartre
    on, 113–15, 119–21, 170–71, 216–17n.
    18, 217n. 19; unlimited, 57, 115–23,
    125–29, 145–50, 156, 165, 168, 171,
    183; of war, 5–6, 145, 148, 150, 153,
    165, 172–74, 184, 213n. 7, 222n. 16,
    228n. 10

Walzer, Michael, 12–13, 228n. 12
"war on terrorism," xii, 179–80, 182–83,
    185, 229–30n. 1
Weisberg, Richard, 196n. 15
World War I, 1, 98, 103, 161, 164,
    227n. 8
World War II, 5–6, 9, 20, 53, 56, 86, 89,
    91, 98, 104, 138–39, 182, 199n. 7